Everyone Eats

Everyone Eats

Understanding Food and Culture

E. N. Anderson

NEW YORK UNIVERSITY PRESS

New York and London

NEW YORK UNIVERSITY PRESS
New York and London
www.nyupress.org

Library of Congress Cataloging-in-Publication Data
Anderson, Eugene N. (Eugene Newton), 1941–
Everyone eats : understanding food and culture /
E.N. Anderson.
p. cm.
Includes bibliographical references and index.
ISBN 0–8147–0495–6 (cloth : alk. paper) —
ISBN 0–8147–0496–4 (pbk. : alk. paper)
1. Food habits. 2. Food preferences. I. Title.
GT2850.A6644   2004
394.1'2—dc22   2004014366

New York University Press books are printed on acid-free paper,
and their binding materials are chosen for strength and durability.

Manufactured in the United States of America
c 10 9 8 7 6 5 4 3 2 1
p 10 9 8 7 6 5

*To all the unknown men and women who created
the staple foods and the cuisines of the world:
our greatest and least known benefactors.*

*With special thanks to my
(fortunately less obscure)
mentors, especially
Paul Buell
Jack Goody
Solomon Katz
Sidney Mintz*

Contents

Introduction
Everyone Eats

Everyone eats rice
Yet no one knows why
When I say this now
People laugh at me
But instead of laughing along with them
You ought to step back
 and give it some thought
Think it over, and don't let up
I guarantee the time will come
When you'll really have something worth laughing at
 —Ryokan, *Great Fool: Zen Master Ryokan*

1

The eighteenth-century Zen poet Ryokan probes us on many levels. He is most concerned with the ultimate questions: What is life? Why live? Is there such a thing as life or existence? Indeed, if you ponder those, you will find much to laugh about. . . .

But there are more immediate, if no less laughable, questions posed by this innocent-seeming verse. Why do we eat what we eat? How did "rice" become synonymous with "food" throughout so much of eastern Asia?

We may further ask, How many of our foodways are determined by biology, how many by culture? Why do we love spices, sweets, coffee? Why do the British and the French not only eat so differently but also tease each other so mercilessly about it, century after century? The British call the French "frogs," to which the French respond that "the English have a hundred religions and only one sauce."[1] Why did pizza zoom from total obscurity to favorite American food in only a few years?

In fact, human foodways are a complex result of the interaction of human nutritional needs, ecology, human logic or lack of it, and historical accident. Humans make food, but, as Karl Marx said of history, "they do not make it just as they please" (Marx 1986:276). They construct their foodways within limits set by biology, economics, and psychology. There is an infinite number of possible dietary regimes, but no dietary regime can long endure if it does not provide protein, carbohydrates, fats, vitamins, and necessary minerals.

Ryokan also stimulates us to ask, Who made these decisions? Who developed the staple foods that support us? Who created the wondrous variety and complexity of cuisines that so greatly enrich our lives? The answer is thought provoking, and this time the humor is subdued and gentle. No one knows the names of the great inventors. We know the names of a few latter-day chefs, but food history—unlike the history of war and violence—is generally a history without names. Whoever developed bread wheat—a complicated, difficult hybrid—benefited humanity more than any named hero; yet we have no clue as to his or her name or language, though we know every detail of the lives of arch-villains like Stalin and Hitler. The unknown Mexican indigenous people who developed maize gave life to countless people. We know nothing about the maize breeders, though we know the names of the conquistadors and generals who massacred their descendents.

Millions and millions of humble, gentle, caring human beings—farmers and homemakers, innkeepers and famine relief workers, lovers and helpers—gave us the benefit of their insight, brilliance, creativity, and labor. To the familiar record of oppression and exploitation, they counterpose a hidden record of generosity, concern, and responsibility. We do not know who they were. We know nothing about them. They live on, but only in the silence of bread, the calm of a bowl of rice, the joy of wine, the light of a cup of coffee.

Strange immortality! To help so much, to pour the goodness and care of life into the most neglected and most important of everyday things, and then to be forgotten. Perhaps they did not care; perhaps they felt that fame is for those who have nothing better to leave.

Even their modern descendents, whose names we know, are not household words. From the late unlamented twentieth century, almost everyone knows of Madonna and Elvis, but few indeed recall E. V. McCollum or Albert Szent-György (the discoverers of vitamins A and C, respectively).

Ryokan, in other poems, poses the classic Buddhist opposition between the glory, fame, and transience of kings and the obscure but enduring world of the common folk. Those ordinary people must survive the wars and famines that their rulers unleash. Somehow, those ordinary people have not only kept their loved ones fed; they have steadily improved crops, recipes, and cultures. One can only repeat, in their memory, that most poignant of all food metaphors: "Ye are the salt of the earth"[2] (Matthew 5:13).

2

Savoir pour prévoir, prévoir pour pouvoir. (Know in order to predict, predict in order to be able to do something.)
—Attributed to Condorcet (France, eighteenth century)

Knowing about food is fun, but there are more cogent reasons to worry about understanding foodways. At least 15 percent of the world's population does not have enough to eat (Farley 2002). The figure rises to 18 percent of those in developing regions. UNICEF reports that almost 30 percent of children are undernourished (UNICEF 2002). Most of the hungry are in areas of war and unrest, or of massive disease epidemics, especially AIDS epidemics. Conversely, many people have too much, or at least too much of the wrong things. A far larger percentage of the world's people has too little iron, or too little vitamin A, or folic acid deficiency (a common cause of horrible birth defects); even iodine, easily added to salt, is deficient in some areas (UNICEF 2002). The problems of hunger, of obesity, and of malnutrition are among the world's most serious concerns. Diabetes, heart disease, cancer, and other diseases owe much of their prevalence to poor eating habits.

Humanity has succeeded—only recently—in providing enough food for everyone. The planet produces enough for all, for the first time in human history. Yet, undernutrition continues. Much food is lost in storage or distribution. Much more is wasted by careless people. Most important of all, those who need it are the poor who cannot afford it.

The future is cloudy. Rampant population growth threatens our hard-won food security. Environmental damage is an even more serious and immediate threat. Most unfortunate of all, however, are the wasteful eating habits of those who can afford to ignore the poor and the needy. Too much grain that could go to the poor is fed to chickens and cows. Too much farmland is producing luxury crops of no nutritional value. Too much of the world's fish catch is thrown away because rich buyers accept only a few luxury species. Too many people who should be eating fruits and vegetables are living largely on highly processed foods, especially bulk starch, oil, and sugar.

In all these matters, we need better understanding so that we can provide better food and encourage better use of it (Brown 1995, 1996; Smil 2000). Our basic nutritional needs, and some very broad preferences, are set by biology. Environment can modify the needs somewhat, but cannot change the basic biology; we all need protein, vitamin C, and so on, no matter what we think or believe. Preferences, however, are notoriously subject to cultural and social forces.

Most studies of food, until recently, concentrated on production and took consumption for granted. This has changed with the rise of nutritional anthropology (Bryant et al. 1985; Counihan and van Esterik 1997; Goodman et al. 2000; Goody 1982) and food history (Davidson 2000; Flandrin and Montanari 1999; Kiple and Ornelas 2000). This changes our understanding of what to do about world food problems. Until recently, the sober literature stressed producing more, and convincing people to eat more healthily. Yet, consumption is not a simple function of production. Consumption determines what is produced, by creating effective demand (i.e., basically, the actual buying or otherwise acquiring of food). Production and consumption determine each other. Since cultural and social factors have an enormous influence on consumption, it follows that culture and society are more important determinants of production than studies of production usually imply.

Thus, recent works often deal with the entire *food system,* looking at production, distribution, and consumption as part of a single process. That is the approach used here. I follow a biocultural approach. This involves paying close attention to human biology, to culture, and to political economy, all at once—recognizing that all are necessary and important determinants of food systems (see Goodman et al. 2000; see also Goodman and Leatherman 1998). The biocultural approach contrasts with narrowly biological or narrowly cultural ones. Foodways simply cannot be explained by simple nutritional considerations, or by simple cultural ones (such as symbol, meaning, or text).

The alternatives to a biocultural practice theory are two. First, there are strictly ecological and economic theories that see foodways as determined by biology—human nutritional needs, instincts, and environment. Second, there are theories that see Society and Culture as monolithic structures, separate from biology and (usually) divorced from the ordinary actions of mere mortals—who are expected to be the "bearers" of culture, not its creators. These two types of theory have dominated nutritional anthropology at various times in the past but are now rather widely seen as inadequate. We need to combine them into a biocultural synthesis to get at why everyone eats.

Society is made up of individuals interacting with each other to try to satisfy their various needs. "Culture" is a word used by anthropologists to refer to the rules, customs, and other shared plans and behaviors that result from this interaction. The understanding of society as interaction, and of culture as the knowledge that dynamically flows from that interaction, goes back to Kant (if not earlier); it was developed as a theory of society by the nineteenth-century Kantian social scientist Wilhelm Dilthey (1985) and his student George Herbert Mead (1964). My own understanding of it is practice oriented and draws on theories of culture as practice (Bourdieu 1977, 1990; Lave 1988). I see both economics and ideas as growing out of practice—out of interactions that are repeated and repeated until people develop from these interactions the generalizations that we know as "foodways" or, more broadly, as "knowledge" and "culture." Such practice has to be informed by at least some concept of the need to stay well nourished. Practice is structured by class, gender, ethnic, and regional identities, as well as by historical accident and incident, including sheer fads.

It is easy to understand why impoverished Mexicans ate maize until recently and have now switched (locally) to white bread; these were and are the cheapest foods available. It is not so easy to understand why slightly more affluent Mexicans love chiles, avocados, and tamarind. The chiles are nutritious as well as tasty, but they hurt the mouth, at least until one is accustomed to them. The avocados are nourishing also, but expensive, and they were a rather unpromising candidate for domestication when they were brought into cultivation thousands of years ago. Tamarind, a newcomer to Mexico from Asia, is sour and strange flavored—not the sort of taste one would expect to see spreading like wildfire among ordinary people. Nobody knows how it managed to do this in Mexico, especially since it is not popular elsewhere in North America.

In this book, I rely heavily on examples of this sort—revealingly complex cases that may or may not be explained as yet.

The immediate urgency of writing about food is provided by widespread hunger among the poor, and also, among the less poor, widespread and increasing obesity and its sequelae (such as diabetes, hypertension, and other problems, in those genetically susceptible). Foodways also provide us with an almost perfect case study in social theory. Unlike sex habits, they are easy to study. Unlike religion, they are grounded in obvious biological fact; no one can deny the reality of food or of starvation. Unlike politics, they are not often the subject of highly polarized and violent debate. They rank with kinship—social scientists' favorite institution for cross-cultural study—in being universal, well recorded, and usually highly structured.

Basic human biology sets limits—very wide limits—for what we can eat. No one will use strychnine as a staple food, or construct a diet lacking in vitamin C. Basic biology also makes some regimens more likely than others; where grain abounds, people will rarely overlook it. However, biological, economic, and ecological realities underdetermine foodways, except in desperate cases. Starving people will eat anything available, but anyone above the desperation threshold exercises considerable choice. Even quite hardscrabble communities and societies can have very complex, elaborate foodways, often structured by religion and other abstract symbolic systems.

Food is used in every society on earth to communicate messages. Preeminent among these are messages of group solidarity; food sharing is literally sacred in almost all religions and takes on a near-sacred quality in many (most?) families around the world. It also carries messages about status, gender, role, ethnicity, religion, identity, and other socially constructed regimes. It is also, very often, used in even more fine-tuned ways, to mark or indicate particular occasions, particular personal qualities, particular hangups and concerns. It is subject to snobbism, manipulation, and debate. It has served as a source of metaphors for writers and artists from ancient Egypt and Mesopotamia on down to Marcel Proust, James Joyce, and D. H. Lawrence, to say nothing of films like Ang Lee's *Eat, Drink, Man, Woman.* (If there is one omission I most regret in the present book, it is the lack of a section on food in art and literature; I am simply not qualified to go there.)

Many anthropologists explain cultural ways by recourse to functions—usually fairly simple, straightforward functions such as providing food, getting money, protecting the group, or keeping the society together (Malinowski 1944; Turner and Maryanski 1979). Optimal foraging theory (see chapters 2 and 3) is a functionalist theory. Functionalists often see culture as an adaptive mechanism, allowing people to survive and reproduce. They are concerned with nutrition, mating, and child rearing, economics, social conflict, and harmony. Other anthropologists see culture as a complex network of symbols and symbol systems, and see the anthropologist's task as one of interpreting and explaining these meanings. They see culture as communication. They are thus concerned with art, music, traditional literature—in short, texts. Foodways, for them, become texts to interpret and analyze. Many, perhaps most, anthropologists see these explanatory styles as complementary, not exclusive. In general, the more they see humans as united by broad, general concerns based on common human genetics, the more they look toward biological functionalism; the more they see humans as dramatically different from each other because of profound cultural differences, the more they involve themselves with meaning and experience. I see them as the two wings of the bird of social theory; without both wings, equally developed, the bird doesn't fly. People everywhere have to deal with the full range; they have to get food and shelter, but they also have complex personal lives heavily informed by language and belief. Experientially and phenomenologically (to use the long words), people are simple functionalists sometimes, complex meaning-generators at other times. One can follow Mennell et al. (1992) in classifying foodways explanations as functionalist, structuralist, or developmental (broadly historic and political-economic). However, structuralist explanations do not capture all the interpretive, meaning-based explanations in the field.

The result, often, is a rather delightful chaos. Humans are not simple, uniform, easily understood creatures. One corollary is that the present book is not tightly organized around one theme. A more unified work would ensue if foodways were all ecology (Harris 1985) or all political economy (as the Marxists hold) or all cognitive structure (Lévi-Strauss 1962). But they aren't. Foodways can only be understood holistically, with just about every aspect of human life taken into account. Daily practice brings together many disparate determinants, from need for vitamin A to desire to emulate the rich and famous. Unity is provided by the fact that people must integrate into one meal, or one snack, or one shopping trip, the satisfaction of many needs: health, affordability, social and sexual life, a sense of control, and, last but not least, enjoyment. No computer on earth could run a program optimizing the satisfaction of all these. But people are brilliant approximators, and they manage to integrate all those goals—not perfectly effortlessly, but successfully enough for everyday purposes.

This book is not a textbook or basic reference work.[3] I hope for readers in classrooms, but I am more hopeful of readers in the vast world outside academia and outside scholastic pursuits. Many encyclopedic and comprehensive works on food already exist (notably Katz and Weaver 2003 and Kiple and Ornelas 2000). I have tried to minimize repetition of easily available information. Standard sources, including my own works, are not summarized in much detail. I have concentrated instead on less well-known material, and especially on my own observations and unpublished research. I have included as much as I can from my own experience—verifying published material when I could not do the research. This means that, among other things, China, Maya Mexico, and the Mediterranean area—the areas I know reasonably well—get a good deal of attention, while other areas—including India (for which see Achaya 1994, 2002) and northern Europe (see Adamson 2002 and references therein)—get short coverage. I have included a good deal on hunter-gatherer foraging and on scent, but I have regretfully left to others the task of going in detail into matters like obesity and anorexia, where my expertise is not sufficient to allow me to add much to the many excellent works available.

One of the best ways to improve world nutrition is to pick up the best ideas from the thousands of cultures that humanity has developed. Each culture encodes a vast amount of knowledge of local foods: how to identify them, prepare them, grow them (if they are planted), and so on. Each culture has its ways of enjoying food and of constructing foodways as social entities. We need to appreciate these ways far more fully. We need to see "other people's foods" as not merely exotic delicacies, to be eaten for variety, but as sources of ideas for saving the planet. Time is short, ecological disaster is at hand; we have no time to lose. The only cost-effective, time-effective way to broaden our food systems enough to insure nutrition through the twenty-first century is to draw on these vast existing stocks of knowledge. We have no guarantee that this will be enough to put us over, but at least it will help; we need to investigate all possibilities. "Valuing diversity" should not be merely a buzzword for schoolkids. It is a life-and-death matter.

Ultimately, the better we understand why people eat what they eat, the better we can feed the world.[4]

> If these sleeves
> of my black robe
> were only wider
> I'd shelter all the people
> in this up-and-down world
> —Ryokan

1

Obligatory Omnivores

1

> Only those who can appreciate the least palatable of vegetable roots
> know the meaning of life.
> —Hung Tzu-ch'eng, *A Chinese Garden of Serenity*

The long and circumstantial story of human evolution explains much. It explains why we need, and want, so much variety in our diets. It explains why we crave sugar and fat. It explains why we can adjust to such a range of regimes. It explains specific nutritional needs: vitamin C from our fruit-eating heritage, protein in quantity because of our large size, active life, and long history of eating not only meat but also high-nutrient plant foods like beans.

It does not, however, explain the specifics of human diets. In fact, it explains why there *are* no such specifics. Humans have been selected for three key things:

- the ability to live on anything we can bite (with our relatively small teeth);
- the ability to learn, reason, and plan;
- social life, including conformity to local group ways.

Thanks to that single complex of abilities and faculties, we can figure out how to leach poisons from nuts, how to cook down sinews to make them edible, how to mash bones and boil them for marrow, and, ultimately, how to grow, process, and distribute the thousands of domestic crops. A particularly interesting accomplishment, considering it was done thousands of years ago, was the domestication of life forms we could not even see: the yeasts and bacteria that are now necessary for making bread, beer, wine, and other common foods.

Humans are fond of ascribing their success in populating the world to their great intelligence. At least some of the credit is due to our adaptable guts. Humans manage on almost anything. The Inuit lived until recently on seal and whale meat. The staple food of Roti, in Indonesia, is palm sugar (see the excellent account by Fox 1977). Termites are vital to survival in central Africa. Salmon provided perhaps 80 percent of the food of the native nations of northwestern North America. Many groups to the south of them lived largely on acorns. And Americans today subsist on food so indigestible that American zoos have had to prevent visitors from feeding the animals; the junk foods that zoos sell to people can be fatal to the other zoo inmates (as explained by warning signs at the San Diego Zoo).

Withal, we cannot compete with true specialists in surviving on one thing. Unlike the koala, we cannot digest eucalyptus leaves. Unlike the cat, we cannot live on mice. We do not have squirrels' internal enzyme laboratory, which lets them devour mushrooms fatal to us and to most other mammals. We cannot even fall back on grass, as horses do. Our eating apparatus, so ready to adapt to new and strange foods, cannot deal effectively with such common matters as cellulose, tannins, or large bones. We can eat only relatively soft, chemically simple items.

We come from a long line of primate generalists. Our ape ancestors lived in Africa, a land of dramatic contrasts. Not only does it have lush rain forests, glacial mountains, vast swamps, parched deserts, and game-rich savannahs; it often has them all in the same area (O'Brien and Peters 1999). In parts of East Africa, a highly mobile hominid could visit all five of those habitats within a few days. When I first visited Africa, I expected vast sun-baked plains and deserts, relieved in some areas by rain forests. But, especially in the Rift areas, I found an incredible variety of scenery packed into small areas. Any hominid, in a daily feeding range, would almost inevitably move through several habitats. Diverse habitats with much woodland, especially riparian habitats, are the most promising for human evolution (Bromage and Schrenk 1999, esp. O'Brien and Peters 1999).

Some six or eight million years ago, the common ancestor of chimpanzees and humans was living a sleepy, contented sort of life in the forests of Africa. We now have some skulls from this period, indicating that the human line may have branched from the chimpanzee-gorilla line by seven million years ago. This idyll was not to last. By five million years ago, the continent was facing ever drier conditions. Lightning fires swept

One place it all began. Olduvai Gorge, Tanzania, where human remains reveal two million years of human evolution. Louis and Mary Leakey and their associates excavated here over many decades, finding a long sequence of hominids. The gorge is named for the abundance of *Sansevieria,* called *olduvai* locally. It is an aloelike plant that supplies a good, hard fiber from the leaves. *Photo by E. N. Anderson, 1998*

through droughty forests, creating vast openings. Grasses, previously humble members of the plant community, exploded in abundance. Tough and resilient, able to regrow from root stocks when grazed, these plants took over most of the continent in the next few million years. Either the drying up of the continent (Vrba et al. 1995) or the very change and diversity itself (Potts 1996), or both, selected apes that could live in diverse habitats and lifestyles.

Chimpanzees retreated with the forest, there to evolve into Rousseau's Savage—for his Savage was, in fact, the chimp (Rousseau 1983 [1782]:204–6). Rousseau saw these animals as powerful, wild, sociable, unencumbered by the trammels of civilization (and *not* "noble"; he did not use the word). So indeed they are. And, like most higher primates (Milton 2000a, 2000b, 2000c), they eat a diet far higher in vitamins and minerals—and also in odd and varied plant chemicals—than the diet of

ns. Chimps live largely on fruits and leaves, and their intake
ch as vitamin C is many times that of most of us. They eat
...d hunt monkeys on occasion, but they are not well adapted
to meat eating; a small amount of saturated fat sends their cholesterol levels very high (Mestel 2002:A20). Humans can eat more meat without this problem, especially when they are young; this is clearly an adaptation to a higher-meat diet. But humans, too, form too much cholesterol when they eat too much saturated fat from animals.

Other apes of the original lineage began to adjust to drier conditions in East and South Africa. We have skeletons more than four million years old now, from the Great Rift, that vast fracture zone where Africa almost tore itself apart before giving up and opting (geologically) for unity. These skeletons—*Australopithecus* and its apparent ancestral form *Ardipithecus*—are apelike: the animals were small (three or four feet tall), with limbs still adapted for tree climbing and brains the size of chimps'. Their bones and skulls are small and light. They ate a varied diet with seeds, meat, and other items (recent findings and opinions are conveniently reviewed by Vogel 1999). They too evidently got far more nutrients and phytochemicals in their diets than we do today.

Most interesting of all, their teeth are small and diverse. They do not have anything like the savage canine tusks of chimpanzees and gorillas. Their teeth, in fact, are very much like our own. The one striking difference (leaving aside certain technical obscurities) lies in the molars: Australopithecines were grinders of vegetable matter. Their molars are large and millstonelike. Their tiny front teeth were adapted to nipping off vegetation, and not to much else; the work was in the back, where powerful jaws and strong, heavy teeth ground tough vegetable matter down. On the other hand, the early Australopithecines were not very specialized as vegetarians either, and there is no doubt that they—like chimpanzees—ate small animals, eggs, termites and other insects, and any other animal food that couldn't defend itself.

Several species have been described for the Australopithecines, but there may have been, at first, only one slowly evolving lineage. Somewhat more than two million years ago, this lineage branched in at least two directions. This process was presumably the result of continued climatic change in the direction of a drier and more variable climate. Once again, some authorities stress the "dry" side, some the "variable"; we do not know enough to decide which was more directly important, so the cautious researcher opts for both factors.

Australopithecine and early *Homo* fossils have been found largely in river valleys, where forests along the rivers alternate with marshes and lakes, and where savannahs, deserts, rock cliffs, and mountains may all surround the river and marsh landscape. Lions, hyenas, hippopotami, antelopes, giraffes, and hundreds of smaller animals and birds abound. Wild figs, grass seeds, berries, oily palm fruits, and a wealth of edible roots and tubers can be reliable sources of food, but only if one follows a complex round, moving from resource to resource as ripening progresses. Australopithecines probably lived in the riverine forests, but spent more and more of their time in the more open environments as dry climates and fire-maintained savannahs spread.

One branch of the Australopithecines grew larger, with thick skulls and enormous molar teeth. This "robust" branch, represented by *Australopithecus robustus* and *A. (robustus) boisei,* died out in a million years or so. Apparently, the robust Australopithecine line evolved to exploit the river-and-savannah plant world by eating more and more of it. They lived to process tough, resistant plant material. They made a good living at it for about a million years, but a combination of factors—progressive drying, fire, predators, and very possibly some hunting by *Homo*—finally wiped them out.

The other branch, which led to modern humanity, took the opposite path; presumably the process of "disruptive selection" was working here. Their molar teeth grew smaller, yet their bodies grew larger. By that time, the members of this branch were within the category we recognize as *Homo.* Several species have been described from around two million years ago (MYA); whether these species are valid or merely members of one highly variable population remains to be determined.

After 1.7–1.8 MYA, as the wisdom teeth shrank, the brain suddenly began to grow, much faster than the body. There followed a sustained, spectacular increase that is without any known parallel in all geologic history. In a million and a half years, the brain increased in size by almost 400 percent. Such a rate of evolution is rare enough for any organ; for the nervous system, it is unique (according to present knowledge).

Moreover, the growth was not a mere expansion to keep up with the body. The whole brain expanded, but the real explosion occurred in the frontal lobes and a few other specialized structures. This, of course, is the system that gives us what we like to call "higher thought"—actually a fine-tuned complex of abilities that enable us to combine exceedingly complex social life, highly adaptable and learning-based foraging, and, above all, the integration of emotional drive with a sophisticated ability to weigh many factors in making decisions. It also gave us the abilities to do calculus, invent computers, compose grand opera, and use nuclear weapons and "smart" missiles on each other. These latter creations certainly show how adaptable and flexible the human brain is; obviously, from very early times, it had the potential to do far more than hunt and gather.[1]

Robin Dunbar (1993) notes that social animals have larger brains than their nonsocial relatives. The larger and/or more complex the group, the larger the difference. Humans, with brains almost four times the size of chimps', would be expected to have social groups proportionately larger; Dunbar figures about 50 to 150 people. This is an educated guess, but it fits uncannily well with a number of estimates of the size of the typical face-to-face, intimate, manageable social group among humans today. However, people also aggregate into much larger groups, up to millions in modern times. This aggregation seems to rely on socialization by slightly older peers in early adolescence (Harris 1998; Peter Richerson, personal communication, 2000). Whoever gets to the teenager just breaking out of the family's tight grip—be it school, military, gang, or national service—tends to win a lifelong allegiance. This makes possible civil society, in the sense of some real identification with and responsibility toward a group much bigger than 50–150 close associates.

Our lineage evolved from the small, small-brained *Homo* forms (*Homo habilis*, etc.) through the larger and brainier *Homo erectus* to modern *Homo sapiens*. Various intermediate and transitional forms, as well as local side branches, have been dignified by other species names, but they seem to reflect minor variation. Most of the real action took place in *Homo erectus*. This is a "temporal species"; it evolved into *Homo sapiens*. It is, basically, a name given to that slice of human history in which the brain grew from 400 cubic centimeters (at most) to almost its modern size of 1,400. The same period saw the social group increase from perhaps 20 to the abovementioned 50–150 (or, at least, some comparable level).

2

Brains are incredibly costly. The human nervous system makes up only 3 percent of body weight but uses fully 25 percent of basal metabolic calories. This means that (if you are resting) 25 percent of blood flow must go to the head, and that, in turn, means that 25 percent of heat loss is from the head (given our thin scalps); no wonder we have long, thick hair up there. Moreover, in conditions of stress, the brain is protected; it gets first call on the blood and the heat. As outdoorspeople proverbially say, "if your feet are cold, put on your hat"—because your head is draining the heat from the rest of your anatomy. Activity increases blood flow generally, and may increase flow to particularly active parts of the body, so you can always stamp your feet—but your head will still need 25 percent of overall flow, so carry a hat or keep your hair long.

On top of this, a woman must provide enough milk not only to permit her baby to grow but also to permit it to develop this enormous, demanding brain. Human infants are born with very small brains (roughly the size of a chimp brain), since erect posture and a huge pelvic opening cannot go together in this world, and a small pelvic opening means a small head. Therefore, most brain growth has to be outside the mother's body—to a degree otherwise found (in mammals) largely among marsupials.

Our fully erect posture and striding walk have other costs. A dog with a broken leg can manage on the other three. A human with a broken leg needs help.

Finally, there is that gut, so adaptable yet so unable to handle really difficult materials. Here we differ less from the chimps, who are rather similarly equipped. We have a moderate-sized stomach, a moderately long intestinal tube, and a digestive apparatus that can handle moderate but not overwhelming amounts of fats or proteins. By contrast, a true carnivore like a cat has a shorter, straighter, smoother intestinal array, while a true vegetarian like a koala or langur monkey has much longer, more convoluted intestines. Human intestines are closely comparable to those of other omnivores, such as swine. Nothing more clearly shows our omnivorous heritage (see Mann 1987).

Noteworthy, also, is the ability of the human stomach to expand. Few mammals can eat more at a sitting than humans can. Today, this ability goes unappreciated except at seasonal feasts (such as Thanksgiving or Id-al-Fitr), but in the old days it was our ace in the hole. Humans could gorge when they had the chance, and live off stored fat for days.

We probably evolved from an opportunistic vegetation eater that ate some animal food (*Australopithecus*) to an opportunistic specialist in high-nutrient foods: meat, eggs, shoots, tubers, nuts, seeds, honey

(*Homo*). The early hominids would have been as adept as we are now at shifting from dead animals to starchy tubers to oily fruits, depending on what their range afforded them at the time. The average human of one million years ago probably lived largely on tender young plant material, got at least 10–20 percent of calories from meat from hunting and scavenging, ate many insects and loved them, dug up roots and tubers during bad times, and gorged on anything and everything edible when a good patch was found. Most of the meat would have been from small animals, insects, and carrion. Five hundred thousand years later, more hunted game and fewer small animals would have been in the picture, and perhaps by then cooking was important, rendering available a vast range of roots, tubers, and seeds such as beans. Fifty thousand years ago, when modern *Homo sapiens* was established throughout most of the Old World, hunting was more important, but taming fire had probably made cooking-dependent plant foods even more so. Carrion, coarse shoots and leaves, small seeds, and the tougher insects were falling out of the picture. Various views and topics related to early human nutrition are well treated in various sources (the most recent, at this writing, is Ungar and Teaford 2002); meat has been the focus of a superb collection of papers, *Meat-Eating in Human Evolution,* edited by Craig Stanford and Henry Bunn (2001), which greatly advances our understanding of carnivory among modern primates and ancient humans as well as among us moderns.

The shift to more meat, often credited with allowing brain expansion by providing high-quality food, has recently been confirmed from an odd direction: tapeworms (Hoberg et al. 2001; Shipman 2001). Human tapeworms are derived from those infesting hyenas, lions, jackals, and (more rarely) other scavenger/hunters of the African savannah. Their intermediate hosts there are wild pigs (including hippopotami, basically overgrown pigs) and antelopes (modern populations are more apt to catch them from domestic pigs and cattle). Apparently, humans became infested with these tapeworms at about the time that *Homo* appeared. The assumption is that this is the point at which people were eating enough meat regularly enough to keep the transmission links going.

There are three reasonable explanations for this pattern of development. First and least likely, the sudden change at 1.7–1.8 MYA could represent the invention of cooking and its use to tenderize a wide range of plant materials, such as tough tubers. This has been advocated by Richard Wrangham and others (Pennisi 1999), but there is no evidence for it, and we really have looked enough to find evidence if there was very much out there. If hominids were using fire in a controlled way and on a large scale, they left astonishingly little record of it.

Second, the sudden change could represent the progressive addition of more meat to the diet, as humans became better at scavenging leopard and lion kills and hunting small animals. The idea of humans evolving as vulturelike scavengers (Blumenschine and Cavallo 1992) is piquant. Recent research makes it seem likely that humans (like lions and hyenas) both scavenged and hunted. Stone tools were being made by this time and were being used to butcher animals. Tools begin to increase in sophistication and variety by the 1.7 MYA date.

The problem with the hunter theory (at least its extreme forms) is that, as full-time carnivores, we are failures. We do not have the canine teeth or the shearing carnassial cheek teeth that a cat or dog has. We do not have claws or even much arm strength, and early tools were not the finest of hunting equipment.

Moreover, we cannot live on lean meat (Cordain et al. 2000; Kelly 1995; Milton 2000b). For one thing, it is low in calories and hard to digest, thus providing real problems for an animal that has to run a brain that takes as many calories as a good-sized dog. For another, our kidneys cannot handle the nitrogenous wastes produced by digesting it. They get overloaded, and if they do not fail the heart fails through trying to push more and more blood through them. Too many people find this out too late during the recurrent fads for high-protein weight-loss diets. Finally, humans need a great deal of vitamin C and other nutrients that are notably more abundant in plant foods than in meat. The early tools, though adequate for butchering, were not spectacularly good for hunting, and were not good enough to be a fully adequate substitute for the lack of carnassial teeth; surely we would have evolved better if we had been carnivores. It does seem likely—in fact, certain—that the rise of *Homo* went with a rise in meat eating, but that seems almost a byproduct of something else: a general improvement in overall foraging skills.

In my view, the only credible theory of human dietary evolution is that the early hominids just became better and better at omnivory. They got better at finding meat, both by scavenging and by hunting, but also at finding roots, seeds, shoots, eggs, and anything else edible. Termites, for instance, were a resource; they are large and abundant in Africa, and are still a popular food. Stone tools from 1.8 million years ago, in South Africa, show marks attributed to their use in breaking into termite mounds ("Dinner in a Mound" 2001). The only way an animal with a huge, demanding brain can survive is by using the brain to figure out how to draw on a wide range of good foods to get the most nutrition with the least effort. At this, we are superb (as will appear later). No doubt, early hominids were beginning to understand the art of comparing a dead elephant five miles off with a patch of seeds only one mile off. How big an elephant balanced out how many seeds? When was it worth the extra four miles?

There is every reason to believe that this sort of foraging ability entailed another skill: the ability to fine-tune a social foraging plan. This is the skill that led, much later, to the rise of modern civilization. A large social group can scatter out all over the landscape. When one member finds a rich patch of food, he or she can summon the others. Surely this was one way language developed—to make it possible to explain ever more clearly what food was available when, and how many people it would feed.

The larger the brain, and the larger the social group, the larger and richer the patches had to be. It takes a very large and rich patch indeed to feed a whole group with brains all burning several hundred calories a day. Moreover, the robust Australopithecines (and other animals) had already sewed up another potentially possible lifestyle: individual foraging for small, numerous, widely dispersed patches of food. The robust Australopithecines ate roots, nuts, and other tough plant matter, wandering the savannahs or woodlands in search of coarse vegetation. Such foraging for large volumes of low-value food does not encourage large social groups. Selection will not produce or maintain a big brain on such a regime.

Early *Homo,* by contrast, would scatter over the landscape in hopes of finding a dead elephant, a fruiting tree, or a termite nest swarming with winged forms. Most important of all would have been areas recently cleared by fire or flood (Kortlandt 1978 argues especially for recent rains and floods). Such areas regrow rapidly with tender young vegetation, and are often selectively colonized by berry bushes. (The berry is a fruit type adapted to dispersal by birds and animals, and is often developed by plants that need to hop from burn to burn.) Moreover, recent burns and other regrowing habitats attract animals, both small and large, and are thus ideal hunting spots; in fact, most hunting peoples selectively burn tracts of land for this reason. Regrowing burns and floodplains concentrate, in one place, all a human needs: tender young leaves, berries, roots, and vulnerable game animals. This would be a rich patch indeed, and no sane human would neglect any one resource to go after another. Concentrating on either meat or plant foods would be suicidally foolish. People would go through the habitat eating anything they could bite or swallow. Their watchword would have been the one we used to say (when hungry enough) in Texas: "I'll eat anything that won't eat back faster."

Fire must have been an important part of the adaptation. Perhaps fire was first used not for warmth or for cooking but for burning brush to open hunting grounds. Fire drives game, eliminates thorns and brush, kills poisonous snakes, and generally makes the country better for people. Above all, it creates new burns that quickly regrow with berries, beans, tender shoots, and other things people want to eat. It is easy to start. Therefore, all hunting and gathering peoples use fire on a large scale, except those in environments that are almost impossible to burn. Campfires and cooking fires require special knowledge and a great deal of care and control; such knowledge was probably learned through starting wildfires. Fire thus became the first tool of environmental management. It still is the most important one—but now the burning is often controlled within an internal combustion engine.

Planning for a social group's daily foraging fine-tuned our skills in conscious, rational thought. Such skills could easily and naturally be put to use in developing storage, food-processing, and even environmental-management plans. Burning and other manipulations trained humans in conservation and scheduling of resource use, and thence, ultimately, came agriculture. From such things as planning to leave a resource for later, so as to get a more perishable one today, humans developed concepts of storage. From the task of bringing foods to a central area, where less mobile members of the group were waiting, humans developed the systems of distribution and reallocation that later became "economics." Some processing—crushing bones, cutting up meat, leaching bitterness from nuts, grinding seeds, mashing tough plant material—must have taken place in such central areas. Increasing sophistication in these is obvious over the long-term archeological record.

Cooking, as noted above, renders tough tubers digestible. Starches like inulin—very common in tubers, and virtually indigestible to humans—are broken down, by prolonged cooking, into sugars that we can digest. But this is not all. Cooking also breaks down tendons and muscle fibers. It detoxifies many foods—or compounds in foods—that are poisonous in the raw. It softens all manner of stems, leaves, and fruits. It opens the shells of mollusks. It kills bacteria and molds that would otherwise cause disease.

Claude Levi-Strauss (1964) pointed out that many South American native peoples see cooking as the invention that made humans human. After all, ants and bees have societies; parrots and other animals can learn to talk. Clothing, the invention that got Adam and Eve out of Eden, was not an issue to these South Americans, who wore virtually nothing. Only cooking distinguished human persons from nonhuman animals.

The modern ecologist has to agree with the South Americans. Of all the inventions of the human animal, fire and its use to process food has been the most important—the one that changed our lives most and brought us irrevocably into a new and different world. It may have been one of the major factors behind the final stages of human brain evolution.

The importance of social, omnivorous foraging was first stressed by Glynn Isaac in the 1970s (Isaac 1978, 1979; cf. Lovejoy 1981). He theorized that early hominids brought food back to a "base camp," a relatively permanent and stable inhabited site. There is, however, no need to imagine such a specific scenario. Groups could also have roamed at will, reassembling at night and planning where to move next. No doubt such discussions helped in the evolution of language. Groups that could be more specific and detailed about planning routes and routines might have grown faster and spun off more descendents. Eventually, we have arrived at a world in which thousands of people can get together in social groups and enjoy it thoroughly—a world in which food is traded worldwide.

The evolution of sociability in the human line parallels the evolution of social life among canines, crows and jays, bee eaters, geese, and other lineages. Typically, in these groups, the less social species forage for widely distributed resources in more or less homogenous environments, while the more socially complex species live in harsh or unpredictable environments where food tends to occur in big clumps or patches. It is somewhat thought provoking that this is especially true of those social animals that have strong, long-term pair bonds between mated pairs. (Contrary to some claims in the literature, humans are normally pair-bonded animals,[2] though they can be otherwise with ease.) The conventional wisdom, since Darwin and even before, has been that pair bonding is largely about raising young in situations where a single parent cannot reliably find enough food while also protecting the young. An animal that must feed a fast-growing brain and protect a young one for fifteen years or so is obviously a good candidate for pair bonding.

Perhaps the huge social groups characteristic of humans arose the way they have in jays and crows: by aggregation of family units and then by expansion of the whole concept of society. Early Australopithecines pre-sumably lived in smallish groups, consisting of a small core of closely re-lated males or females and their mates and young. The larger the group, the more it could forage for rich patches, defend itself, and share skills and knowledge (in child rearing as well as foraging). I suspect that small kin groups evolved more and more ability to clump together into larger aggregations when food afforded. Chimpanzees do this; they may have evolved it independently or may retain an ancestral condition shared with the human line. Eventually, people evolved enough social skills to allow them to aggregate into huge social groups that included many nonkin. This would require evolving true sociability: the friendliness, generosity, openness, and trust that we extend even to strangers. It would also re-quire evolving an ability to deal with "cheaters," deadbeats, aggressive individuals, psychopaths, and other hard cases. In general, humans are trusting and friendly to strangers, but quick to turn against any stranger that does not reciprocate. Humans are even quicker to turn against any member of their own group that does not play by the rules! (The ways this could lead to a highly developed moral sense have been the subject of some delightful speculation, e.g. Petrinovitch 1995; Cronk 1999.)

Humans show the kin-based roots of sociability and morality in a number of ways. Human traits such as collective defense, generosity, and constant gossip (cf. Dunbar 1993) make good sense in the context of a family, or even a small group. They are not necessarily so rational when groups become large and kin ties become weak. Thus (one assumes) hu-mans invoke family metaphors in teaching morality: "All men are broth-ers," "the sisterhood of women," "the human family," and so on. Con-versely, humans work hard to dehumanize hated enemies (Staub 1989).

Particularly interesting, and relevant to food, is the tendency of hu-mans to conform to the behavioral norms set by senior or more powerful members of the group. This makes excellent sense when it is a case of chil-dren imitating parents. It is less sensible when it is a case of subjects imi-tating rulers. It is irrational when it is a whole nation imitating movie stars.

Language seems especially adapted to communication about social matters, as Robin Dunbar has persuasively argued. Among other things, he has shown that most conversation today is about face-to-face social is-sues—gossip, in short. The need for such complex social fine-tuning would have increased with group size, brain size, and the need to forage widely for high-quality foods. It is sometimes alleged, by linguists, that language must have been "invented" at some recent point in the past. This is clearly not the case.[3] The human lips, tongue, vocal cords, and throat are massively altered to allow complex linguistic production, and the human brain has specific centers for language processing (though they are also useful for some other purposes, and evidently arose from simpler and less tightly entailed structures). These are all enormously different from anything a chimpanzee has, and bespeak a very long period of very active evolution. Human communication took a long time to reach its present level of complexity, and the change was gradual. Social foraging had much to do with that—though social problems such as finding a mate must have been major factors as well.

Many writers over time—most recently the "sociobiologists" and some evolutionary psychologists—have alleged that we are city dwellers with cave-dweller instincts. However—leaving aside the fact that people have very rarely lived in caves—it is obvious from the record that humans evolved not to be "cave dwellers" but to be adaptable, flexible, and quick to learn. Our "cave dwellers" genes allowed Einstein to develop his theories and Edison his inventions. Our ways of loving, worshiping, and—of course—eating are just as far from the Australopithecine condition as our math and electric systems are.

We evolved to keep looking, as creatively as possible, for the next good place. That is the human story.

3

Modern hunter-gatherers vary enormously in their diet. In the high Arctic and Subarctic, they live almost entirely on meat, since there is not much else to find; this means they have to get much fat, since lean meat is not a viable diet by itself (Cordain et al. 2000). In inland California and the Great Basin, they lived largely on seeds and tubers. In pre-agricultural Netherlands, they had a diet based on salmon, deer, eels, shellfish, hazelnuts, and berries (C. Meiklejohn, personal communication, 1978)—an enviable diet indeed. The !Kung San of the Kalahari, until recently, lived largely on mongongo nuts (*Ricinodendron rautanenii,* rather similar to hazelnuts or macadamia nuts). Australian aborigines lived on a wide variety of plant foods. People are versatile animals, and have always been (see Kelly 1995). There is a clear trend, long known in anthropology, from almost entirely animal foods in high latitudes down to overwhelming dependence on plant foods in low latitudes, especially in dry areas where animals are few (Keeley 1998; Kelly 1995). An exception is rain forests, which are similar to subarctic forests in that most of the plant biomass is tied up in wood, and people have to hunt; but rain forests are such poor habitats for hunter-gatherers that doubt has been cast on whether they were inhabited at all in pre-agricultural times (Bailey et al. 1989). Keeley (1998) points out that latitude, and plant-rich habitat in general, account for most of the variance, as opposed to population pressure or cultural preference.[4]

Most recent authorities believe that the vast majority of hunter-gatherers in the past lived largely on plant foods or, locally, on fish and shellfish. The ethnographic record might seem to suggest otherwise (Cordain et al. 2000; Kelly 1995), but that is because ethnographies have overemphasized hunting. In particular, hunting is overemphasized in the work summarized in the Human Relations Area Files (HRAF), a huge compendium of ethnographic records of human cultures. This is partly because of the natural bias of male ethnographers in the Indiana Jones era of anthropology. It is also partly because many of the surviving hunter-gatherer cultures were in refuge areas where plant growth was too poor to tempt settled farmers: the Subarctic, the High Plains, the South American Chaco.

Also, many contemporary hunter-gatherers are not actually independent and self-reliant societies; rather, they are specialized meat suppliers to settled agricultural peoples. This accounts for the heavy meat harvest of the Mbutu of Africa, the Agta of the Philippines, and other groups. These peoples live not so much by hunting for food as by hunting for meat to trade for agricultural staples. Even the San of southern Africa, the prototypic hunter-gatherers of anthropology textbooks, were in contact with agricultural peoples and often traded extensively with them (Wilmsen and Denbow 1990; cf. Solway and Lee 1990 and Headland and Reid 1989 for a balanced view of the whole issue).

Finally, there are outright errors in many published sources (especially those based on the HRAF material), and they seem to be systematically promeat—that male bias again. For instance, Kelly (1995:66) estimates that the Haida of the Queen Charlotte Islands of British Columbia obtained 20 percent of their food from hunting land animals and 60 percent from fishing (the rest from gathering plants). I have worked with the Haida on the Charlottes, and can testify that this is flatly impossible. Before deer were introduced around 1900, there were no large animals on the Charlottes except a few bears (large and dangerous) and a tiny (now extinct) relict population of caribou. The population of the Haida, on the other hand, was high, at least eight thousand people. They could not possibly have gotten even 10 percent of their food from meat. In fact, they lived almost entirely on fish. Similar if less extreme overweighting of land-animal meat is evident in all the Northwest Coast societies in Kelly's sample. His estimates of the role of animal food in California Indian diets also seem far too high.[5]

Hunters and gatherers range from almost entirely meat-eating to almost entirely vegetarian. The average is certainly not the 50-50 proposed by Cordain et al. (2000; see Milton 2000b), but, on the other hand, it seems beyond question that the average hunting-gathering group ate more meat than the average agriculturalist group. Hunting peoples often got well over 20 percent of calories from meat. Even the modern American, carnivorous by inclination but agricultural by dependence, gets only about 10 percent of calories from meat.

If one were to calculate an average for 10,000 BC, one would have to decide whether to average *societies* or *individuals*. Many societies but few individuals live in high latitudes or in tropical forests. The vast majority of humans would have lived in the lush plains, steppes, and woodlands. At a wild guess, I would bet the average for *societies* would be 20–30 percent animal foods (meat or fish), the average for *individuals* more like 15–20 percent. Moreover, fish probably was far more important than meat. Almost all groups near a sea or a large lake or river depended heavily on fish and shellfish. Very, very few depended overwhelmingly on mammal meat; only the Arctic and Subarctic Native Americans and the Native Americans of the Argentine pampas are known to have so depended. They maintained exceedingly low population densities. The Ice Age hunters of Europe and probably a few other areas almost certainly lived mostly on meat also, maintaining fairly large populations, but even they ate more plants than was once thought (Mason et al. 1994). Elsewhere, "Man the Hunter" (Lee and Devore 1962) may have hunted successfully and happily, but "Woman the Gatherer" (Dahlberg 1981) was producing most of the calories.

The degree of human sociability remains truly astonishing. We are by far the most social animal. Ants and bees have nothing like a modern city. The human genetic program specifies that we will crave human contact, want to be in societies, and want to do everything needed to keep ourselves in our social scenes.

Darwinian theory predicts that we will prefer close relatives to others. Evolution is based on a tautology: the genes that leave the most descendents leave the most descendents. "Fitness" is measured by how many of one's genes are actually passed on. All the excitement lies in just how the fitness is maximized.

Obviously, it is best maximized by raising a lot of children. However, it is also maximized by helping one's relatives raise a lot of children—just so long as that does not come out of one's own children's hides. The unmarried aunt who helps all her sisters and brothers raise their children is thus doing her own genes a favor. Commoner than unmarried aunts, and equally useful evolutionarily, is the constant trading of favors that goes on within families: mutual babysitting, food sharing, resource loaning .

An individual should therefore sacrifice himself or herself for his or her children, if they are old enough not to need that individual's care. An individual should also theoretically be prepared to sacrifice self for a large set of brothers and cousins. One's sibling shares half one's genes, so, in an ideal Darwinian situation, a childless person who can save three siblings by sacrificing his or her life certainly should do it. In the real world, choices are seldom so simple, but people do regularly die for their families. The more closely related they are, the more they are ready to sacrifice time, effort, or even life for each other.

This allows us to speak of *kin selection,* a shorthand way of saying that kin can often maximize everyone's Darwinian fitness by sticking together and helping with the total gene pool.

Yet, people also regularly sacrifice themselves for perfect strangers, and even for abstractions like Religion and The Flag. They even jump into icy rivers to save strangers' pet dogs. Similarly, although stepparents are far more likely to abuse their stepchildren than biological parents are likely to abuse their young (Daly and Wilson 1999), the vast majority of stepparents and adopting parents take perfectly good care of their stepchildren. The "cruel stepmother" is common enough to be a stock figure of folktales, but she is not a majority case. Why are we so fond of adopting or stepparenting children to whom we are not close kin? Why do we usually treat them as well as we treat our genetic descendents?

Perhaps one reason (not very satisfying to a hard-core selectionist) is that we actually share over 99 percent of our genes with all our fellow humans; the human species is an exceptionally uniform one, with astonishingly little genetic variation. Geneticists calculate that we went through a genetic bottleneck about two hundred thousand years ago (give or take many thousands of years). This is often phrased as descent from a single "mitochondrial Eve" in southern Africa, but actually it means we descend from a small founder population that may have been very widely dispersed. In any case, the result is that we are so close to other humans that sacrificing oneself to save a lot of strangers is not at all foolish from the point of view of inclusive fitness.

Also, it is almost certain that, over time, many fairly sizable groups fought it out or competed, the more solidary being more successful. This might lead to a form of "group selection" (Sober and Wilson 1999). Yet, contrary to the impression one gets from some literature, out-competing and killing one's fellow humans is not always a good way of maximizing fitness. Nature is not particularly "red in tooth and claw," and "survival of the fittest" does not mean a dogfight. The trouble with fighting is that many of the fighters get killed. Moreover, while the tougher members of the species are out there fighting and dying, there are other, less tough individuals staying home "making love not war." It is pretty obvious who will leave all the descendents and thus win the selection sweepstakes.

Humans are not the most peaceful of animals, but do not deserve the frantic exaggeration of their violent nature in books with titles like *Demonic Males* (Wrangham and Peterson 1996; see devastating review by Dolhinow 1999). As a social species, we fight a lot but get along enough to form huge, complex social groups. This is not biologically surprising; as we have seen, many other omnivores manage it, from crows to wolves. Social behavior has to be beneficial to individuals, or more accurately to individual genes and genetic lines, to continue. This causes a paradox— why doesn't everyone cheat? There are many answers, including a supposed skill at detecting and stopping cheaters (see, e.g., Atran 2002; Cronk 1999). People are fair at "cheater detection," but con artists still make a good living. Suffice it to say that cheating stays uncommon enough to allow social life to exist, in crows as in humans.

A separate point, not directly relevant here but important for understanding, is that disease (infectious or degenerative) is, and probably always has been, the major cause of death in humans—especially children, who are thus removed from the breeding pool before they have a chance to pass their genes on. Thus it is the major selective force acting on humanity. This is far too often forgotten.

4

In all this, there lies a most valuable lesson. Recently, a host of authors, some competent, most not, have rushed to tell us that genes are destiny—that we are the slaves of our "selfish genes" (Dawkins 1976),[6] which force us to carry out countless highly specific behaviors. We have also heard that genetics, not parenting, determines child behavior (J. Harris 1996—who, in fairness, adds peer-group influence), and there are still a few racists maintaining long-disproved theories of biological difference. The media speaks of "fat genes" and such.

Nowhere are genes more genuinely determinative than in nutrition. Unlike "IQ" (whatever it is) and aggressive behavior, our body's needs for iron, vitamin B1, and lysine are really genetically given and tightly specified. Our tastes, too, are heavily influenced by genetics, as we shall see; fat and sugar are just the beginning.

Yet, individuals vary enormously in their needs (Williams 1956). Close relatives are closer in body chemistry, of course, but even newborn identical twins differ slightly, because of differences in the womb environment. Also, the human body, adaptable as always, can adjust to great differences in nutrient intake. This seems to be true, for instance, of vitamin C. In north China and south India, poor people had until recently no easily available sources of vitamin C, at least during winter, yet they survived (see Anderson 1990 for the Chinese case). They seem to have developed a very C-sparing physiology. (Many animals that cannot synthesize vitamin C still maintain appropriate levels of it in spite of eating very little of it; Hughes 2000:757). Conversely, devotees of "megadosing" with vitamin C seem not to be gaining much benefit from these higher doses (see summary by Hughes 2000:760); apparently the body adapts in that direction too. Similar, if less spectacular, adjustments are recorded for protein, fats, and other nutrients.

The same is more true for behavior. Smiles are basically genetically determined; they are derived from a widespread mammalian appeasement gesture. However, among humans, they can be called up or modified at will, giving us everything from the car salesman's forced grin to the Mona Lisa's cryptic expression. Aggression depends on situations and decisions about them. Intellectual ability, even insofar as genetically specified, does not determine one's survival, or even one's welfare; many a genius goes through life unnoticed, and many a fool has posed for a great mind. No one lives long without food. No one can choose to do without vitamin

B1. No cultural construction or social convention can decouple iron deficiency from anemia.

Yet, tight genetic entailment of nutritional needs has not stopped humans from varying enormously in their foodways. There are hundreds of different staples (from whale blubber to palm sugar), tens of thousands of eaten species, hundreds of thousands of recipes, billions of variants on them. Any good Ukrainian cook can make several variants of borsch, each of them able to supply most or all the nutrients we need—and that is only one dish in one country.

The problems with the genetic-determinist theories are simple.

First, and *critically important: genes do not specify final results; they guide development.* They are packets of information, and what they code is not behavior or even physical appearance, but the assembly of proteins. They guide the body's patient construction of enzymes and fibers and neurohumors from stray bits of carbohydrate and amino acid. They guide the assembling of molecules into cells and cells into final systems.[7]

Second, in humans, genes usually code for flexibility—for an ability to develop along alternative channels. They code for a body that can adapt to many environments, and a brain that can learn, plan, revise, and change. This is not some sort of mystical process. The genes actually code for specific types of growth and change in specific neurochemicals and neural linkages. When we have employed our genetically given ability to make the transmission of certain molecules easier and easier along one pathway, while harder and harder along another, we have learned something. This is no more wondrous, no more surprising, than the genes' coding for adaptability in vitamin C metabolism.

To be sure, there are certain behaviors that are very tightly specified. A human cannot keep his or her eyes open while sneezing, or stop breathing for more than a few minutes. One cannot stop one's heart at will. So the genes can do hard-wiring when they have to. However, it isn't the human way.

Our genes, then, specify broad contours of behavior. They make it easy for us to learn certain things—languages, faces, maps—while other things are much more difficult to learn. It is easier for a computer (one with no built-in biases) to multiply billions of million-digit numbers than for it to recognize a face after several years' worth of changes. Yet humans find the latter a trivial chore. Hunters and gatherers think nothing of following a complicated route for miles, after rain and vegetation growth have totally changed the appearance of the landscape.

Sharing may have evolved as a reproductive strategy. Giving out food has the useful spin-off that food can be, and often is, exchanged for sex. Of course, this is a sure way to make Darwinian selection go into overdrive. Among the Ache of Paraguay, the best hunters leave the most children. Many of those children are by women married to someone else. No one has stepped forward to replicate this study in the elite restaurants of Paris or Beverly Hills—but only because no one needs to.

A million years of this, and we find humans who are self-sacrificing, generous, and fond of starting soup kitchens and food banks.

Nowhere are we more prone to give than when there is food to share. I have walked in, as a perfect stranger, to countless hungry households in odd corners of the world, only to be offered the best in the house and welcome.

Our social feeding is not entirely unique. Wolves manage some degree of social feeding, though with a rigid dominance hierarchy. Chimpanzees eat socially, and even have some concept of "eating"—socially—versus mere "feeding" (de Waal 1996). Closest, perhaps, are the acorn woodpeckers studied by Walter Koenig (Koenig and Mumme 1987; Koenig, personal communication, 1997). Large groups of these birds cooperate in storing acorns and sharing them out. They also cooperate in raising each other's young, using the acorns as a back-up food resource for themselves. Like humans, they plan ahead and conserve, drilling pits far in advance and then storing acorns in them for up to years at a time. Like humans, they share with open-hearted generosity and cooperate to drive off thieves. Like humans, they are fond of competing noisily with each other over trivial social matters, such as who gets the favored perch. Koenig showed that this all arose from straightforward kin selection.

People dying of starvation tend to become selfish toward the very end. A harrowing account of this is given by Colin Turnbull in *The Mountain People* (1972). At first Turnbull thought the behavior of the Ik was cultural, but he later learned of Ancel Keyes' experiments with conscientious-objector volunteers during the Second World War, and other treatments, which show that people normally respond this way to extreme famine (C. Turnbull, personal communication, 1975).

The most thought-provoking thing here takes us back to genetics. It appears that our genes really do tell us to get selfish when things are desperate. In that case, it follows that they are telling us to be unselfish and generous the rest of the time. Surely, this would make old Ryokan laugh.

People are *really different*. The extreme selfish-gene theories of Dawkins, Wrangham, and others predict the behavior of mountain lions, eagles, and cheetahs, but cannot possibly predict the behavior of humans. No matter how hard you try, you cannot get a bunch of mountain lions to sit down at a table together and eat politely. The sociobiologists can explain why people often act like rats, but they cannot explain why people sometimes act like humans.

This being said, it is the individual or kin group that forages most successfully, not the one that fights most successfully, that is in the best position to raise the most children.

This perception gives us "optimal foraging theory." Individuals are expected to forage optimally, i.e., to find the most calories or (better) the most adequate overall diet for the least effort.

There have been countless tests of this theory among nonhuman animals, and—to make a long and fascinating story short—most of them forage more or less optimally. It is amazing to watch warblers or flycatchers adjusting their insect-hunting behavior to circumstances. They can take account of competition, of newly available resources, and of shortages. Even more amazing is the performance of some small wasps that lay their eggs on caterpillars, which the wasp larvae then slowly eat from within. The female wasp can assess the size of the caterpillar, calculate exactly how many larvae it will support, and then lay exactly that number of eggs—all female except one, so there will always be one and only one male per brood (Hannah Nadel, personal communication, 1982). If an animal with a microscopic brain can do that, obviously humans must be very good at the job. Other primates, too, are superb choosers of the best foods and the best routes to the best sources of the best foods (Milton 2000a, 2000b).

Indeed, hunters and gatherers do forage fairly optimally (Kelly 1995; Smith 1991; Smith and Winterhalder 1992). Given that they need, and prefer, fat, and that they have other pressing concerns (mates to keep, children to protect, lions to avoid . . .), they forage very efficiently indeed (cf. the important exchange on optimal foraging theory between Hawkes 1993 and Hill and Kaplan 1993). Close studies of surviving hunter-gatherer groups in remote environments, such as the Hadza and San of Africa and the Ache of Paraguay, reveal that actual foraging comes close to computer models of optimum regimes. By and large, they get the most calories for the least effort, and they get all the nutrients they need, making special provision for those that are not more or less automatically obtained by eating a balanced diet. (The conclusions are rendered somewhat tentative by the fact that all these peoples have, and have long had, extensive contact with agricultural groups, and get some weapons and/or food therefrom. The Ache were once agricultural themselves, and still trade with farmers.)

Fat is often the most problematic of these. The Ache of Paraguay, who are otherwise among the classic "optimal foragers," display an inordinate fondness for armadillos, largely because these animals are fat, and animal fats are not easy to come by in the Chaco. Recall that those successful armadillo hunters leave a disproportionate share of genes.

Eric Smith (1991) showed that the Inuit of Hudson Bay usually hunt in such a way that they expend minimal effort and resources for maximum yield of meat, except that they prefer sea mammals to fish, at least in part because the sea mammals are fat. They thus tend to miss fishing opportunities that would provide more calories (but not more fat) per unit of effort than the sea mammals. But there is more: reworking some of his data, one finds that the Inuit he studied could have done even better by staying home, making crafts for sale, and buying food with the money—not hunting at all. The lure of the hunt seems to have been "irrational" but compelling. Of course the store-bought food would not have been so nutritious, so perhaps the hunters were right to ignore it.

Hunters and gatherers can usually assume that anything they can find will be a reasonably balanced diet. They are foraging on nutrient-rich items: berries, small animals, nuts. Optimal foraging breaks down as agriculture becomes intensive. Plants make starch easily, and farmers find it easiest to grow starchy and low-nutrient foods like maize and potatoes. Less affluent rural residents may not be able to get much beyond such bulk starch staples. They may know how to eat to stay optimally nourished, but they can rarely afford the foodstuffs. Optimal foraging for sheer calories becomes more and more distant from, and even antithetical to, foraging for optimal nutrition.

The modern urbanite, foraging in the supermarket, is faced with the hardest choices of all. There are thousands of items. The cheap, easily prepared foods are exceedingly non-nutritious, while the nutritious foods are not particularly cheap and take some serious cooking. White bread and candy bars contrast with stew meat and broccoli.

There is another consequence of our primate heritage and hypertrophied brain: we are blessed and cursed with an insensate craving for sweets and fats. These are high-calorie, easily digestible foods that are most easily found in a rich patch following a burn. We seem especially fond of sweet-sour foods—which, in nature, would be ripe fruits and berries. We love animal fats and vegetable fats equally. It has been said, in defense of the "hunter" theory noted above, that humans "all like meat." They don't. Lean meat, such as game, is apt to be singularly tough and tasteless. Some do like it, but what we all like is fat. We love the taste of it, the feel of it, and above all the full, good sensation in the stomach when some high-energy lipids are down there. Thus, what passes for "meat" in American restaurants is basically fat, held together with an absolute minimum of protein fibers: bacon for breakfast, hamburger and hot dog for lunch, and prime rib roast, T-bone steak, or tenderloin for dinner.

The situation in the rest of the world is comparable: gourmet foods are fatty. Now that we know fatty meat is sometimes bad for us, many simply become vegetarian or near-vegetarian rather than face lean meat. Meanwhile, vegetable fat consumption has skyrocketed all over the world, and vies with fatty meat as an indicator of economic improvement. This is not new; our early hominid ancestors knew and relished vegetable fats in the form of nuts, seeds, and oily fruits such as the fruit of the African oil palm.

Our cravings for sweets and fats made sense when it motivated us to look for such things, as well as for berries (often rich in vitamin C), bone marrow (rich in minerals), and other highly nutritious items. Such desires have become less functional in modern times, when technology allowed refined sugar and vegetable oil to become the cheapest calorie sources. Today, our inherent fondnesses fit all too well with the logic of profit seeking.

5

So the human tendency to crave certain foods is biologically grounded.

So is the human ability to regulate intake, and individuals differ in their ability to control themselves. However, this does not mean that anyone is doomed by a "fatness gene" or saved by a "willpower gene." These myths are the darlings of the media, especially the mass media (see, e.g., Nash 2002, in *Time* magazine, for a typical account—paying lip service to behavior, and then settling in for several pages of gene blaming). Even journals that should know better, and write better, overemphasize the hard wiring (*Science,* for example; the special section of 7 February 2003, pp. 845–60, gives the same lip service to exercise and diet but focuses on genes and hormones). Recall that genes code for adaptations to environment, not usually for fixed responses. Genes give us a back brain full of desires and a front brain full of abilities for rational planning. At best, we use the latter to balance, accommodate, and deal with the former. We figure out how to get what we want, at the least cost.

Predictably, humans differ enormously in their genetic equipment for metabolizing food. Efficient metabolizers turn food (especially carbohydrates) into fat with ease. This may cause them sorrow today, but it was the salvation of their ancestors. Such efficient metabolizers are disproportionately abundant among peoples with long, recently ended histories of seasonal hunger. By contrast, poor metabolizers stay healthy and thin today, but will starve if famine comes. Similarly, some people are naturally active and fidgety, some quiescent; culture and experience affect how these tendencies are expressed.

The desires—which also differ in strength from person to person—are for bulk calories, for fat, for sweet and sour-sweet, and for salt. These are obvious survival needs. The body detects them in a number of ways. Salt, for instance, is monitored by the hypothalamus (a tiny structure in the back brain). When blood levels fall below a certain point, the hypothalamus sends out messages that make salt taste good. Also, we tend to get used to a particular level of salt consumption; eat a lot, excrete a lot; eat little, conserve that little. Other needs are more complicated to monitor. Satiety—just the feeling of having enough—is so complex that no one has it quite figured out yet. Physical fullness of the gut, blood sugar levels, knowledge that one has eaten, and many other hard-to-compare indicators are all involved, and all are complex accommodations of genetics and past experience. Our craving for sourness, or possibly for a sour-sweet taste blend, is poorly understood. It is an adaptation that leads wild primates and human hunter-gatherers to seek out vitamin C sources. Among modern humans, it drives a fondness not only for vitamin C–rich foods but also for pickles, lemons, and soft drinks—none of these being particularly good vitamin C sources.

Chocolate is not an aphrodisiac, does not have miraculous power over premenstrual syndrome, and does not soothe. What it has is simply a formidable combination of fat, sweetness, flavor, and stimulant (theobromine—a variant of the caffeine molecule).

Alcohol also has a wide appeal, but an uneven one. For complex reasons, some people reject it, many appreciate it in moderation, a few abuse it seriously. The latest fad is to maintain that alcoholism is genetically determined, but having every genetic predisposition in the book will not make an alcoholic out of a devout Muslim raised in a devoutly Muslim community; the individual may never see alcohol in his or her lifetime. Conversely, I have studied certain unfortunate communities where every adult abused alcohol, genes or no. Immigrant communities change their alcoholism rates over time to approximate their host communities' rates. Thus, again, genes are not destiny.

When it comes to new foods, our genes pull us in two directions (see chapter 7). Especially as children, humans are very diffident about trying new foods. The condition is known as "neophobia." However, unlike lab rats, which are notoriously neophobic animals, humans are also fond of trying new things. We love variety. The same old taste gets dull. This is why so many staple foods are bland and tasteless. One cannot get tired of something with no taste or texture to notice. By contrast, even salmon and lobster pall after a while; there are old records of workers protesting when these were served day after day.

Food processing firms have learned to take advantage of the human cravings for sugar, salt, and fat by putting enormous quantities of these in processed foods. A large percentage of modern food consists either of sugar in virtually pure form, or of some tasteless or near-tasteless starch base used as a carrier for fat and for sugar or salt (cf. Schlosser 2001). Such food is now appropriately called "junk food," a term translated into various languages (*comida chatarra* in Spanish, for example). No one has accurately defined this category, but in general it refers to overpriced snack food that is low in nutritional value and high in sugar and/or fat. Candy, chips, pretzels, cakes, and cookies afford obvious examples. Ronald Reagan's administration in the 1980s was properly censured for promoting ketchup as a "vegetable" for school lunches; ketchup is sugar and vinegar, with purely token amounts of tomato and flavoring added. Close reading of the "ingredients" list on the label always shocks naïve buyers of frozen dinners, fancy breads, and other ready-made foods. The goods almost always turn out to have formidable amounts of salt, sugar, fat, and bulk starch, and astonishingly little else. Anything called fruit juice has to be real fruit juice, by United States law, but most buyers do not realize that "fruit punch," "nectar," "cocktail" and the like are basically sugar water; sometimes they contain some fruit juice, often they contain none at all. Thus does junk food subtly invade our homes, and thus do the giant corporations take advantage of human instincts.

All this makes it easier for people to grow obese. However, we have given food a very bad rap. The major problem for most obese people today is not overeating but underexercising.

In the United States, for instance, calorie consumption has dropped, over the last century, from an average of thirty-three hundred per adult American per day to a mere twenty-eight hundred. (This is actually a rather tricky figure; food "disappearance" is much higher than that, but involves a lot of plate waste. Twenty-eight hundred is an estimate.) Yet obesity has skyrocketed. A third of Americans are overweight. People weigh far more than they did in 1900. This is dangerous; heart disease, cancer, diabetes, and other degenerative conditions are much more common among the obese. According to a note on page 58 of the September 4, 2000, issue of *Time,* adult-onset diabetes, in particular, has tracked the rise of obesity, growing from 4.9 percent of the population to 6.5 percent in the 1990s, as obesity grew from 12 percent to 20 percent and overweight from 44 percent to 54 percent ("overweight" means over the life insurance tables' allowance for no-risk weight, "obesity" means fifty pounds over same). The situation in the rest of the world is comparable. Obesity has skyrocketed in Latin America too (Eberwine 2002) and, indeed, in most of the world—at least among urbanites (Nash 2003).

Politics is to blame as well as lack of exercise (Nestle 2002; Willett 2002). The food industry is powerful, influential, and well connected in the halls of education and government. It can push high-calorie, low-nutrient foods in schools and even via the U.S. Department of Agriculture.

Perception is involved. People tend to believe they eat better than they really do; they eat less fruit and vegetables and dairy products, more fatty and sugary snacks and other unhealthy items than they realize (Squires 2002).

In 1900 we were farmers and blue-collar workers; only the few idle rich had a chance to get fat. Thus fat was idealized, and such behemoths as Diamond Jim Brady and his love Diamond Lil were the targets of emulation. Today we are computer programmers, store clerks, secretaries. We drive instead of walking and turn on the gas instead of chopping wood. We are almost all urban, and much of our habitat is too crime ridden for walking. Only the rich can afford gym membership and mountaineering vacations. So obesity increases. The evidence is not all in, but I am convinced that lack of exercise, not genetics or excessive junk food, is the major culprit. Suing McDonald's is wrong-headed; better sue the

TV set, or the government that fails to provide safe places to walk and play.

Moreover, people idealize what is expensive and hard to get. In West Africa and Oceania, where inadequate and starchy food was the rule, fat is beautiful. In the modern city, thinness is idealized, and the bird-boned anorexic becomes the supermodel. Women (and some men) continue to subject themselves to diets so extreme that the body rebels. They often suffer serious malnutrition, particularly when the diet slides over into anorexia nervosa, a serious condition with its own characteristics and etiology.

This is no way to lose weight. The natural, human way is to eat a huge amount and exercise a huge amount. We evolved as hunter-gatherers, ranging ten or twenty miles a day, carrying food back to camp, and fighting off the odd lion or enraged buffalo. We should be eating more than thirty-five hundred calories a day, and working it off. We also evolved in a world in which fats, salt, and sugars were rare, and were valuable; now that they are all too common and cheap, we must be careful with them.

Therefore, if you are blessed with a fat reserve:

First, learn to love it, or at least some of it. Think of what will happen if famine strikes, or if you get seriously ill with a chronic disease. A threadlike supermodel in a famine is a dead supermodel. Let us be blunt: our standards of beauty are pathological and unsafe.

Second, cut out the junk calories. Read the labels on processed foods.

Third, eat well, and exercise to burn up any "excess" calories. Even in a jail cell, one can do weight lifting and gymnastics. New standards from the U.S. government encourage much more exercise, rather than calorie restriction, for all of us—an hour of exercise per day is recommended (National Academy of Sciences 2002).

Fourth, note that cravings for complex carbohydrates and for protein are weak at best. Whole-grain bread, lean meat, and above all beans and vegetables are the salvation and best recourse of the prudent eater. One does not overeat on these; one overeats when fats, salty foods, and sugars are on the table.

Food pyramids are well enough in their way but do not do the job; so far, they do not incorporate such major concerns as saturated vs. unsaturated fat, processed vs. unprocessed carbohydrates (white vs. whole-grain bread, and the like), or full fat vs. reduced-fat dairy products. Nor do they differentiate between really superior vegetables like broccoli and so-so vegetables like lettuce and potatoes. They do not provide adequate guides (partly because they have been worked over by the food industry; see Mestel 2000; also Nestle 2002 and Willett and Stampfer 2003). In general, food education campaigns have had their problems, not least because of the politics above mentioned (Nestle 2002; Willett 2002). The modern omnivore is best advised to eat as much like a hunter-gatherer as possible, and to exercise accordingly.

2

Human Nutritional Needs

1

Human needs are far more than physical requirements. Dan Jantzen, the distinguished biologist, has said that human needs are "food, shelter, and sex" (Jantzen 1998). If only it were that simple. Shelter by itself is no adequate way to stay warm; one needs fire, clothing, and materials for repair, at the very least. Sex is only the beginning of reproduction. Among humans, five minutes of sex leads to fifteen years or more of hard child-rearing work.

Food, likewise, is complicated. (For this and what follows, I have relied on Kiple and Ornelas 2000 and, especially, Shils et al. 1999; see these sources for more details). We do not need simply "food"; we need a vast range of nutrients. We also use food to provide feelings of security, control, communication, and nurturance.

The average "reference human" (a 72-kilogram [150-pound] adult), if active, needs about three thousand calories a day, as well as a large but variable amount of water. Around sixteen hundred of those calories go to support basal metabolic activities: heartbeat, digestion, and such, including those four hundred calories for the nervous system.

The rest go into activity. Some adults get by for long periods (famines or hungry seasons) on little more than the basic 1600.[1] Audrey Richards described people virtually hibernating during the dry season in the starved lands of interior Zambia (Richards 1939, 1948), and similar conditions existed in north China in winter in the bad old days. Metabolism slows, activity ceases; people lie down until food arrives. At the other extreme, lumberjacks in the old hand-logging days in the north woods needed five thousand to six thousand calories, and consumption of seventy-five hundred calories/day has been reported (though there was probably some waste going unnoticed). I recorded consumption of five thousand calories/day by fishermen dragging heavy nets in winter storms on the South China Sea. Chill temperatures as well as heavy activity force the body to burn more. Just as they can adapt to famine, humans can adapt to chronic cold by running up calorie consumption. They also adapt to high levels of food intake by using the food less efficiently or, perhaps, by harvesting vitamins from the intake and letting much of the rest go rather poorly digested.

Muscle uses thirty to fifty calories/pound for basal metabolic functions; fat uses only two. Thus, the more muscle you have, the thinner you can stay. Extreme dieting wastes muscle, and restored body weight after such loss often takes the form of fat.

Nervous, fidgeting people may use a few hundred calories/day more than tranquil people. Conversely, some people use fewer calories because they have notably more efficient metabolisms than others. In traditional societies they were lucky; they could survive while the others starved. In modern society they are unlucky; they get fat. They also, often, get diabetes. Adult-onset diabetes is often associated with highly efficient carbohydrate metabolism and high sugar intake. Alcoholism may be associated with this metabolic type.

Worldwide, most calories are from carbohydrates. In fact, outside of a few hunting societies of former times, almost all human groups get most of their calories from that source. (Many hunter-gatherer societies, and some postindustrial societies like that of the United States, get as many or more calories from fats and oils.) The great staples of world commerce, such as wheat, maize, potatoes, rice, and sugar, are all carbohydrates.[2]

Carbohydrates are needed, but apparently only in small amounts, though worldwide they are the overwhelmingly major source of calories. Complex carbohydrates (starches are the main ones humans can digest) are better for human bodies than are simple ones (sugars, and some very simple or highly refined starches).

Carbohydrates are carbon chains with the general formula CHO. The standard basic one that we use for ordinary metabolism is glucose, $C_6H_{12}O_6$. Some other simple sugars have the same empirical formula but different structure; fructose is one structural form (the levorotatory) of the same compound. (Glucose is the dextrorotatory; galactose is yet another variant). The human body converts fructose and galactose to glucose for metabolic purposes.

Short-chain compound sugars include sucrose—ordinary white sugar. It breaks easily into a molecule of glucose and a molecule of fructose. Maltose breaks into two glucose molecules.

Lactose is broken by digestion into glucose plus galactose. Human babies are born with the enzyme lactase, which performs this cleavage. However, most humans stop producing this enzyme around age six to ten. Thus most adult humans cannot digest lactose (Patterson 2000). Like other undigested sugars, it causes diarrhea and flatulence, and, in large quantities, outright sickness. Small amounts of milk are tolerated; more leads to indigestion. However, Europeans (especially north Europeans) and East Africans have depended on fresh milk so long that they have evolved the ability to keep producing lactase throughout life. Presumably, children without lactase did not thrive, as fresh dairy products became more and more vital as staple foods—though at least some humans can also adapt to high-milk diets by continuing to produce lactase when they would not otherwise have done so.

Outside of Europe and East Africa, most humans cannot eat fresh dairy foods. Even in Mediterranean Europe, most cannot; in East and Southeast Asia, virtually all cannot, even after long exposure. But they have learned to make microorganisms do the enzyme work. Fermenting milk into yogurt, cheese, and the like involves breakdown of lactose by *Lactobacillus* bacteria. Yogurt is generally made by *L. bulgaricus*. (Other *Lactobacillus* species give us salami, sauerkraut, and San Francisco sourdough bread.) Thanks to yogurt making and other processing, peoples in West and Central Asia and the Indian subcontinent depend on dairy foods, though only 10–20 percent of them can digest lactose (see Patterson 2000:1060).

Some Arctic-dwelling humans—as well as some birds, such as starlings—have lost the ability to produce sucrase, and thus cannot digest ordinary sugar (sucrose; see Draper 2000).

There are longer-chain sugars, mostly indigestible. Stachyose and raffinose, in beans, cause the indigestion and flatulence associated with beans, because we can't digest them.

Still longer chain carbohydrates (polysaccharides) are starches, and these we can digest, breaking them into glucose. Potato starch is particularly easy to digest, and thus can cause a "sugar rush."

Still longer chains include things like lignin and cellulose, indigestible to higher animals. Ruminant mammals, termites, and other such creatures have symbiotic microorganisms that do the digestive work.

Proteins are carbon-nitrogen structures. They are made up of chemically combined amino acids. An amino acid is a carbon atom to which are joined an $-NH_3$ basic ion; a $-COOH$ group; a hydrogen atom; and a more complex fourth blob, different in each amino acid. Compared to carbohydrates, they are difficult for plants to make, and difficult to digest.

Protein, per se, is not actually a physical need. What we need are eight of the amino acids that are the "building blocks" of proteins. Since amino acids do not often occur in nature except in the form of proteins, the term "protein" is used as shorthand for this requirement. The body makes the other fourteen or more amino acids it needs, and all its proteins, from the basic eight. Proteins, when eaten, are first broken down by digestion into the component amino acids, then reassembled in the cells of the body into whatever proteins we may need at the moment. The "reference human" needs about two ounces of protein a day, about what you get from six ounces of meat or a cup of beans. This "reference human," recall, is an active, large adult storing up supplies for times of stress. (Disease, burns, etc., may lead to mass drawdown of bodily protein supplies.)

The amino acids most commonly deficient in food are lysine and methionine. Grain is usually low in lysine, beans in methionine; a combination of the two (or use of a high-lysine grain like the Guatemalan corn mentioned above) provides better nutrition. It has long been noted that almost all cultures that have spent a long time at high population densities have figured out ways to combine beans and grains: *kichri* (bean-grain mixes) and *dal* (split lentils or beans) with rice in India, bean curd and rice in China, *pasta e fagioli* (pasta and bean soup) in Italy, tortillas and beans in Mexico, and so on. The value of protein to the body is only as great as the value of the most deficient amino acid. Liebig's Law of the Minimum applies here: If you need to build tissue and have everything except one nutrient, you can't build the tissue. The least adequately supplied nutrient sets the Liebig limit. Thus a person getting all her protein from grain may seem to be getting enough protein, but in fact may be getting only two-thirds as much as she needs.

The balance of amino acids in a given food is called the "protein score." The more perfect the balance of amino acids for human growth and tissue repair, the higher the score. This is a rather arbitrary measure, though the concept is clear enough. Various authorities score foods in different ways. Usually, human milk, being ideal for humans, is assigned a score of one hundred. Egg white runs around ninety-six. (Sometimes egg white, or even whole egg protein, is scored as the one hundred mark—in which case the whole table has to be redone.) Muscle meat runs around eighty-five. Grain and beans go around sixty-five to seventy-five; rice is rather high in score, soybeans are protein-rich but low in score. Potatoes have some of the best plant protein, scoring around seventy-five to eighty. (Different laboratories report different scores, and different potato varieties have different scores.) Grain-bean mixes run around seventy-five or even higher. The belief that vegetable proteins are "incomplete" is pure myth. The only really incomplete proteins (lacking one or more essential amino acids and thus scoring zero) that one meets in everyday life are gelatine and casein—both *animal* proteins.

Note that the protein score has nothing to do with the *amount* of protein in the food. Leaf protein is very high scoring, but most leaves have so little available protein that they are very poor sources for a hungry human, though alfalfa sprouts and other young leaves of protein-rich plants are better in this regard. Conversely, beans have low scores but are high enough in total protein to be widely called "the poor man's meat."

The body requires fats—or, more accurately, linoleic and linolenic acids. Usually, people need only trace amounts. The exceptions are women who are pregnant, or, above all, lactating. Human milk is quite fatty. Producing it thus requires fat in the diet and, usually, fat stores in the body. A woman's body is programmed to store about twenty pounds of fat during pregnancy; this is a reserve that is drawn on for lactation. In addition, a lactating woman needs to get about 7 percent (at least) of her calories directly from fat.

The popularity of animal foods cross-culturally is explained by desire for fat better than by the value of the protein (Michael Baksh, personal communication, 1983, 1992). People love fat. Left to themselves, they tend to select exceedingly high-fat diets. Arctic peoples may get 80 percent or more of their calories from fat, during good times. Perhaps it is only cost and habit that keep other cultures from joining Americans, Greeks, Inuit (Eskimos), and Northwest Coast Indians in using fat as a main staple. Animal fats are, of course, notoriously bad for the circulatory system—especially if one is male, genetically prone to make a lot of "bad cholesterol," and getting on in age.

Fats are made up of fatty acids, fats being esters ("salts" of the acids). These are CHO chains like carbohydrates, but with a -COOH tail at one end. Digestion breaks them down into the component ions, with lipase being the key enzyme. Fatty acids divide into saturated (all carbon atoms bonded to four other atoms), monounsaturated (one of the carbon atoms double bonded to one other carbon atom—so these atoms have only three atoms attached to them), and polyunsaturated (several of the carbon atoms double bonded). Saturated ones include lauric, palmitic, and myristic acids, which are considered bad for health (at least among sedentary persons), and stearic acid, which is not known to be implicated in health problems. Dairy foods and palm oils are high in the first three; beef is high in stearic, and thus less of a problem for the heart-disease candidate.

Monounsaturated fatty acids include oleic (the major one in olive oil) and several other fatty acids. Polyunsaturated ones are primarily linoleic, linolenic, and derivatives thereof. Linoleic is one of a class of closely related "omega-6 fatty acids" (two double-bonded carbon atoms). Linolenic and its relatives, "omega-3 fatty acids," are associated with very low heart disease rates. On the whole, polyunsaturates are found in plant foods, but omega-3's abound in the marine food chain, and thus in marine animal fats—being especially common in salmon, mackerel, herring, and some marine mammals. Most plant polyunsaturates are omega-6, but omega-3's are common in flaxseed, walnut, and evening primrose seed oils, among others. It appears that linoleic, linolenic, and probably arachidonic (another polyunsaturate) are necessary for humans (see Jones and Kubow 1999). Hunters and gatherers got more omega-3's than most of us do today, and thus had a better balance in their diets, presumably with good effects on health (Eaton et al. 2002).

Consumption of walnuts and similar nuts, and of marine animal fats, is associated with lower blood cholesterol and thus lower circulatory-system disease. The dangers of a high-fat diet are due to overconsumption of saturated fatty acids, and perhaps to a high ratio of linoleic to linolenic acid among the unsaturated ones. With more linolenic acid, protective and compensating mechanisms kick in. Heart disease rates are low among even the most assiduous of marine-animal-fat eaters—the Inuit, for example. Eating linolenic acid by itself apparently does not protect against heart disease; one must eat it and/or its metabolites in natural foods.

The ratio of "good cholesterol" (high-density lipids, or HDL) to "bad cholesterol" (low-density lipids) is also affected by this. It depends on total consumption of unsaturated fats as opposed to saturated fats and, rather surprisingly, carbohydrates. A high-carbohydrate diet is worse than a diet with appreciable saturated fat (Mensink et al. 2003). Moreover, one saturated fat has a virtuous role here: lauric acid, a short-chain fatty acid that is common in coconut oil and some other tropical vegetable oils, raises overall cholesterol, but largely by raising HDL. This may explain the anomalous heart health of those Polynesian islanders who consume many coconuts.

2

Vitamins are the next important class of nutrients. Vitamins are defined as complex chemical compounds that must be eaten, but only in small amounts. The first to be discovered was vitamin B1, but the vitamins begin with A because it was the first to be scientifically described, analyzed, and named (by E. V. McCollum and associates, in 1913; see Ross 1999:305). Casimir Funk coined the term "vitamine" (with final "e") about the same time. Only later did scientists refine the concept (and the spelling), adding the B vitamins and then the rest.

Vitamin A, like many nutrients, is poisonous in overdose. Many deaths have occurred from self-medication with megadoses of vitamin A or from eating the livers of polar bears and other large arctic animals that concentrate huge amounts of vitamin A for the long polar night. Vitamin A (like iron, copper, arsenic, etc.) illustrates the value of the old Greek concept of moderation, and the worthlessness of the modern attitude that "if X is good, 10X is ten times as good."

Vitamin A is needed for general physiological functioning, and more specifically for seeing in dim light, since rhodopsin (the chemical in the rods of the eye) is made from vitamin A by a simple, direct metabolic change. Deficiency shows itself first in night blindness, a condition that impairs the lives of millions of people today. Deficiency in childhood can lead to permanent total blindness; therefore, charitable agencies such as the Helen Keller Foundation have taken a very active role in getting vitamin A to outlying regions—often by encouraging the raising of carotene-rich foods. Vitamin A is not usually eaten, however; we get most of our vitamin A from carotene, especially beta-carotene. Another simple change turns it to vitamin A in the body. Carotene is abundant in carrots, of course—and in other bright orange or deep green foods: orange sweet potatoes, red peppers, leaf vegetables, etc. (The orange of oranges and the red of beets are not from carotenes.) There are actually several carotenes, beta-carotene being the main feedstock for vitamin A. Yellow maize has some, but other grains don't. Carotenes and some chemical relatives appear to protect against cancer; at least, consumption of carotene-rich foods is associated with low cancer incidence, but consumption of large amounts of beta-carotene and vitamin A, by themselves, is not.

Vitamin A itself occurs mainly in liver, also in some other organ meats and in milk, and to a small extent in meat. Vitamin A deficiency is especially common in areas where rapid modernization has led to a change in diet, with store-bought foods replacing traditional fruits and vegetables, or in areas where sheer poverty forces people to depend on starch staples. Vitamin A is fat soluble, and eating it without any fat means that the eater does not digest it—it is excreted unused. This is a problem for some poverty areas where carotene-rich foods are common enough but fats are rare. It used to be a problem for people taking vitamin pills, but now the A is bonded to a fatty acid in the pills.

B vitamins are a series of chemically related water-soluble vitamins. They are necessary to the whole body, but lack of them tends to show up first in nervous system functioning.

B1 (thiamine) is common in most foods, but much of it is lost when grain is milled. Thus beri-beri (thiamine deficiency, leading to neurological damage that typically is characterized by paralysis of the feet) is a disease of polished rice and white flour. Flour is usually sold enriched today, with the major B vitamins put back in, but this is not universal. Enriched rice is, unfortunately, not the rule worldwide. Polished rice has only about half the thiamine of whole-grain rice; this has been a major problem in many rice-dependent areas. A fair account of beri-beri is found in the *Shang Han Lun,* a Chinese text of the second century AD (though its final form was not set until perhaps 500 AD); the book advises curing it by eating fresh, varied foods (Chang 1981).

B2 (riboflavin) is common in the same foods as other B vitamins, and rather rarely deficient by itself. If it is deficient, the other B vitamins are too, and probably several other nutrients. Thus it may be passed over in silence here.

B3 (niacin), by contrast, is one of the world's most serious vitamin problems. It is rather widespread in foods, but is often milled out like thiamine (though to a less serious degree). The real problem is that it is chemically quite active as a base. It reacts with strong acids in foods (such as oxalic acid) to form compounds that human beings cannot digest. The worst problem comes when the diet is rich in phytic acid, a strong acid found commonly in seed coatings and husks and in many leaves, especially where phosphorus is abundant in the soil. (The plants use the acid to store phosphorus. See Weaver and Heaney 1999, esp. p. 147.) The phytate radical of the acid bonds with the niacin. This is classically a problem with maize eaters, because corn is low in niacin and high in phytate. Avitaminosis B3, known as *pellagra,* is thus classically called "a plague of corn." It was common in the old South, in Italy, in Romania, and elsewhere. It is a serious danger in Africa and north China today, as maize becomes more important due to its high yields. One of the most unpleasant conditions imaginable, it is characterized by the "four D's": diarrhea, dermatitis, dementia, and death. Agonizing pain often accompanies the mental deterioration.

The Mexican Indians found a trick that saved the pre-Columbian world from pellagra. They boiled maize with lime (calcium oxide, not the citrus fruit) to soften its hard kernels. This boiling process produces the familiar *nixtamal* of Latin America. The lime, of course, reacts with the acid and neutralizes it, saving the niacin and minerals (Katz et al. 1974). In other areas, including the pre-Columbian and post-Columbian South of what is now the United States, wood ashes were used with the same effect. Lye in the ashes neutralized the phytate.

Hard maize kernels had been selected, in turn, as a protection from weevils. In the American Southwest, weevils were not a major problem, so the Indians grew softer corn. This meant they were less prone to process the maize, though the Zuni did process it with alkali from alkaline springs, and other groups used wood ashes. Nutritional deficiencies had much to do with the fall of the great pueblos of the twelfth and thirteenth centuries. Some of these deficiencies may have been due to overmuch phytate in the maize, though there were also sheer shortages of food, as drought impacted an overused ecosystem.

In more recent times, maize meal in Mexico has sometimes not been lime treated, resulting not only in inferior tortillas but also in a resurgence of vitamin and mineral deficiency. I was told in Yucatan that this happened in particular when U.S. maize meal was imported or used in food aid. Today, the major Mexican food purveyors are careful to use lime in processing their corn meal.

Not only maize but also wheat and soybeans, as well as many other seed foods, are rich in phytate. Thus, people in areas where these are important foods can only flourish if they have processing techniques that destroy the phytate. Leavening in bread does this. Yeasts metabolize the stuff and destroy it, so yeast-raised whole-grain wheat bread has half (or less) of the phytate of unleavened bread. Unleavened whole-grain bread is also associated with metal deficiencies, including zinc deficiency in Iraq, for the same reason: phytate takes up active metal ions. Making soybeans into tofu (bean curd), soy sauce, miso, etc., gets rid of the phytate. Historically, soybeans did not become an important food till such processing technologies were established, since the Chinese realized they were nutritionally inferior (before processing). Soybeans have other serious problems (iodine-bonding chemicals, etc.) that are also reduced or eliminated by processing.

B6, B12, and other minor B vitamins are rarely deficient in diets. An exception is folic acid, a B vitamin necessary in large quantities for fetal development. As its name suggests, it is found abundantly in leaves, but it is also found in other fresh foods. It is thus common in natural foods. However, life on a modern processed diet often leads to deficiency, which in turn can lead to defects in neural-tube development in the fetus, as well as other problems for all ages (Herbert 1999). It is estimated that as many as a third of the pregnant women in the world are deficient in folic acid, though one serving of relatively vitamin-rich fruit or vegetables provides enough (Herbert 1999:444). Folic acid has become a major concern of maternal- and child-health workers and advocates, and is being widely distributed. My wife Barbara, a maternal- and child-health specialist, proselytizes for it wherever she goes.

B12 is necessary for iron metabolism, and lack of it causes anemia. This vitamin, more technically known as cyanocobalamine, is deficient in extreme vegetarians, since it is not found in true vegetable foods. It is, however, found in fungi, especially yeasts. Brewer's yeast is the richest source (though there is a controversy on how available the B12 in yeast is to human digestion). Vegetarians have learned to sprinkle it on their food, or—in other cultures—to use various fermented products rich in yeast, such as soy sauce, south India's sourdough foods, and—best of all—beer. Old-time beer was not strained and clarified, as it is now; such processing eliminates the yeast. I have had rice beer in Malaysia that had to be eaten with a spoon. The rice mash was full of yeast.

Vitamin C is a special problem for higher primates. Most other organisms make their own, metabolically. (Guinea pigs are among the few others that do not, which is one reason they are so popular as lab animals in nutrition studies.) The ability to make vitamin C was probably lost because we were eating fruit and leaves, and primates who wasted metabolic effort doing unnecessary vitamin making left slightly fewer descendents. In any case, the body uses up vitamin C stores fairly rapidly: in a few weeks or months. The result, if no further vitamin C is taken in, is scurvy—once one of the most dreaded of all conditions, and a virtually inevitable corollary of long residence on shipboard or in jail. Long winters led to scurvy in the days before modern transport made fresh food available. Vitamin C being necessary to all bodily processes, scurvy is really a breakdown of the whole bodily machine. Skin deteriorates; rashes,

Vegetable seller, India. Small-scale marketing remains a desperate need for people, especially women, around the world. *Photo by Barbara Anderson, 1997*

dry flakiness, and eventually fissures and scaling patches develop. Wounds and illnesses don't heal. Teeth loosen; gums deteriorate and develop painful sores.[3] A very painful death eventually supervenes.

The main sources of vitamin C are fresh plant materials. Those with the highest levels include the acerola or Barbados cherry, the lemon guava, green and red peppers, and certain other fruits. Rose hips from *Rosa rugosa* are extremely high, but most other rose hips are not particularly rich in C. Grain and other dry foods are lacking in vitamin C. White potatoes are the only important starch staple that has it. Meat has a little in the blood (but not in the actual muscle tissue), and organ meats (especially liver) can be high in vitamin C, but an animal diet is usually not an adequate source. Arctic peoples eat stomach and intestinal contents of animals such as reindeer, and so survive.

Vitamin C is easily destroyed by oxidation, dissolved by water, and otherwise wiped out, so it is lost when food is dried, heated, pickled, boiled with the water thrown away, or destructively processed. Thus, people must have access to fresh foods. Before James Lind popularized the use of lime juice to prevent scurvy, in the eighteenth century, ships often lost most of their crew on long voyages (Hughes 2000).

Vitamin D is necessary to calcium metabolism, and deficiency causes bone problems (rickets or osteomalacia). Sources include sea animal livers, D being a fat-soluble vitamin like A. It is normally manufactured by the skin in the presence of ultraviolet light, and thus is a dietary necessity only for people who live in foggy or long-night areas (e.g., the industrial slums of England in winter) or who live indoors all the time—especially dark-skinned people, since melanin blocks ultraviolet rays. Veiling and seclusion of women in extreme Muslim areas like Libya leads to vitamin D deficiency. (Incidentally, veiling and seclusion of women is *not* Koranic or religiously enjoined by Islam; it is a habit picked up from Christian communities in the early Islamic period.) Vitamin D deficiency—rickets in children, osteomalacia in adults—is characterized by weak bones. It has resurfaced as a problem in the United States, due to indoor lifestyles (Stokstad 2003).

Vitamin E is necessary to most body functions but is so common and is needed in such trace amounts that it is virtually never deficient in humans (despite the dishonest claims of certain "health" food promoters). Vitamin K is necessary to produce the chemical that allows blood to clot. It too is almost never deficient. Both these vitamins are fat soluble.

3

The human body needs at least fifteen mineral nutrients, but few are of broad anthropological interest. Things like vanadium and arsenic (the ultimate proof that many a necessity is poison in overdose) are needed in such small quantities (if at all) that they are picked up without anyone noticing.

As for the major mineral nutrients, phytic acid is again a problem. Being a fairly strong acid, it bonds tightly with the more chemically active metals. Thus iron, calcium, zinc, copper, manganese, magnesium, and some minor metal nutrients are rendered undigestible, and can even be pulled actively out of the body's preexisting stores.

Iron (Fairbanks 1999) is often deficient even in the absence of food phytate. It is necessary mainly for hemoglobin—the chemical in red blood cells that carries oxygen to the tissues—and deficiency causes anemia. Women are at particular risk, since menstruation almost doubles the

Faces of malnutrition and hope, Bangladesh. Malnourished woman and child in desperately resource-short area of Dhaka, Bangladesh. Behind her is a squash vine, trained up a shack built of salvaged boards and scraps. The vine promises much good food to come and suggests that even under the worst circumstances, people find creative ways to survive. Unfortunately, gardening here was inhibited by the landlord—he was afraid that it would establish de facto land-tenure rights and challenge his power. *Photo by E. N. Anderson, 1999*

iron requirement and pregnancy and childbirth triples it. Thus, iron supplements are routinely supplied to expecting mothers. In traditional societies, iron was once supplied by an omnivorous diet high in small animals, fish, leaves, and the like. The shift to grain agriculture and the rise of dense, impoverished populations have been devastating. Today, it is estimated that over 80 percent of women of child-bearing age in India are anemic. Indian spices are often high in iron—that is one reason for the spicy Indian diet: people early learned that spices prevent the weakness and pallor we now know as anemia. But most women in India have trouble affording much spice or, indeed, affording anything beyond minimal grain staples.

The main iron source for most people is vegetable tissue, with leaves being a rich source—but this is precisely the area where oxalic, phytic, and other acids are a problem. Even without them, iron is hard to digest unless already in animal tissues. Humans can absorb only a small percentage (as low as 2 percent) of the iron in vegetable sources. Thus meat and especially blood and liver are valuable. Billions of people manage to survive without much animal protein, but they tend to get anemia, especially if they are women of reproductive age.

Conversely, too much iron is also a bad thing. The level of supplementation needed by a woman for childbirth is dangerous for an old man. This has led to a major worldwide controversy over whether to begin iron supplementation of common foods. Currently, it is not done, and reproductive women need iron pills.

Another problematic active metal is calcium, necessary in enormous quantities for bone growth, but (like iron and most other metal nutrients) potentially dangerous in overdose. Calcium deficiency is one cause of osteoporosis—bone deterioration with age—which is common among the elderly, especially among women who have not exercised much and who did not build up good bone mass in youth. Calcium, too, is subject to blotting up by phytic acid, as noted above. Moreover, it must be in proper balance with magnesium, potassium, and phosphorus in the diet for proper nerve function and bone growth. This makes calcium nutrition very complex (Weaver and Heaney 1999; Seely 2000; Spencer 2000). Authorities can reach opposite conclusions. Seely (2000) thinks that ancestral humans ate little calcium and we are now eating too much. Spencer (2000) thinks the exact opposite. For the record, Spencer is correct—in the main—about the high-calcium diet of ancestral humans. But some early humans ate very little calcium. So both of them may be right, for different people at different times.

Salt—sodium chloride—is necessary to human life. Being concentrated in only a few spots (outside of the ocean), it is a major stimulus for trade. Many a traditional group was forced to produce all sorts of valuables in order to be able to obtain this vital need. Loss of salt often causes death among people working or traveling in the hot sun. This gave Death Valley its name; ironically, the explorers in question died among salt-rich plants, and any local indigenous person could have told them they could have saved their lives by browsing a bit. They didn't ask.

Salt is yet another nutrient that is dangerous in overdose. At least in genetically susceptible individuals (apparently a large percentage of humanity, and some other primates, are at least somewhat susceptible), it brings on high blood pressure (see Kotchen and Kotchen 1999).

Iodine is another problem, being deficient in many of the world's soils. Iodine is needed in only one of the body's chemicals: thyroxin. However, this is a critical compound; it is the hormone, secreted by the thyroid gland, that regulates growth—including brain growth. Marine products (sea salt, sea food, and especially seaweeds) are good sources, but people far from the sea often suffer. The dreadful effects of iodine shortage were superbly described by L. Greene (1977, 1980). He studied an area in the Andes where iodine was almost lacking in the soil. Cretinism—mental and physical deficiencies caused by iodine deficiency—seriously affected a third of the population. Many victims could at least herd sheep, but many could do nothing but sit on the floor. Greene was able to bring in iodized salt, ending the problem for those he could reach—but the problem is a worldwide one. Iodized salt has eliminated iodine deficiency in most areas, but junk food and processed food tend to use noniodized salt, and the problem is cropping up again.

4

Males and postmenopausal women are more at risk for heart disease than reproductive-age women, because estrogen is a protector from atherosclerosis. (The world's most fortunate few women can now opt for hormone replacement therapy after menopause, thus protecting themselves. This is not an option for the majority of women, still sunk in poverty and oppressed, even in the area of nutrition, by gender discrimination. Moreover, hormone replacement therapy now appears to have its own costs, and its value is debated.) Many plants, notably beans, contain estrogen-like chemicals, and these may lower the heart disease rate. High soybean consumption, for example, is associated with low heart disease incidence.

The danger of saturated fat was established in cross-cultural epidemiological research by Ancel Keys, back in the 1950s (Keys 1980). It has been confirmed in countless studies since. Initial fears that consumption of cholesterol would lead to too high a level of blood cholesterol have not been supported by evidence. Apparently the body handles cholesterol perfectly well; it is the saturated fats that are the problem. Much more needs to be learned about the whole question, including the roles of various types of unsaturated fats. Hydrogenated vegetable oil—margarine and the like—is significantly worse than any natural saturated fat. The "trans" fats created by hydrogenation seem genuinely damaging to the heart. Following this finding, American snack firms and fast-food chains have been sharply cutting back on their previously heavy use of hydrogenated oils (Allen 2002).

Some foods, like coconut, have almost exclusively saturated fatty acids. Others, like peanuts, have saturated, monounsaturated, and polyunsaturated oils in roughly equal amounts. Finally, such oils as safflower are almost entirely polyunsaturated. There is a weakly supported claim that polyunsaturated oils are better for the heart than monounsaturated oils. However, people who eat great amounts of monounsaturated oils tend to live long and stay healthy. This is most famously true of Mediterranean inhabitants; olive oil may be special. In Keys's studies, South Italians and Greeks—olive oil eaters—stayed heart-healthy much longer than North Italians, to say nothing of Dutch and Finns.

The Mediterranean diet (Albala 2000; Matalas 2001; Shils et al. 1999) is also rich in flavinoids (in particular, carotenes), now known to be associated with resistance to cancer and heart disease (Nijveldt et al. 2001). Red wine proved to be good for the heart and probably preventive of cancer, and indeed a very moderate consumption of alcohol (one ordinary drink a day) is associated with better health and longer life (Klatsky 2003).

Oat bran and other sources of soluble fiber, including beans, lower blood cholesterol; oat bran and beans together do better than either one separately. Oat bran became a fad a few years ago, but was added to muffins and cereal in such minute amounts that no one benefited much. You can buy bulk packaged oat bran and use it in bread, a pound of it to five or ten pounds of flour; it works fine. You can then eat enough of it to make a real difference.

There remains much to clear up about all this. Several friends of mine were involved in a study of Polynesian migrants to New Zealand (thanks to Tony Hooper, Ed Plummer, and Corinne Wood for the following information). Polynesians eat a lot of saturated fat because of their dependence on coconuts, which are actually the staple food of some islands. Yet they rarely get heart attacks back home. In New Zealand, they move toward a diet of white bread, potatoes, candy, pizza, and so on. Their

Fish from the coast, Hong Kong. The woman had bicycled from the coast to an inland village with these fish. Today, the transportation is better but the wonderful fresh fish have long succumbed to pollution and overfishing. *Photo by E. N. Anderson, 1966*

saturated fat consumption actually goes down dramatically, but their heart disease incidence goes up just as dramatically. There is something protective about the healthy, exercise-filled life in Polynesia, and something dangerous about the sedentary life abounding in refined foods.

At least some of the difference is fish. Fatty fish are rich in omega-3 fatty acids, which protect against cholesterol buildup. Polynesians eat a lot of fat fish: bonito, mackerel, scad. Similar fish protect Arctic and Northwest Coast Natives in North America. Seals, whales, salmon, smelts, and other common foods of the North are rich in omega-3 fats. Heart disease is rare. The basic omega-3 fatty acid, linolenic acid, makes little if any difference; other omega-3's seem to be the ones that count (see Conner 2001).

Other foods, including island vegetables and fruits, may also have a piece of the action. Factors at work could also include stress and lack of exercise in New Zealand. We really do not fully understand the whole picture at this time.

It now seems clear that cabbage-family greens (broccoli, brussels sprouts, turnip greens, and the like) reduce the incidence of cancer, and they may well reduce heart disease. Carotene, high fiber, and other chemicals (no one is sure which) are apparently involved. There is much to learn about the value of greens in general. Other foods will no doubt prove valuable. Yogurt has been rather equivocally implicated in lowered heart disease incidence. Walnut and pecan consumption reduces heart disease risk. One controlled study found that daily consumption of these nuts was accompanied by heart disease incidence a striking 50 percent lower than in comparable nonconsumers (Joan Sabate, personal communication, 2000; it is only fair to note that Dr. Sabate's study was supported, in part, by walnut growers—but I trust his objectivity and accuracy). Other nuts seem to have similar effects, from preliminary research (Joan Sabate, personal communication, 2000). Many other traditional and favored human foods probably work.

Another chunk of the difference is diabetes. Diabetes, untreated, usually brings about death from heart or kidney failure. Rapid change from the almost sugarless diet of Polynesia to the sweets-loving world of New Zealand is a shock to the system. Polynesians are rather susceptible, genetically, to Type II diabetes—as are Native Americans, Native Siberians, and many other traditional rural peoples of the world. James Neel long ago hypothesized that they carry a "thrifty genotype" that enables them to metabolize carbohydrates very efficiently. If this is the case—it is controversial—it is a fine adaptation to harsh surroundings with erratic food supplies, but a most unfortunate trait in the modern world, because it makes its bearers more vulnerable to diabetes and to alcoholism (Cudel 1994). The modern diet is rich in short-chain carbohydrates, ranging from sugar to alcohol to potato starch. Changing to such a diet has been accompanied by a skyrocketing incidence of diabetes in Mexico and in Hong Kong, and above all among Native American peoples.

The Akimel O'odham and Tohono O'odham (the peoples that European settlers called Pima and Papago) of Arizona were virtually free from diabetes until two generations ago. Before the twentieth century, they had lived on desert foods such as mesquite meal, wild greens, and cactus buds and fruits, and on traditional crops: maize, locally grown wheat, beans, squash, chiles. In the late nineteenth and early twentieth centuries, they lost most of their land and almost all the water needed to irrigate what land they kept. After World War II, they were progressively incorporated into the wider society of Arizona. This led to the expected dietary changes. Alcoholism, previously very rare, become more common. Sugar and white flour replaced traditional foods. Today most adults suffer from diabetes, and life expectancy is falling as the disease extracts its dreadful toll in heart and kidney failure and in necrosis. Return to traditional diet reverses much of this, but is difficult to effect (Cudel 1994).

Tohono O'odham in Mexico were slower to change, but are rapidly catching up. This may presage a vast disaster in Mexico, where most of the population has considerable Native American ancestry. Already, diabetes has become common among the more prosperous of the Maya of the Yucatan peninsula. It is spreading in other groups as well.

This introduces the subject of alcohol. Obviously, alcohol in large doses is a deadly poison. Death from alcohol poisoning is common. Death is also not infrequent among alcoholics forced to go "cold turkey"; withdrawal from physical addiction to alcohol is extremely harsh. (We are not talking about a "drinking problem" of two beers a night here; we are talking two pints of vodka a day.) Heavy drinking, even without frank addiction, is associated with heart disease, cancer (alcohol is quite carcinogenic), and much else. However, small amounts of red wine (a small glass per day, best taken with food) protect against heart disease, and apparently white wine and beer do too. This is not so much because of the alcohol as because of various tannins and other compounds. One would expect that what the British call "real" beer and the Americans call "microbrewery" beer is better in this regard than the ordinary tasteless, mass-produced brew, which has little in it beyond alcohol and a lot of water.

Proneness to cancer also varies with heredity, but it too is manipulable by diet (see Kroes and Weisburger 2000 for an overview). Antioxidant vitamins—vitamins A, C, and E—destroy many carcinogens, and are thus a good thing to eat in quantity. The cabbage family (once again) stars here. The phytoestrogens in beans protect against some cancers as well against heart disease. Tomatoes, cooked, appear to act against prostate cancer, mostly by keeping up the lycopene levels in the prostate; lycopene is concentrated in tomatoes and prostates, a rather odd pair. A number of other anticancer foods and drugs are claimed in the literature, with varying degrees of believability. The same foods seem able to prevent Alzheimer's disease, though more research on this matter is necessary.

This is a healthy sign; for a long time, it seemed that more and more foods were turning out to *cause* cancer. By the 1980s, people were saying, "Everything causes cancer," and thus were not bothering to avoid the

very few things that really are risks. No common foods are serious carcinogens in the class of tobacco and alcohol. Nitrosamines in poorly
salted fish appear to cause nasopharyngeal cancer (Anderson et al. 1978).
Nitrosamines in grilled meat, soy sauce, and other food products have
been implicated by association with various cancers, but do not appear to
pose much risk. One potentially very serious risk is aflatoxin in spoiled
peanuts and similar products. Some aflatoxins are extremely prone to
cause liver cancer. But no one eats spoiled peanuts voluntarily, and the
tiny amounts of aflatoxin in foods like peanut butter present minimal
risk.

There are tiny amounts of toxins in many common foods, such as
parsnips, arugula, and many herbs such as sage and comfrey. No one eats
a bushel of parsnips a day.

The extent of poisons in natural foods has been exaggerated in some
quarters—especially by people who argue in favor of using artificial additives or of allowing pollution, claiming that nature is full of poisons already. This argument is justified if the additives in question are safe (most
are), but as an argument against fighting real pollution, it does not make
the grade. First, it isn't true. People are usually good at detoxifying the
few really dangerous things they eat. Second, if the claim were true, it
would mean we should be *more* careful about pollution, not less. The
toxic load on our poor, suffering bodies would become insupportable.
The precautionary principle—"first, do no harm"—tells us we should
still minimize the risk. More to the point, we can voluntarily abstain from
parsnips (indeed, most of us do), but we usually have the pollution
dumped on us whether we want it or not (see also Fox 1997; Nestle
2002).

Long life is gained through eating a varied diet, rich in high-fiber vegetables—including those trivially "toxic" ones. Long life is not gained
through living in a polluted environment. Pesticides, hormones, and
artificial coloring and flavoring agents add little at best; we do not need
them in the food supply. Feeding antibiotics to livestock, for instance, has
led to the evolution of bacterial strains that resist a very wide spectrum of
antibiotics, and are therefore a huge danger to humans—already at risk
from a host of drug-resistant pathogens. McDonald's has now stopped
buying antibiotic-fed beef (Drexler 2003).

Mediterranean peoples live long, healthy lives, even under harsh circumstances. Keys (1980) tells of watching centenarian peasants on the island of Crete putting in a full day's hard work in the fields and coming

home cheerful. They lived on bread, yogurt, and olive oil. In general, the Mediterranean diet is based on heavy consumption of grains (often whole grains), fruits, and vegetables, with olive oil as the fat source and most animal protein coming from fish or yogurt. Cheese and meat are allowed in small quantities.

Some years ago I attended a meeting to plan and propose a similar East Asian diet, based on rice and wheat with a huge consumption of cabbage greens and soybeans, use of various unsaturated oils, and—again—fish as the main protein source; East Asians do not traditionally eat cheese or, indeed, any dairy products. One could easily concoct a Tohono O'odham diet, a Mexican peasant diet, a Polynesian diet, or a South Indian diet that would be similarly healthy. In fact, just about any diet from the traditional and poor parts of the world would do—except for the diets of the Central Asian steppe nomads and other pastoralists who formerly lived largely on milk and meat. Indeed, most traditional diets are notably healthy, having been perfected by countless generations living with at least occasional scarcity and want. DeVore and White (1978), among others, have advocated preservation of, or return to, traditional diets. This is "a consummation devoutly to be wished," as Shakespeare said in a very different context, but it is not always practical; the desert-dwelling Tohono O'odham are reviving their traditional diet, but other groups find themselves in city slums, eroded farmlands, or other environments where the chance is lost.

Carotene-rich vegetables, especially those of the cabbage family, are uniformly and consistently associated with longer life and lower incidence of heart disease and cancer. Berries, especially strawberries, raspberries, and blueberries, are less conclusively but quite suggestively linked. Most intriguing is a recent finding that brains age better in lab rats who eat blueberries (Azar 2001). Senile dementia is lessened and delayed. Of course, no one particularly wants brainier rats, but the hope is that this generalizes to humans. At worst, it provides a good excuse for eating blueberries.

Several areas of the world have been claimed as "long life" areas. Dan Georgakas, in a delightful book called *The Methuselah Factor* (1980), debunked several of the claims in question. The Hunza of northern Pakistan gained a reputation for health because no one saw sick people among them. Actually, they kept their sick indoors—the climate is fierce. When a medical doctor visited Hunza, he found as much sickness and early death as one would expect in that part of the world. The long-life claims of the Abkhazians, the people of Vilcabamba in Ecuador, and many other communities have been similarly debunked.

One may note, also, the recent attention paid to southwest France, the longest-lived part of the western world. The people of the area eat much butter, cheese, and paté, so there are claims that such foods are "not so bad." The truth, however, is that the southwest French lived hard lives when the current oldsters were growing up. Diet ran heavily to whole grains and fresh vegetables (Strang 1991). Exercise was inevitable for most, and came in the form of sixteen-hour days on the peasant farm. Only the richest could afford much meat or butter. It was under those harsh circumstances that they developed their toughness. We can predict that the current generation, raised on butter and cream, will live shorter lives for it.

Elie Metchnikoff, the elucidator of the immune system, noted that Bulgarians lived long, even in the bad old days when poverty and disease were rampant. He ascribed this to yogurt. He was partly right, but we now would add their fondness for fresh vegetables and fruits and their poverty-forced abstinence from meat, sugar, and cheese.

Japan is the longest-lived country in the world (along with Iceland), and its longest-lived people are found in interior mountain villages where exercise is forced on one by the terrain, and where the diet is (or recently was) largely unpolished rice, fresh vegetables, and soybeans. South China has some similar but slightly less longevous villages, notably among the Zhuang (Thai-speaking) peoples of Kwangsi.

3

More Needs Than One

> Were one to go round the world with the intention of giving a good
> supper to the righteous and a sound drubbing to the wicked, he
> would frequently be embarrassed in his choice, and would find that
> the merits of most men [and women] scarcely amount to the value
> of either.
>
> —David Hume, "Of the Immortality of the Soul"

Food may or may not be a source of more pleasure than sex, but it does
have one advantage: it is easier to study. Observing people's sex lives is
Not Done, at least in societies known to me. Americans love to talk ob-
sessively about their sex lives, but their honesty may lag well behind their
talkativeness, and one is not allowed to check by observation.

Food, by contrast, is normally a public matter. There are some societies, all very food-short ones, in which eating is a private or even secret
matter. In the vast majority of societies, however, eating is done in an
open, sociable fashion. One eats with family, friends, workmates, or the
general public. Cafés have large picture windows or, better still, tables
right out on the sidewalk. Feasts are wide-open, general-invitation affairs. Food markets and restaurants are open to the world, and are often
the centers of activity and life for the communities that support them.

Human needs go far beyond nutrition. Inevitably, people use food to
satisfy many needs beyond those for simple nutrients. Food is used to
communicate, to reassure, to affirm religious faith. Throwing tomatoes at
a politician signals something; taking holy communion signals something
very different.

For convenience, we may begin with a somewhat modified version of
Abraham Maslow's classic list of the broad classes of human needs.
Maslow (1970) began with the biological needs of all organisms, then

progressed to the "higher" needs that come with an enlarged brain and, ultimately, with the human condition. For lack of a better way to make sense out of the wellsprings of human motivation, beginning with life-and-death need groups is at least convenient. I follow Maslow, though I have rearranged and revised his table on the basis of information that has come out since 1970.

All needs are complex. We have seen, above, that the need for "food" is actually a whole set of needs for protein, carbohydrates, and almost three dozen other nutrients. Our other needs are equally broad and complex.

1. *Nutrition.* This has been covered above.

2. *Temperature regulation.* One normally thinks of "clothing and shelter" here. However, food is important, and usually the most important thing, in maintaining body temperature. It is the fuel we burn. Many groups exposed to rough weather adjust by developing high and fast metabolic activity so that they can burn food instead of having to wear layers of clothing. When I worked with the Nuu-chah-nulth of western Canada, I noticed that they ate a great deal but wore very light clothes when working in the almost permanent cold rain of their habitat. (This rain soaked everything, so heavier clothing would have been worse, not better.) Before the twentieth century, they used to drink straight whale oil by the cupful. They had adapted. Their bodies had learned, through experience, to burn more calories to keep warm.

We are all aware, on a more trivial level, of the value of hot drinks and cooling drinks. Hot soup on a cold day provides immediate body heat as well as calories to withstand the cold.

3. *Dealing with sickness.* Staying healthy is an obvious life-or-death need for any organism. Diet therapy is found commonly in all cultures. Chicken soup is a well-nigh universal recourse in case of colds. Mint tea is a highly effective stomach medicine, and almost everybody knows it.

Food-borne infections (notably *Salmonella,* but also *E. coli, Listeria,* and dozens of others) are abundant even in rich countries. The United States has about seventy-six million cases a year, including five thousand deaths (DeLauro 2003). According to a note on page 10 of the September 2003 issue of *The Nation's Health,* global food standards have been adopted but have not had time to have much effect.

4. Sleep and arousal. Humans need sleep. In fact, we need a whole cycle, from deep sleep to dreaming sleep to drowsy awaking to bright-eyed alertness.

Sleep is easily manipulated by food. For most of us, thankfully, a full meal or a glass of wine remain adequate, preferable to a sleeping pill.

Arousal is more interesting. We rarely think of it as a problem, yet an enormous percentage of international trade in foodstuffs—up to 15 percent of the value of international trade in foodstuffs, in past years—is in foods whose sole value is to wake us up: coffee, tea, cola, and other caffeine sources (Anderson 2003).

Perhaps best covered under this head is the concept of food as sheer "fun," but that takes us into a much more exotic realm, a realm not necessary for "life" but certainly necessary for "living": aesthetics.

5. Sex and reproduction. No foods actually work as aphrodisiacs (though "Spanish fly"—a cantharide beetle preparation that irritates the urethra and thus creates something between desire and discomfort—is used in Moroccan cooking). However, every culture has its body of lore about "aphrodisiac" foods, and countless books have been written about them (Benedik 2000). Most obvious candidates for (purely mythical) "aphrodisiac" value are the penes and testes of notoriously randy animals: bulls in Europe and America, seals and deer in East Asia, and so on. Everything that looks even slightly like testes (oysters . . .), penes (asparagus . . .), or female genitalia (peaches . . .) has been credited with "aphrodisiac" properties.

An ancient Mediterranean belief credits nut candy with such powers; nut lukum (a gelatinous candy) is now almost universally labeled "Turkish Viagra" in Turkish bazaars, and Morocco has a commodity sold to tourists as "Moroccan Viagra," made of honey with almonds and argan nut oil.

All of these foods can sometimes work if the eater believes strongly enough. Nothing is more responsive to the placebo effect than the sexual function. A gentleman observed selling tap water as "Viagra" in one Mexican city probably obtained a success rate not far behind the genuine article.

Infant and child nutrition is a far more complex and serious matter than aphrodisiasis. One has to worry about nursing infants, weaning them, and deciding how to feed them as they grow older.

Breastfeeding, in particular, has been a problem going far beyond nutrition. Mother's milk remains by far the best food for babies (on this and what follows, see Blackburn and Loper 1992; Cunningham et al. 1991; Naylor 1997; Quandt 2000; Rebar 1994; Wellstart 1992). Cow's milk is quite different in composition, having less sugar and less available iron. Human milk is rich in vitamin C, which humans must take in, but cow's milk has almost no vitamin C because calves synthesize their own. (Conversely, cow's milk has more B vitamins, because calves grow faster and need to build tissue systems quickly. And horse milk has more sugar, whale milk more fat, reindeer milk more protein . . . every mammal has the milk its own babies need.)

Even making up formulas with all these ingredients added does not solve the problem. Mother's milk and colostrum stimulate the formation of the immune system and include poorly understood substances that stimulate brain growth; a bottle-fed baby has a poorer immune response, and, all too often, a poorer brain than he or she might have had. Bottle babies are more prone than are breastfed ones to allergies as well as to disease. New discoveries about the benefits of breast milk have been coming out every year recently—too fast for formula manufacturers to track the new findings.

This problem becomes acute in areas where clean water is not available. A bottle made up from powdered milk or formula, with dirty, contaminated water, is the lot of many babies in the Third World—and even in parts of the United States. Such babies die at appalling rates.

The problems with bottle feeding have been recognized for decades but have not been adequately addressed, in spite of countless resolutions (e.g. World Health Organization 1994) and countless initiatives, such as the "baby-friendly hospital" initiative (Wellstart 1996).

The problems are two (Pelto 2000; Van Esterik 1989, 1992, 1997). First, aggressive marketing by formula-making companies such as Nestlé has led to a widespread belief that formula is "better" than, or at least as good as, breast milk. Reactions have included widespread boycotts and public criticism, but the problem is only partially solved. There are, of course, a few women who cannot nurse—but the vast majority of non-nursers have chosen not to, very often because they were manipulated by hospitals and formula makers.

Second, modern lifestyles are not baby friendly. In particular, employers, especially in the sweatshops of the Third World, have been extremely unwilling to make time for breastfeeding. (Many sweatshops do not even allow bathroom breaks except at lunchtime.) The employers get a few more minutes of work out of women employees, but society pays an appalling cost. More widespread if less damaging is the failure to provide quiet places and other public support for nursing. Many hospitals—significantly, those that receive large donations of materials from formula companies—still make it difficult for new mothers to nurse. There are even residual pockets of absurd puritanism. Not to go beyond my own experience: the manager of a bookstore near my home recently expelled a nursing mother for her "scandalous" behavior. The bookstore in question has a huge display of lurid and kinky pornography at child's-eye level.

As a result of all this, babies do not get optimal nutrition in the United States or most of the urban Third World. It is the most civilized and least civilized areas of the world that unite in treating mothers and babies decently; western Europe joins the surviving traditional rural societies (such as my Maya friends in Quintana Roo) in holding stalwartly to breastfeeding.

Of all the ways that human nutrition could be improved, promotion of breastfeeding is the most critical, the most urgent, and (as of this writing) probably the least pursued. (See further discussion of child feeding in chapter 9.)

6. Control needs. It has been shown (Anderson 1996; Langer 1983; Schulz 1976) that humans have a genuine biological need to feel in some control of their situation. Without it, they die. Humans *must* feel safe and secure, above all. This is not just a matter of physical safety. It is more important for people to feel accepted, approved, and socially grounded than to feel physically secure. Food is conspicuously important in demonstrating both types of security.

Anorexia nervosa, bulimia, and similar eating pathologies are apparently due in large part to problems with control of self and self-image (see e.g. Bordo 1997; Bruch 1978; Prescott 2000). Genetics and other factors may be involved in these dreadful conditions, which now affect millions of people—the vast majority of them young women. Standards of beauty, perfectionism, and an extreme overdevelopment of the control need combine to produce a life-threatening commitment to being thin. The extreme thinness that has been idealized in western cultures for the last thirty years is particularly dangerous to women's health; even if they do not get anorexia, they often starve themselves to the point of amenorrhea, and they have no fat reserves to draw on in case of sickness or emergency. Other societies have fatter ideals. It has been frequently noted that fatness is idealized in cultures that are short of food, while thinness is idealized where bulk calories are easier to find than good exercise facilities (Anderson 1988; Brown and Konner 1998). Many other factors, both genetic and environmental, clearly enter into the anorexia pattern; many books have been written about this issue, and the full explanation of the phenomenon is not clear.

However, contrary to some published claims, anorexia nervosa is not unknown in other cultures. It is widespread in the world today (Prescott 2000). It may have been common during the Middle Ages, judging from the harrowing tales of self-starvation in the lives of saints, but the cultural climate was different and the question remains open (Prescott 2000:1003).

More clear are literary descriptions. The great Chinese novel *The Story of the Stone* (Cao 1973–1986) describes in excruciating detail the progressive wasting away of the heroine, Lin Daiyu, who exhibits a perfect clinical picture of typical anorexia. Raised in luxury but overcontrolled and subjected to perfectionist expectations, the young woman refuses to eat and denies feeling hungry, as part of her painful rebellion against control and subjection. Other sources, including traditional Japanese and Russian literature, include less clear but still suggestive accounts.

Part of feeling in control is understanding one's situation. Learning, study, and scholarship are thus, in part, outgrowths of a basic need to know where one is in the world. Even lab rats, when introduced to a new environment, cannot rest till they have explored every part of it. Humans are far more complex. The endless quest for knowledge is motivated by many things—from need for food to the sheer pleasure of seeking—but it is fundamentally an outgrowth of the same urges to explore, understand, and control.

7. Social needs. Finally, the "highest," and by far the most serious, of human needs are the social needs. The need for human company is a life-or-death need for infants, not only because adults provide care but also because caregivers provide love. We know this from experiments with other primates but, more directly and poignantly, we know this from countless horrific stories of abuse and neglect in homes and orphanages. Children with their other needs satisfied die if they do not get loving, nurturant care. If they get only a small amount, they live, but are terribly damaged. The importance of society to adults needs no elaboration. Nor does the fact that food is important in sociability. What does require discussion are the complex ways in which food is manipulated in social contexts.

These interact with the control needs; hierarchies and social insecurity are outcomes of both. Food becomes a symbol of comfort, home, and love. Thus many an eating disorder is traced to a family problem related to lack of these. Psychologically devastated people very often overeat or starve themselves. At the other end of the scale, people find deep meaning (Frankl 1959, 1978) and what Maslow rather vaguely called "self-realization" in their work for family, friends, and others. Frankl shows that such meaning is vital to survival and health.

Sociability and autonomy conflict in us all, guaranteeing that humans will never be satisfied and will always have to make hard choices. Theories that focus on practice, dialogue, and negotiation have been applied to the business of eating (cf. Bourdieu 1977, 1990; de Certeau 1984; Heldke 1988; see also Curtin and Heldke 1992).

Food is thus not an end in itself, but a means to many ends. Food as fuel is a means to the goal of being able to survive and accomplish. Food as social facilitator is not an end in itself; the end goal is the social life that the food facilitates. Food as fun might be considered an end in itself, but the actual goal is not the food but a sensation of arousal, or sometimes a feeling of snobbish gourmetship.

With so many needs to satisfy, and so many foods that can be used, it is difficult indeed for any human to calculate a perfectly optimum foraging strategy. We simply don't have the brains to work it out, unless we are in a place where we have to eat everything we can bite (as among the Ache of Paraguay) or where there is nothing to eat except two or three things (potatoes and buttermilk in old Ireland). Moreover, we have to trade off control against sociability, pleasure against health, and much more—this in a constantly changing, shifting world.

So we approximate. Humans are born approximators, and are at their best when trying to balance off all those needs at once. They can find ways, almost without thinking, to handle all those wants and needs in a single meal.

Many food studies in recent years have been vitiated by extreme "social constructionism," the idea that society or culture "constructs" all that we believe and do. A corollary, sometimes traced, is that the powers-that-be in society construct what we do, inevitably making things worse for us (this is an exaggerated and oversimplified form of a point argued—with subtlety and convincing evidence—by Michel Foucault, e.g. 1970). Some writers appear to believe that society or culture determines every belief—that nutritional needs are socially constructed, not biological.

However, nutritional reality cannot be ignored. Moreover, individuals, not cultures, construct their own foodways, for their own reasons. What culture does is provide a wealth of knowledge and rules on which to build. Cultural information is merely one input into the construction process. Individual intention and agency (and, no doubt, some subconscious or unconscious factors too) determine actual food consumption.

That said, it is true that the powers-that-be not infrequently persuade or force people to eat particular things in particular ways. Foucault could have found as much evidence for this in foodways as he did in his studies of the history of sexuality. However, people can learn and resist. The result is a negotiation, not a stable and fixed "construction."

Recent studies from the strongly constructionist point of view have had one very good result: they have directed attention to the full complexity of cultural/social views of foods. If foods are symbols, used in communication, then one would expect to find the encoding and decoding of messages sent by food to be extremely complex and interesting. This is, indeed, what recent scholars do find.

4

The Senses
Taste, Smell, and the Adapted Mind

A walk with a dog can reveal much about scent preferences. While the human enjoys the scent of flowers, resins, and fresh foliage, the dog delights in seeking out garbage, carrion, and excrement. Indeed, the dog often perfumes itself with these substances, by rolling and rubbing its shoulders in them.

Explaining foodways may reasonably begin with explaining scent preferences. What we usually call "taste" is actually smell. The actual taste receptors on the tongue detect salt, sweet, bitter, and sour, as well as the taste of MSG (a taste called "umami"), but not other taste characteristics. Everything else—meatiness, rose and saffron flavors, scorched tastes, yeasty and fermented notes, and all—is processed by scent receptors in the nose. Food vapors ascend through the nasopharynx from mouth to nose, there to be analyzed. Thus, to understand food "taste," we have to understand smell.

The scent preferences of the dog are easily explained. Dogs are scavengers; they are attracted to the scent of their food. They are also acutely sensitive to the odors of other dogs. Pheromones in excreted materials are a major channel of canine communication.

The reasons for the human's preference are less clear. We know much more about the dog. Humans do not usually eat flowers, nor do they eat much foliage. Of course, humans also show sensitivity to, and appreciation of, the smells and tastes of typical human foods, but when humans wish to create a beautifully scented environment, they almost invariably fall back on floral or resinous smells. Moreover, the smells and tastes we favor in foods are an odd set. Spices, herbs, onions, garlic, chile peppers, and sharp condiments such as mustard have a worldwide popularity that runs far beyond their small contribution to human nutrition. (Incidentally, this chapter concentrates on food, because it is in a book about food, but everything said below goes for perfume as well. When all other animals want to smell each other's body scents and pheromones, humans almost universally prefer to smell flowers and resins on each other. The scents of perfume are all volatile oils, and the favorite ones, like the favorite flavors of spices and herbs, are usually intensely antiseptic.)

The fragrant substances that humans appreciate are almost all volatile oils. These are light molecules based on ring structures.[1] They evaporate easily, and hence are available to the nose. Most of them are found in plants, where they usually serve protective functions—repelling insects, killing bacteria, and the like. They do not correlate with edibility or poisonousness in plants. Humans like certain oils and resins that are described in English by adjectives such as "spicy," "minty," "piny," and "floral" (Gibbons 1986; Moncrief 1966; M. Stoddart 1990).

It is easy to tell apart the species of sage (*Salvia*), for instance, by smell, because each species has its own mix of the two dozen or so volatile oils that commonly perfume plants of this genus. Volatile oils—and, to a lesser extent, resins—are therefore the most efficient guides to use in sniffing one's way through the environment.

Most of the "tastes" we favor in foods are actually the scents of volatile oils. By contrast, the foods that actually give us most of our nutrition—starches, raw meat, leaves—evoke little scent response in humans. We like the tastes of grain, nuts, beans, and meat, but we are relatively insensitive to their smells in the natural, raw state. Fruit is the great exception—an exception easily explained by our primate heritage. We evolved from a long line of fruit eaters, all acutely attuned to the chemicals secreted by ripe fruit (Milton 1993). Pure carbohydrates, proteins, and fats are essentially tasteless and odorless to humans. Simple alcohols have a weakly detectable scent. Humans also react to a range of molecules associated with foods—but, typically, these are reactions to smells released or created during cooking (see McGee 1984, esp. 608–9), a process probably invented after humans had evolved to reasonably modern biological status. (Animals burned in wildfires do *not* smell like well-cooked meat. The skilled cooking that produces good smells almost certainly came late in the human story. Recent evidence of the use of fire by *Homo erectus* is highly equivocal [Balter 1995] and certainly does not prove careful, controlled cooking.)

In *The Adapted Mind* (1992), Barkow et al. argue that widespread and deeply felt preferences may be innate. We are a learning animal, and genetic mechanisms in higher primates determine learning systems rather than instincts (Barkow et al. 1992), but nothing can be learned unless the neurological capability is present.

Later in the same book, Profet argues for the evolutionary importance of taste (Profet 1992)—sweetness attracts us to fruit (cf. Mintz 1985); bitterness repels us from poisons. Morning sickness in pregnant women is, in Profet's theory, due to the need to reject anything that could harm the embryo. In addition, Orians and Heerwagen (1992) and Kaplan (1992) argue that human preferences for particular landscapes are indeed founded on instinct. In short, human preferences seem to have biological bases.

Even the *ability* of humans to detect particular volatile oils is of interest, and is certainly a genetically determined matter. Why should we have evolved, or retained, the ability to smell these items at all? As Richard Axel has recently written,

> around 1,000 genes encode 1,000 different odor receptors. . . . Given that mammalian DNA probably contains around 100,000 genes, this finding indicates that 1 percent of all our genes are [*sic*] devoted to the detection of odors, making this the largest gene family thus far identified in mammals. The enormous amount of genetic information devoted to smell perhaps reflects the significance of this sensory system for the survival and reproduction of most mammalian species. (Axel 1995:156)

It seems beyond possibility that such a huge genetic system would not be fine-tuned by natural selection.

Sociobiological and "adapted mind" explanations should, ideally, fulfill two conditions.

First, the behavior in question must be universal among human groups, or at least so widespread and ancient that diffusion is not a likely explanation for its worldwide presence.

Second, the behavior or trait in question should not be more parsimoniously accounted for by the operation of common sense. If everyday human rationality would lead to a given behavior, the burden of proof is on anyone advancing an innatist explanation. A very large range of sociobiological explanations, in particular, are in deep danger from Occam's razor. An intelligent primate can easily figure out social arrangements associated with mating, marrying, rearing young, and finding food. Invoking an evolutionarily complex genetic history for every human behavior is, at the very best, unnecessary. Presumably it is easier for a large-brained primate to change and fine-tune behavior through learning than through evolving fixed action patterns (under rigid genetic guidance) for all behavioral traits.

Many authors, notably Engen (1981), conclude that human preferences in scent are strictly learned. Even Engen, however, admits that musk may possibly have some form of innate appeal (Engen 1981:167, 1991:71).

However, recent research suggests strongly that there is an innate tendency (mechanism unspecified) for humans to find some scents attractive and others unattractive (Ehrlichman and Bastone 1992), and that this is evident even in infants (e.g. strawberry and clove being liked very early in life; Schmidt and Beauchamp 1992). It will probably never be possible to separate "nature" from "nurture" in many cases of smell preference (cf. Doty 1991; Kniep and Young 1931; Moncrief 1966), but, in general, it seems that humans dislike a range of toxic chemicals (many of them "aromatics" based on benzene ring structures), and it seems certain that humans have an innate liking for volatiles associated with fruit, flowers, foliage, and plant life in general.

Culture, however, certainly plays an enormous role in defining what smells "good" and what smells "bad." The question is not whether smell preferences are genetic or cultural, but how genetic ability and cultural preference interact. Taste preferences, like other bases of foodways, are a biocultural phenomenon. Biology sets the broad parameters; culture fine-tunes the actual patterns of behavior.

In fact, it appears that humanity's acute sensitivity to, and fondness for, these volatiles has a medical explanation.

Paul Sherman and Jennifer Billing (Billing and Sherman 1998; Sherman and Billing 1999) point out that common spices, herbs, chile, and garlic contain potent antimicrobial and antifungal chemicals. They surveyed world use of such compounds and found that they are most used in areas that have major problems with food spoilage—largely tropical lands, the hotter the spicier. From my own research, I can add that extra-tropical areas with a fondness for spices and "hot" foods are characterized by rural poverty and dense populations, major risk factors for foodborne diseases. So Sherman and Billing argue that people have learned over the millennia to use spices and other chemicals as preservatives and disinfectants. This argument is powerfully confirmed by the extremely widespread and important use of these and other volatile-oil-rich plants in traditional medicine (Etkin 1986, 1994).

Food and borders, Azrou, Morocco. Spices from
around the world in a country market. *Photo by
E. N. Anderson, 2000*

Among the most easily detected odors are the smells of mint (menthol
and related chemicals), thyme and its relatives (thymol and relatives), and
cinnamon (cinnamomeol), to say nothing of the well-known fragrances
of rose, lavender, nutmeg, vanilla, sagebrush, and many more. Humans
can smell these in very low concentrations.

The taste for spicy, herbal, and floral volatile oils is widespread. Billing
and Sherman (1998; Sherman and Billing 1999; Sherman and Flaxman
2001) provide full surveys and documentation (see also Engen 1981;
Moncrief 1966; Serby and Chobor 1992, passim, esp. Ehrlichman and
Bastone 1992). The same basic list seems to provide the basic food flavor-

ings and perfumes in every culture that uses such things. The almost obsessive craving of historic Europe for spices (see, for example, Toussaint-Samat 1992) is not unique; Africa (especially North Africa), west Asia, India, China, Japan, and other regions also imported, and import, spices at great expense. The pre-Columbian civilizations of Mexico independently developed a large spice trade, involving allspice, chiles, chocolate, vanilla, epazote, and dozens of other aromatic plants. Chocolate, like coffee, may owe much of its popularity to its caffeine (and theophylline) content, but it is significant that chocolate is fermented (and coffee is roasted) to bring out the flavor. Fermentation and roasting change the chemistry of the volatile oils, making them appealing to the human nose. The explosive success of chocolate around the world certainly owes something to its taste.

Sherman and Flaxman (2001) indicate that onions, garlic, and allspice are almost totally destructive to food-poisoning bacteria, while many other spices, including chiles, are not far behind. They also point out that meat dishes are almost always more highly spiced than nonmeat ones; meat is more prone to incubate dangerous bacteria than vegetables are.

Many or most of the volatiles in question are bacteriocidal or at least bacteriostatic. Others act against fungi, protozoa, and internal and external parasites (Claus 1956; Grieve 1931; Lewis and Elvin-Lewis 1976; Trease and Evans 1978; Tyler et al. 1981). Among the most potent is thymol, still widely used as an antiseptic. Lavender owes its place in the linen closet to its value as a repellent of moths and other insects. Menthol, cinnamon oil, nutmeg oil, rose oil, eucalyptus oil, citrus oils, citronella oil, and many others have been used in antiseptic and insect-repellent preparations. Sage, for instance, has been used in antiseptic medical preparations (Claus 1956:282) as well as folk medicine. Sandalwood oil, cedar oil, juniper oil, and cade oil, all from popular incense or pleasant-smoke plants, are also effective antiseptics that were widely used in medical practice until recently.[2] The allyl sulfates that give distinctive flavors to onions and garlic are also bacteriostatic and insect repellent, and are almost universally liked. There appears to be no more widely used flavoring than onions. Many volatile oils, such as citronella oil, are insect repellent or insecticidal. Peppermint oil, for instance, is intensely insecticidal, killing 85 percent of mosquito larvae in one set of trials ("Minty Insecticides" 2000). Marr and Tang (1992) have shown that *Zanthoxylum*, a genus whose species are very widely used for flavoring and spicing in East and Southeast Asia and the New World, contains powerful insecticides. Among these are anethole and caryophyllene, both intensely aromatic volatiles found in several other widely liked spices and herbs. In fact, they take their names from their occurrence in dill and clove, respectively.

Many volatiles have stimulant and digestive activity in humans. According to my personal observation (and Grieve 1931), mint is used throughout the world for stomach aches; this is because of the volatile oils it contains, which have carminative, stimulant, and antiseptic properties (Claus 1956:278–79; Tyler et al. 1981:116–21; "carminative" refers to digestive aids that combat flatulence). Menthol, the most obvious ingredient in the mints, is antiseptic and antipruritic (Tyler et al. 1981:120–21). Cinnamon, cardamom, fennel seeds, and many related spices are widely eaten for the carminative and digestive effects of their volatile oils (Grieve 1931; Lewis and Elvin-Lewis 1976; Stobart 1970). Most of the volatiles, especially those of spices, have rubefacient (reddening, i.e., circulation-stimulating) and cleansing effects on the skin. An example is carvone, whose D- and L- forms smell like caraway and spearmint, respectively (Engen 1981:6).

Sherman and Flaxman (2001) have extended Profet's argument that pregnant women with morning sickness frequently avoid spicy food. Morning sickness is widely held to be a protective mechanism, causing women to reject possibly toxic or teratogenic chemicals in foods. Spices are strong stuff, and could be dangerous. Proof is not at hand, however.

Primates appear to use aromatic plants in a "medical" fashion. Chimpanzees have been observed to seek out and feed on herbs known to have medical properties but no significant nutritional value (Baker 1995; Wrangham and Goodale 1989). Mary Baker, in her field studies of *Cebus capucinus* monkeys, has made extensive observations of use by these animals of citrus leaves and fruit, and other intensely aromatic leaves (the genera *Citrus, Clematis, Piper,* and *Sloanea* are used; Baker 1995). Capuchins crush the leaves and rub themselves thoroughly with them. Since citrus oils have some bacteriostatic and insecticidal action, it is very possible that the ultimate purpose of this behavior is to combat fleas, skin diseases, or the like. Other monkeys have been observed using related species, and even lemon-flavored candy (Baker 1995:7). Humans have learned to use many of these leaves for the same purpose.

In this realm of self-care, the human animal has more problems than the monkeys do. Thin body hair, long head hair, and copious perspiration form an intractable combination. Moreover, humans are unable to lick or chew many parts of their bodies, and cannot even scratch some parts. This is an effect of upright posture and relatively inflexible spine. All of these factors lead to a particularly pressing need for grooming and for use of substances that discourage bacteria and insects.

The olfactory center lies deep in the lower brain. It is ancient in structure and function. It is richly connected to the limbic system, the wellspring of mood and emotionality and a key structure in memory processing. Thus, familiar smells evoke remembered moods in a peculiarly powerful way (Engen 1988; Gibbons 1986; Lawless 1991; Moncrief 1966; Rouby 2002; Serby and Chobor 1992, passim; Stevenson and Boakes 2003; D. Stoddart 1988; M. Stoddart 1990). The scent of madeleines dipped in tea evoked the memories that led Proust to write *A la recherche du temps perdu* (see discussion in Engen 1988, 1991). Stevenson and Boakes (2003) have shown that smell and memory are very closely connected, neurologically and experientially, and have developed a highly sophisticated model of how this works.

Scent was once thought to operate by a "lock and key" system. Certain molecules were said to fit (like keys) into certain molecular receptors (the locks) at the ends of highly specialized nerves in the nasal passages. The truth is now known to be more complex. Molecules are carried into receptor cells by specialized proteins. Particular populations of neurons respond to particular chemicals. The experience of scent emerges from the response of these neurons; their interaction with each other; and the response of the brain to the highly complex message they send (Anholt 1992). "Trained persons can distinguish among at least 10,000 odors upon presentation out of context, while for some experts (e.g., perfumers) this number can be as high as 100,000" (Chobor 1992:356).

Mice exposed through early life to particular chemicals greatly increase their ability to smell these (Wang et al. 1993), due to sensitization of neural pathways or to actual neuronal growth. The same is almost certainly true of humans.

The olfactory system is sensitive to certain chemicals and not to others.[3] Moreover, among those it can detect, it is far more sensitive to some than to others. This ability has clearly evolved, and clearly been subjected to natural selection. Animals have widely differing smell capabilities, and these can usually be correlated with their feeding habits. Birds, for instance, are not usually well equipped in this regard, but turkey vultures (*Cathartes aura*) are very sensitive to carrion smells (McCartney 1968:95; Stager 1964 and personal communication, 1957).

Sheepdogs have at least twenty times as many scent receptors as humans do (Engen 1981:20–21). Syrotuck claims that various dog breeds have anywhere from twenty-five to forty-four times as many smell receptors as humans (Syrotuck 1971:13). There is some evidence that humans can smell more things than this implies, and that there is actual repression of scent awareness at higher levels of the human brain. Certain pathological conditions, including adrenal cortical insufficiency, may release the human potential in this regard, allowing affected individuals to live in a doglike world of scents (Henkin 1967; Sacks 1987:156–60; these observations need to be replicated).

Humans can detect extremely low concentrations of butyl mercaptan, a chemical occurring in rancid butter, rotting ginkgo fruit, and other putrefying fatty substances (Engen 1981:4). Sensitivity to butyl mercaptan is a full four orders of magnitude greater than sensitivity to ripe fruit scents (Cain et al. 1992:287). Sensitivity to chemically related compounds associated with spoilage is almost equally high. Most of these smells are perceived as "bad" by adult humans in most cultures. However, experimental and observational data indicate that humans do not instinctively react one way or another to these smells; disgust must be learned (Angyal 1941; P. Rozin 1987, 1988; P. Rozin and Fallon 1981). Humans may have evolved as scavengers (Blumenschine and Cavallo 1992), and thus may once have found such smells delightful. Indeed, "high" game and cheese in Europe, "stinking beancurd" in China, and fermented fish sauces in Southeast Asia are culturally approved. The same smell can be experienced as disgusting if experimental subjects are told the smell comes from decay or feces, attractive if they are told it comes from cheese (Ehrlichman and Bastone 1992).

Learning, of course, greatly influences scent and taste preference (P. Rozin 1982, 1987, 1988; P. Rozin et al. 1986; Rozin and Fallon 1981, 1987; Rozin and Schiller 1980).[4] Even the attractive scent of bacon, noted above, owes more to volatiles in wood smoke (a preservative) than to the pork itself. Many of our most favored food smells (such as frying bacon, fresh bread, and wine) do not occur in nature. Most of human evolution occurred before bacon curing and yeast fermentation were invented or controlled. However, cultural learning leads to highly culture-limited appeal, such as local tastes for particular regional plant foods, or highly localized cultural fondnesses for cheese, fish sauce, pickled cabbage, and hung game. According to research that I have not yet published, these fermented foods are popular only in areas that had to process foods in these ways in order to store them. It is difficult to explain the worldwide appeal of spices and floral scents by recourse to cultural learning.

Several explanations for our affection for herbs and spices do not stand up under investigation.

The notion that spices are used to disguise the flavor of rotten food has long been disproved (see e.g. Billing and Sherman 1998; McGee 1984; Toussaint-Samat 1992). Spices cost their weight in gold in early Renaissance Europe; those who bought them could certainly afford fresh food. In any case, as every cook knows, spices *bring out* the flavors of foods.

Our smell preferences could be seen as a holdover from prehistoric times—a "vestige" in the nineteenth-century sense. This explanation is almost certainly wrong. While primate relatives of humans do indeed feed heavily on flowers, fruits, and leaves, they are not reported to prefer the highly aromatic ones. Often, indeed, the aromatic chemical is associated with toughness and inedibility or with toxins in the plant. Moreover, "vestiges" theory is now widely discredited. Humans diverged from the lower primates many millions of years ago. Our nearest primate relatives, the chimpanzees, depend on leaves, fruits, and meat, not flowers and gums. It would be astonishing indeed if sensory evolution had stood still for all that time, while so much else changed.

Second, perhaps primates are attentive to flowers—both sight and smell—because these indicate fruit in the future. According to this hypothesis, flowers are attended to because they indicate the size of the coming crop. Kaplan (1992) and Orians and Heerwagen (1992) advance this hypothesis to explain our liking for the appearance of flowers. It fails to explain our attraction to their scent, however. We are extremely sensitive to such things as ylang-ylang and rose but not particularly sensitive to the various aromatic fragrances of such major primate foods as *Ficus* spp.

Third, in at least some cases, strong plant smells indicate poison. However, the first line of defense against poisons is the quite different sensory receptor that detects bitterness (Johns 1991; Profet 1992). A few volatile oils are toxic, such as those of juniper, but most are safe, at least in the small amounts usually ingested. Among deadly poisons common in nature, only hydrocyanic acid, with its characteristic flavor familiar from bitter almonds, is easily smelled. Strychnine, botulin, fungal toxins, and other common toxins in nature are not detected by human scent. Finally, toxins that are easily smelled are almost universally considered unpleasant—as any evolutionary biologist would predict.

Fourth, humans apparently try to mask their body scent for hunting purposes and also for camouflage of pheromone smells that might indicate ovulation (Damsen 1993; Dobkin de Rios and Hayden 1985; M. Stoddart 1990). The hunting part of this hypothesis, at least, is certainly true for many hunters, according to my field observations. However, we do not see this as an explanation for attraction to the specific scents considered herein. Hunters do not use such scents to mask body odor; instead, they wash carefully to get rid of as much human odor as possible, and they avoid contact with strong human odors.

There has been a theory that humans wish to reject and deny the animal body, and use smells to conceal this aspect of humanity (Rozin and Fallon 1981). This theory too does not predict what fragrances will be enjoyed.

All the volatile oils described in standard pharmacognosy texts (Claus 1956; Tyler et al. 1981) are intensely aromatic and usually considered pleasant. Human preference for certain flavorings in foods is due to medical concerns. It is a biocultural phenomenon: it is grounded in genetics, but the specific forms it takes are determined by cultural history.[5]

Spices are still a major item of international commerce. Clove, cinnamon, nutmeg, mace, allspice, ginger, cardamom, black pepper, and apiaceous "seeds" (achenes) such as fennel, anise, dill, coriander, and caraway are among the spices whose volatile oils have made them important items in international commerce, used throughout the world, by cooks of literally hundreds of cultures. Current spice trade is one of the world's largest and most far-flung trade networks, involving thousands of tons of botanicals, worth hundreds of millions of dollars, and involving essentially the entire world and all its nations (see e.g. Purseglove et al. 1981, where extensive figures are reported). Two thousand years ago the spice trade was already extensive and involved most of the known world (Miller 1969). The same spices are consistently the ones most favored.

These spices originated in different parts of the world, sometimes quite obscure and remote parts (clove, nutmeg, and mace from the remote outer islands of Indonesia, allspice and vanilla from tropical Mexico). Their success is not due to their association with some dominant culture. Herbs such as mint, thyme, rosemary, basil, marjoram, and oregano are also very widely popular. The Maya of Mexico and Guatemala, for one example, not only had their own native spices (including allspice, which has gone worldwide) but took enthusiastically to most of the above spices when they became available after the Conquest (Coe 1994). Among Mexican native spices were oreganos and mints of quite similar taste to the Old World species. Native onions were also very widely used by American peoples before contact with Europe.

Thus, an inborn fondness for antiseptics, fine-tuned by culture, made history.

5

Basics
Environment and Economy

1

The most basic determinants of foodways are environment and economy.

This is so obvious, and so generally realized, that it is often taken as the whole story (e.g. M. Harris 1974, 1985; Harris and Ross 1987). Much of the present book is devoted to qualifying such a simple view. However, no one can deny that environment and economy have been the main shapers of foodways for most people over most of history.

In the short run, they can be almost totally determinative. Agriculture in less-than-affluent areas is basically a matter of producing a diet that people can afford. This means it must produce the staples that are the cheapest to grow. That, then, is what people eat. They have no choice.

In a cash economy, economics determines which plants or animals can be grown most cheaply, and which will sell at the best price. A plant that grows well but cannot be sold will vanish from a monetized economy. An animal that costs more to rear than it brings on the market will not be reared for sale.

A traditional society, less totally monetized, will reckon in terms of land and labor. The crop that takes the least land will be favored where labor is abundant; rice dominates South China because it produces so much grain per acre, but it demands weeks of work per acre to produce so well (see Geertz 1963). The crop that takes the least labor (per unit output) will dominate in areas where labor is scarce and land abundant. Wheat dominates the north plains of North America, and dominated many plains in the ancient Near East, for this reason.

Overall, traditional societies tend to maximize across nutritional needs. They pick the crop mix that provides the best diet for the least input. They have a high-yield starch staple, a plant protein source, and—

almost always—an animal protein source as well. Usually there is a special oil source. They always have high-yield, vitamin-rich fruits and vegetables that serve as "protective foods," supplying necessary micronutrients and often protective chemicals.[1]

Foodways change for many reasons; changes in ecology and economics are among the most obvious. One of the most interesting changes was the invention of agriculture. Many theories have been advanced to explain this key development (sometimes called a "revolution"); since no one can go back in time to see it happen, we may never know which is correct. Speculation on the reasons for the rise of agriculture is one of the most fertile sources of publication in the realm of anthropology. However, for reasons of space, crop biology and agroecology must regretfully be left out of this account. Fortunately, these matters are very well covered elsewhere. (For some recent surveys, see Cowan and Watson 1992; Heiser 1990; relevant sections of Kiple and Ornelas 2000, above all McCorriston 2000; MacNeish 1992; Piperno and Pearsall 2000.)[2]

Changes at the end of the Pleistocene apparently put in process the development of agriculture, in several parts of the world. The Near East, China, Mexico, South America, and perhaps other areas all independently developed agriculture in the few millennia immediately following the last glaciation. This clearly had to do with the spread and increase of plants in those parts of the world; many other factors were no doubt involved.

A Chinese proverb says, "When you are dying of thirst, it's too late to dig a well." Carl Sauer argued long ago that starving people have no time, energy, or resources; they cannot invent agriculture or develop new crops (Sauer 1952). He proposed that agriculture must have started among reasonably affluent, settled people. This may or may not be so, but at least we can be sure it did not start among the truly desperate. Hunters and gatherers are not as impoverished as many writers still imply. When they do face want, they usually move, a strategy that makes farming even less attractive than it is in good times. Thus farming probably started among people who had enough food; they presumably wanted to produce their favorite foods closer to home.

Sauer's point rules out sheer desperate need as the reason for agriculture. Therefore, others have sought other explanations. Richard MacNeish (1992) pointed out that agriculture started in seasonally dry, warm-temperate, mountainous areas, where many ecological zones were closely packed together and where many seasonal resources encourage storage and husbanding; he further hypothesized that trade between inhabitants of neighboring ecological zones was important. One might suppose that people in one zone wanted to have their special product close to the house, to be available for trading with people from neighboring zones. I think this was indeed the direct reason for agriculture.

It is also clear that ecological shifts at the end of the Pleistocene—notably, plants and plant cover increased in the regions of primary agriculture—obviously set the stage and context. In some areas this meant more moisture and thus better conditions for plants. However, V. Gordon Childe (1951:67) suggested that local drying at the end of the Pleistocene concentrated people around oases, where they would have much incentive to plant grains like wheat, which they had once found locally but now had to grow in the moist oasis if they wanted it. Recent research has dramatically confirmed Childe's model (Leslie Quintero, Philip Wilke, personal communication, 2002, 2003; they are colleagues of mine who have been doing the research in question). Childe also picked up on the issue of trade, seeing it—surely correctly—as essential to the rise of agriculture (Childe 1951:72; he also saw women as the inventors—a long-popular, if unprovable, idea).

Many of the countless other explanations advanced for agricultural origins may have some truth in them, but they do not predict the actual places and times. At present, only Childe and MacNeish predict these, and Childe only for the Near East and possibly Mexico and Peru; domestication in China and elsewhere took place in wetter environments. It is difficult (I believe impossible) to give significant credence to a model that does not predict the times and places.

Did agriculture improve or hurt human nutrition? The conventional wisdom has always been that agriculture provided more food and a more secure livelihood and that this was the reason for its adoption. This idea was challenged and tested in a major research agenda some years ago. The results were stunning and unequivocal. Skeletal evidence showed that, everywhere in the world, hunters and gatherers were reasonably well nourished, but agriculture led to a slow increase in population and a slow *deterioration* in nutrition (Cohen and Armelagos 1984). As numbers increased, people turned more and more to starch staples—not adequate nutrition in themselves. Only very recently, with the rise of refrigerated transport and other modern means of shipping and storing, has agriculture fulfilled its promise of providing really adequate diets to a huge population. Even today, billions of people (not just in Third World nations) subsist on unbalanced diets, too starchy and too thin on the nutrients that hunter-gatherer diets provide in abundance.

In most of the world, the staple is grain, from one or another species of the grass family. (A grain is technically called a caryopsis; it is a fruit consisting of a seed in several layers of thin, dry, tightly adhering seed coats. These coats have a good deal of nutritional value, while the kernel is mostly starch.) Grasses are tough, versatile, and highly productive. Many of them thrive on disturbance and are thus easy to cultivate. Grains have a good balance of carbohydrate and protein, and are easy to store.

Most staple foods that are not grasses are some form of tuber or root crop: potatoes, yams, manioc (aka cassava, yuca, or tapioca), taro, or the like. Again, these must be disturbance tolerant and productive to be good cultivation choices.

Farmers need back-up crops that will succeed if the staple fails. In Europe it is traditional to grow rye, wheat, and barley. The wheat is usually the staple. In a cold, wet year the wheat and barley fail and the rye does extra well. In a hot dry year the rye and wheat do poorly, but the barley flourishes. Very widespread until recently was *maslin* (mixed) cultivation, in which various grains and even peas and the like were all sowed together. If one or two or even three crops failed, there was still something. The grains were often harvested and ground all in one batch, producing bread with varied and interesting flavors (but, often, rocklike hardness).

The staple grains of the world are the clearest and best studied cases to consider. Wheat and barley were the first species to be cultivated (so far as we know). They were domesticated in the Near East around 9000 BC. Presumably they were chosen because they were common, easy to grow, productive, nutritious, tasty, and easy to store. In comparable environments elsewhere in the world—Spain, California, Chile, southwest Australia—little or nothing was domesticated. The Near Easterners could have done as the Californian native peoples did, remaining hunter-gatherers to the last. Or Californians and Australians could have domesticated grains. Californians actually domesticated barley for at least some period, about 2,000 years ago (Charles Mikcisek, personal communication, 1991). The Near Easterners also domesticated sheep and goats. The Californians had similar sheep; why did they never domesticate them?

The Near East and Mediterranean have, besides their staple grains (wheat and barley), a range of plant protein sources: chickpeas, lentils, broad beans, and the like—all cultivated right from the earliest days of agriculture. Sheep and goats, animal protein sources, were also part of the original roster; pigs and cattle came later. Onions, garlic, and a range of vegetables and herbs are protective foods (on the origins and spread of agriculture in the Near East, see Zohary and Hopf 2000).

In China, rice and millets were both early; rice outperformed millets, but did not compete with them for land. Both could be cultivated: rice in wet places, millets in dry.

Over time, people find and develop plants that provide the maximum nutrients for minimal input. As money enters the economy, this often changes; people try for the maximum income for minimum expenditure. We have the historic evidence in China; early staples like various millet species (there were about four species, the commonest being *Setaria italica*, foxtail millet), and early vegetables like mallows and smartweed, were replaced by more productive or more versatile and saleable foods—wheat, Chinese cabbages, and spinach (introduced from Persia early on). When maize came from the Americas, it moved rapidly to replace the last of the millets. Maize also spread at the expense of lower yielding crops in Europe and Africa.

In China (Anderson 1988, 1990), rice yielded high; wheat and millets backed it up. Maize replaced millets when it was found to be more productive. Much earlier, soybeans had similarly displaced adzuki beans. Soybeans, pigs, chickens, and a range of vegetables provided protein. Chinese cabbages provided vitamin-rich greens, and also seed oil.

Africa developed several systems, based on grains (sorghum, a local rice species, several millets, and many others) or tuber crops (notably yams—of the genus *Dioscorea*, very different from the large sweet potatoes called "yams" in the United States; on African cultivation see National Research Council 1996). The rice (*Oryza glaberrima*) inspired the development of a sophisticated rice agriculture, which later allowed rice production to expand in North America, usually with the use of Asian rice but African slaves, who were skilled rice farmers (Carney 2001). Superior farming skills made them prime targets for slave raids and brutal oppression.

The pre-Columbian diet of central Mexico was another optimization across needs. In Mexico, grains were independently domesticated. A form of millet (*Setaria viridis*) similar to Chinese foxtail millet came first, but was abandoned when maize came into favor. Maize was subjected to spectacular changes, making an unpromising grass into a high-yield grain (Coe 1994). A choice was made; millet was displaced. Mexico could have grown millet on lands too dry or cold for maize, as China did, but the competitive advantage of doing so was apparently too small to make it worthwhile.

Maize provided the most calories per acre, and was the staple. Back-up staples included amaranth and chia seeds. The protein staple was the common frijol bean. Animal protein came from turkeys, dogs, fish, and a range of insects. Vitamin-rich crops included tomatoes, chiles, squash, and avocados. No free oil was produced, but the chia, squash seeds, and avocados were rich in oils.

South America domesticated the potato, as well as quinoa (*Chenopodium quinoa*), for starch staples; lupine or *tarwi* (*Lupinus mutabilis*) for plant protein; llamas (*Lama glama*) for animal protein; and squash (*Cucurbita maxima*, different from Mexican squash), peanuts, chiles (native ones, including species different from Mexico's), and many other species for protective foods. Several tuber crops similar to (but not related to) potatoes were important in the Andes, and some still are important there. (On all these crops, see National Research Council 1989.) Andean South America was the only area of the New World in which animal husbandry was highly evolved. Llamas and alpacas (basically, a woolly variety of llama) were the major domesticates. These were herded in high-altitude meadows. In the high Andes I encountered a special llama-herding breed of dog, resembling a border collie but larger—an extremely intelligent, trainable, pleasant animal. I was given to understand that it was a traditional breed; it may even be pre-Columbian, in which case it is the only herd-dog breed native to the New World, and should be carefully preserved. An eating dog similar to the Mexican one was also developed. Small animals were not neglected by the Andeans; guinea pigs were domesticated to provide a family-meal-sized animal.

In the South American lowlands, a different system was established. Sweet potatoes and manioc were important, manioc being the most wide-spread staple. The Muscovy duck (*Cairina moschata*) was apparently domesticated in the upper Amazon. (On lowland South America, see Piperno and Pearsall 2000.)

The very different world of the island Pacific (Polynesia and other island realms) had a similar maximizing solution: taro and other root crops for starch, pigs and chickens for animal protein, coconut for plant protein and oil, and pandanus, taro leaves, and various other vegetables for vitamins. Grain grows poorly or is subject to typhoon wreckage in much of the island world. Root crops produced more food under island conditions, and had the advantage that the edible part was underground; the top could blow away in a storm without a famine resulting. Roots are hard to store, but the islanders developed incredibly sophisticated systems to overcome this limit (see Pollock 1992).

Years ago, Sally DeVore and Thelma White (1978) compiled a book of such optimal solutions, pointing out that most traditional peoples have far better diets—in terms of nutritional value of foods eaten—than modern Americans do. The point remains valid.

However, ecology is never totally determinative. Every environment provides a large range of possible domesticates. It also provides settings in which some of these do much better than others, different settings in which the others flourish, and perhaps some settings in which everything can grow. Given that people tend to experiment, that most environments have a huge range of edible items, and that famines may force people to eat what they usually hate, there is always a place for choice.

Once a staple crop is established, we have what my economist friend Richard Such calls a "lock-in." A pattern continues because it is cheap to replicate and would be expensive, both financially and psychologically, to change. The whole of north European agriculture is based around a highly complex but very efficient system of wheat and small-grain production. From the plow types to the bakeries and pasta factories, everything is set up to deal with wheat. So, although the potato came early and proved far more productive and well adapted than wheat, wheat remains the staple food—except in areas too poor and marginal to afford it. The iron hand of economics forced the impoverished Irish and Poles to live on potatoes in the old days, but they yearned for bread—and now they can afford bread, and are eating fewer potatoes. Potatoes added themselves to the system, but did not destroy it. Conversely, the introduction of wheat and barley to the potato's homeland in Peru and Bolivia did not displace the potato from its primacy among the indigenous peoples there. The potato did better under the conditions of indigenous farming, and the indigenous farmers knew much better how to grow it. Moreover, they had developed countless varieties, adapted to every niche. So wheat and barley flourish in favorable places, but the harsher lands and many of the less harsh areas are potato country still.

At every point there were choices, but progressively tighter lock-ins occurred as systems got more and more fine-tuned and specialized. At the beginning, people could choose to adopt or not, to eat or not, to grow or not. The potato was a very hard sell in Europe. The efforts of many rulers over several centuries were needed to make the folk eat these strange tubers (Salaman 1985). The ecological and economic advantages of the plant were not a guarantee of success.

Historically, shifts in foodways often come from ecological or economic changes. The catastrophic freeze of 1709 that devastated and ruined the olive industry in the higher, cooler parts of south France is a famous example (Grove and Rackham 2001:133; Le Roy Ladurie 1971). More generally, the Little Ice Age, of which this freeze was only one episode, changed agriculture throughout Europe. This sharp cold spell, lasting roughly 1400–1800, led to glacial advances, shorter and cooler growing seasons, and much colder winters. Wheat retreated from the north and east, leaving oats dominant in Scotland and rye dominant throughout most of East Europe. The vine retreated southward, leaving England without a wine industry. Greenland lost its Norse settlers (McGovern et al. 1988). Economic changes followed. Potatoes and sugar beets replaced or supplemented grains in much of north Europe. Beer waxed as wine waned. Diets simplified; the cold weather not only drove out warm-weather crops but also reduced incomes, putting spices and other expensive imports out of reach. Perhaps this had something to do with the loss of spicing from English and, to a lesser extent, French dishes, during the same period.

A new invention, or newly opened lands, or new sources of fertilizer may suddenly make a particular food cheap; consumption goes up, other things being equal. However, consumption may actually go down if the item gets stamped as a poverty food. Or consumption may go up only after substantial advertising campaigns (as with avocados—considered "strange" within my memory) or progress in food processing technology (as with soybeans).

Changes in food production follow general patterns. Yujiro Hayami and Vernon Ruttan (1985) showed that people tend to develop agriculture in such a way as to remove bottlenecks. If labor is in short supply, as in the United States through much of history, labor-saving devices will be invented. If land is scarce, as in East Asia, land-sparing technologies will increase and flourish.

Ester Boserup (1965) argued that population pressure would make people intensify their agriculture. She theorized that people, faced with more mouths to feed, would have to work harder. This does often happen. However, Boserup missed the point that, for intensification, capital must be available and society must be secure. If capital is the missing factor, population growth leads to cheaper labor (or simply starvation) and

Basics of food production, Bangladesh. These fisherfolk are working on a project of the Grameen Foundation. The Grameen Bank, founded by Bangladeshi economist Mohamed Yunus, provides tiny loans or finances small-scale projects, allowing capital-deprived individuals to start small enterprises, usually ones that produce food. *Photo by E. N. Anderson, 1999*

persistently nonintensive land use—as in much of Latin America and Africa. If society is not secure, the powerful seem always to respond to population pressure, or any other pressure, by taking from the weak. Instead of agricultural intensification, one gets war, banditry, or savage oppression. If population pressure alone were enough to cause intensification, Haiti and Bangladesh would be the most agriculturally developed nations, while Canada, Australia, and the United States would be the least. Similar "paradoxes" exist in traditional societies: densely populated aboriginal California relied on hunting and gathering, while agriculture flourished in thinly populated aboriginal New England. Clearly, Boserup's theory is only one part (an important part, to be sure) of a larger picture. Relative prices or availability of land, labor, and capital all play a part. So do taste and inclination, which are in part determined by the accidents and contingencies of prior history.

It is typical, if ironic, to find that luxury crops get much of the attention of plant breeders and agricultural developers, while the staple foods of the poor are neglected. The two great studies of the history of particular crops—Redcliffe Salaman's work on the potato (1985) and Sidney Mintz' on sugar (1985)—both point out that these began their European cycle of development as luxuries. Their luxury status and price made it worth the bother of developing them into the mass staples they eventually became. Today, beef, turkey, and even sturgeon farming (sturgeon produce caviar) gets plenty of research action. Conversely, staple foods of the poor, such as manioc and chickpeas, or millets in Africa (National Research Council 1996), have never received much development attention.

Today, we find that the rich nations are the ones that invest in agricultural research and development. The poor nations usually spend most of their wealth on weaponry (which is one main reason they remain poor). One result is that the luxuries of the rich get the attention denied to the staple foods of the hungry.

A traditional society (with little or no money at the farm level) has one advantage: it is not tightly limited by market pricing. A plant that is hard to grow and impossible to sell may be kept around because it is locally beloved, or because it survives in a famine year. Weeds, not worth selling, may be used simply because they are there. In the Mediterranean region, dozens of mushroom and weed species are eaten (see e.g. Gray 1997). One sees ordinary people (not just the poor or the highly traditional) foraging for greens in the parks, or mushrooms on the roadsides. Such behavior was once found throughout the world, but it has become rare in most cash economies.

Even in solidly market economies, uneconomic but traditional cultivation usually goes on. Many Americans and more Europeans still plant vegetable gardens, though they could often buy the vegetables more cheaply at the store. Vegetable gardens provide a better liked product, to say nothing of healthful exercise and a general sense of virtue.

However, the sad tendency in market economies is for old and choice "heirloom" varieties to disappear. They are squeezed out by new varieties that are cheaper and easier to grow. These often lack the flavor and texture of the old. In these cases, economics plays against ecology. The ecologically sound farmer will maximize the number of crops and varieties, to have a range of options and to hedge against failure. The economically best option in the short run (but hardly ever in the long run) may be to grow only one variety of one plant.

Sometimes, the consumers rebel against monocrop monotony, and force the breeders to bring back flavor and texture to a familiar crop that

Local marketing of staple foods, Azrou, Morocco. Grains and beans of all sorts, as well as spices, pots and pans, and even camels, are for sale on the grounds of the great market at the edge of Azrou. People from the surrounding remote mountains travel to this central town. *Photo by E. N. Anderson, 2000*

had been debased. I have observed this in the case of strawberries, apples, and tomatoes in California in recent years. Today, various specialized clubs and organizations, such as Native Seed Search (based in Arizona), work to save heirloom varieties and sell them to connoisseurs and researchers. Not only food crops but also roses and other ornamentals have their heritage protectors. Of course, this represents only a tiny and rather luxury-level fraction of the market, and the dismal process of biodiversity reduction continues. Even so, one can see that the market can be either destroyer or savior of traditional varieties—according to whether consumers value quality and variety, or short-term cheapness alone.

The worst problem is that most of the world has little choice; they have to buy the cheap food because they lack the money to do otherwise, and, in a world now largely urban, they also lack the opportunity to produce food for themselves. They thus are often exposed to foods that cost very little to produce but can be marketed for high prices: candy bars, sodas, potato chips, and the like. Fresh produce, fresh milk, and good-quality meat and fish are much less available to them; such foods spoil readily and are thus expensive to distribute and sell. Marketers may see healthy foods as appealing only to upper-class buyers; in Los Angeles (as in other American cities, and probably in cities everywhere) fresh foods and health-conscious items are available only in upscale markets, while markets catering to poor neighborhoods often fail to stock even so basic a food as milk (Conis 2003).

On the other hand, traditional local markets still manage to provide good fresh food in many areas. And I have seen dooryard gardens flourishing in the inner-city slums of Dhaka, Bangladesh, and serving as quite literal lifesavers for the desperately poor inhabitants. We often underestimate the potential of urban gardening.

The moral is this: to save the hungry of the world, those who are more fortunate have to dedicate serious efforts. We cannot expect population pressure or desperate need to force intensification.

2

Thus, we can see that explanations in terms of ecology and economics can be disarmingly persuasive without necessarily being right. We will have occasion later to examine such explanations in regard to religious taboos.

A case study of how a dubious ecological explanation can become fixated in the literature is provided by an explanation of the potlatch, an institution universal among the native peoples of the Northwest Coast of North America. The potlatch (the word comes from the Nuu-chah-nulth language of southwest British Columbia) is a ceremony found from Washington State to southern Alaska. It involves feasting and giving away property. The feasting can get very elaborate, with hundreds of recipes (analyzed by Walens 1981); the Northwest Coast peoples are among the few human groups who lack agriculture and have a sophisticated cuisine. Property given away typically includes not only blankets and other useful items but also beautiful art goods; this is one reason why the Northwest peoples have a world-famous art tradition. "Tribes," actually local groups organized by descent and led by hereditary chiefs, compete with each other to see who can throw the biggest and most spectacular potlatch. Countless explanations for this custom have been offered, ranging from the psychological to the social.

In the 1960s, Wayne Suttles (1985 and personal communication, 1987) and his student Stuart Piddocke (1965) proposed a function for the potlatch as it was practiced among the chiefdoms of the Puget Sound–Vancouver area. They hypothesized that it might serve to even out resources. A group with lavish resources would throw a potlatch, inviting all the neighbors, including impoverished ones who needed the food. The impoverished groups, if they got rich in their turn, would reciprocate. Thus, whoever was lucky that year would share the wealth with the unlucky, who would return the favor, and all would be lovely. This was seen (by Suttles, at least) as one side function, not necessarily intended, of an institution that clearly had other purposes as well.

This explanation was proposed with proper caution, qualifications, limitations, and admissions that evidence was not conclusive (Suttles 1985 discusses the whole controversy). Unfortunately, overenthusiastic writers (notably Marvin Harris 1974, 1985) picked it up, extended it to all potlatches everywhere, and treated it as the clear major cause of the potlatch. Harris may have oversimplified and overextended, but at least he discussed other explanations, and said some extremely perceptive things about the whole institution, its complexities, and its evolution. For instance, he pointed out that the potlatch expanded beyond all practical value under the stress of oppression and demographic collapse in the late nineteenth century (Harris 1985). In later popularized versions, all this was also brushed aside. Finally, we come to the modern textbook forms (Beardsworth and Keil 1997:101; Kottak 2003:212–14). Here all subtlety and qualifications have gone by the board, and the potlatch—everywhere—has "the latent and manifest functions of . . . sharing of current food surpluses (particularly of perishable foods) and the provision of a virtual guarantee that [the hosts], in turn, would benefit from feasts with others when their own supplies were short" (Beardsworth and Keil 1997:101, citing popular sources rather than scholarly ones). This exemplifies a point made repeatedly by Stephen Jay Gould (esp. in Gould 2002, passim) that textbooks routinely oversimplify theories to the point of distorting them.

In fact, research findings had not been too kind to the hypothesis. Martin Orans (1975) pointed out the total lack of direct evidence for it. John Pritchard showed that in the northern Northwest Coast (far from Suttles's lands), resources were so uncertain and potlatches took so much advance planning (many years) that no one could target a potlatch to help the poor; potlatches were randomly related to hard times. People who were suddenly faced with shortages could not rely on having a potlatch nearby; instead, they scattered out to stay with kinfolk in other areas (Pritchard 1977 and personal communication, 1984). Most important of all, veteran Northwest Coast expert Philip Drucker provided the real explanation of the potlatch (Drucker and Heizer 1967). Drucker, who had worked with the Nuu-chah-nulth when they still remembered old times, established conclusively that the potlatch validated the title of a chief and solidified support for him in war. The Northwest Coast peoples were among the more warlike groups in history, fighting to take over land and fishing spots or to take slaves. A chief needed all the followers he could get. Since any dissatisfied individual could easily travel to another chief's domain and serve him instead, a chief had to do everything possible to validate his title and hold his followers' loyalty. Generous giving was about the only thing he could do.

An appealing aspect of this explanation is that it fits with other "merit feasts" around the world. In many chiefdom-type societies, competitive generosity, specifically in the form of feasts with gift giving, is the standard way to acquire followers for raiding and warfare. The most dramatic examples are found in the old epics, from *The Iliad* to *The Tain* (the Irish national epic; see Kinsella 1970). The best ethnographic study is probably D. G. Robertson's study of eastern Afghanistan (Robertson 1896), because Robertson was there when the institution was in full glory, warfare and all.

Today, the potlatch still serves to validate title, and to mark and validate life changes (coming of age, marriage, and so on). It does have the incidental function of helping some poor individuals, but invitations are accorded on the basis of personal importance. (In my experience, the people one invites first and foremost are one's fellow chiefs and leaders.)

So, forty years after Suttles and Piddocke, we still have no evidence for their hypothesis (even in its original, local, highly qualified form). Instead, we have a counterhypothesis proven beyond reasonable doubt.

The success of that hypothesis at explaining the institution does not rule out other functions, be they ecological, social, or psychological; people often figure out ways to get multiple uses out of an institution. In fact, I still think Suttles and Piddocke were onto something, if only for the small, highly localized, resource-rich groups of the Sound-and-Straits area. But the potlatch in general is fundamentally a typical case of a worldwide phenomenon: competitive feasting and gift giving, among chiefs, for the purpose of holding onto followers.

As such, it is still a neat example of an institution that uses food for directly functional ends—specifically, in this case, economic and military goals.

6

Food as Pleasure

The beginning and root of all good is the pleasure of the belly, and everything wise or exquisite must be referred back to this criterion.
—Epicurus

Eat till you burst, drink till you pass out; anything more is excess!
—Mexican saying (my translation)

1

We eat largely to stay alive. Most people in the world, most of the time, have to take whatever they can get—usually dull, inadequate, depressing fare. But almost everyone gets to celebrate occasionally, and good food is almost always at the core of good times. For the lucky 25 percent of the world's citizens who can eat when and what they want or at least have *some* breadth of choice, daily fare can be diverse and tasty. Even among the other 75 percent, people often find ways to spice up their stodgy diets by using wild herbs, simple fermentation processes, varied cooking methods, and other clever but inexpensive tactics.

The ancient Egyptians, Mesopotamians, and their neighbors all concerned themselves about good food. The Bible refers to spices, olive oil, fat meat, fruits, and other goods. The ancient Greeks had an extensive gourmet literature, much of it surviving only in quotations (Dalby 1997). The Chinese, of course, are famous for good eating (Anderson 1988; Chang 1977); Yuan Mei in the eighteenth century was probably the most famous Chinese food writer (Waley 1956), as well as being a feminist far ahead of his time. The French gourmet tradition was old before Jean Sangthelme Brillat-Savarin set his seal on it in *The Physiology of Taste* (1925). This book became the Great Work for gourmets—or, as he called them, gourmands, the words having differentiated in meaning only since his time.

It is the nature of humans to take delight in satisfying survival needs. Indeed, any higher animal must find deprivation of food and drink uncomfortable, and satisfaction of the need at least somewhat pleasant. Hunger hurts. Satiation is a neutral state; it feels neither good nor bad (unless one is overstuffed to the point of sickness). The enjoyment comes in the process of moving from state A (hunger) to state B (comfortable fullness). Almost every culture seems to have a saying equivalent to the common English-language proverb "hunger is the best sauce."

It is the same with most simple pleasures. Warmth is not experienced as special unless one is coming in from winter weather. A cool drink of water is heaven when one is truly thirsty; otherwise it is uninteresting. Sex feels wonderful after long abstinence, but usually less so after an abstinence of only a few hours. Evolution has done this to us. Jared Diamond explains it in a book called *Why Is Sex Fun?* (Diamond 1997). Those who did not enjoy satisfying a biological need would not bother to satisfy it, especially if there were costs. Thus they would die out. Sex is "special" because it is not really a physical need for the individual, but only for the genetic line, and because sexual behavior is really risky. Female praying mantises eat their mates, cats easily catch mating birds, and humans kill themselves or each other over love. Therefore, those animals that do not have a passionate sex drive naturally and sensibly abstain, and thus do not pass on their genes. Nature may be red in tooth and claw, but it also forces some fun on us.

Food is different. We eat to survive, not to sacrifice our interests for our children. Still, to motivate an animal to eat and eat well, not only must hunger hurt but also the reward and pleasure centers in the brain must fire up when good food is eaten.

Also, people almost always eat as a social act. Lonely individuals often lose the desire to eat. They simply do not feel hungry. They often starve to death. The charitable organization Meals on Wheels, which takes food to shut-ins, has learned that the delivery person often has to sit with the recipient. Otherwise the food goes uneaten.

Under natural circumstances, we would eat merely to socialize and survive. Food would be merely a means to those two ends. Humans are perverse enough, however, to change a means into an end. Food, like sex, is cultivated for pure pleasure. Nature is often derailed—dismissed outright—from the process. Contraceptives derail the reproductive process. The ancient Romans ate, vomited, and ate again. Today, this behavior is common again. We now judge it harshly, under the name of "bulimia."

The Romans did it simply to maximize pleasure; bulimics today have more troubled and conflicted reasons for their behavior, and are often driven by desperate desire to be thin, or by darker psychological forces. Others deliberately seek out foods with minimal caloric value—a less drastic way of accomplishing the same goal of eating for pleasure rather than for nutrition.

Most or all mammals have inborn taste preferences; this can easily be observed in cattle, dogs, and other familiar animals. We have seen that the human organism is born with some degree of fondness for the sweet, sweet-sour, salty, and fat, as well as for spices. Meat, fish, nuts, and seeds, nutritious and popular almost everywhere, evidently touch some sort of inner chord.

Flavors developed in vegetables and meats by cooking, and in fruit by ripening, seem inherently pleasing (see Harold McGee's classic *On Food and Cooking*, 1984). Preferring ripe fruit makes good sense in terms of primate and plant evolution; the fruit develops good flavors when ripe, so that we will eat it and scatter the mature seeds around. The plant uses nutritional value to lure dispersal agents. It is harder to understand how we came to like cooked food, but perhaps cooking was discovered so long ago that we have had time to evolve a preference. Cooked food tends to be healthier and safer than the raw sort, so there would be selective advantage for this.

Experience appears more important than genetics. Foods we were raised with are typically our favorites. This goes right back to mother's milk. Not only do babies learn to love soft, sweet, milky things; they also learn to love flavors such as garlic and onions, and even the hotness of chile, all of which print through in the milk. Some mothers self-consciously eat their ethnic foods when nursing their babies, so the children will grow up with the right tastes.

Even without such imprinting, children learn to love the foods their parents and older peers prefer. In this, again, we resemble other mammals, which learn their proper foods partly by hanging around with parents and watching what they eat. For many people, "good food" is simply the food they are used to. Americans love white bread, hamburgers, and ketchup, while rural Zambians love mopane caterpillars, millet mush, and hippo meat, because these are "what everyone eats."

Children are most prone to love foods that are used as treats, rewards, and markers of special events (Conner and Armitage 2002). More interesting is the universal tendency to loathe foods identified with poverty and bad times. Children learn with striking swiftness and thoroughness that they should hate such foods. Sweet potatoes are a delicacy in many areas of the world, but are abominated in China and in parts of the American South, because they were poverty foods there. Many of us who remember rationing in World War II cannot imagine how anyone can actually *like* the processed meat product known as Spam, which made frequent appearance on wartime tables in place of rationed meat and thus became stigmatized. Yet Hawaiians, among others, love Spam and use it creatively (see Laudan 1998).

It often happens, through such taste development, that a familiar, everyday food becomes a luxury as times change. Recently, this has been particularly evident in the case of cured fish products, because overfishing has made them rare where they were once the cheapest of protein foods. Salt cod in the Mediterranean, caviar in Russia and Iran, pickled herrings in north Europe, and smoked salmon in Scotland and Scandinavia got into the diet because they were cheap, but now remain important as luxury items in the diets of those who became used to them.

One obvious question, but one with no well-understood answer, is, When do we want the familiar, and when do we want the new? We know that Mom's chicken soup is comforting when we are sick and miserable, while exotic restaurant fare is usually most appealing when we are excited and cheerful and when we are out with adventurous friends. Also, "openness" is a basic factor in personality. Some people (and some monkeys, as well as other mammals) are just more adventurous than others. Often these are the young adults; the old and the very young are more conservative. But, beyond that, people simply differ. The individual who can't wait to try a new ethnic cuisine and the one who would never dream of eating anything but familiar home meals stand at opposite ends of the openness scale.

Someone growing up in London or Los Angeles will have much more chance and encouragement to try new foods than someone growing up in a small, isolated farm town. Someone growing up in a family that values food and tries many new items will be more apt to value good food than one raised on a steady diet of white bread and frozen dinners. (Two of my children rebelled against the "weird" food in our home—but they grew up to be lovers of fine and varied foods. To modify one of the countless proverbs that use food as symbol: even if the apple rolls away from the tree, eventually it rolls back.)

Varieties of potatoes, Cuzco, Peru. Thousands of varieties of potatoes exist in the Andean region, and a single market stall may offer twenty different ones, differing in size and color. Other tuber crops, such as oca and ulluco, are also common; they are little known outside the Andes, but could potentially revolutionize the world as much as potatoes have done. *Photo by E. N. Anderson, 1997*

Aesthetics has much to do with pattern, order, and symmetry. The most basic aesthetic sense is the pleasure derived from recognizing, understanding, and enjoying a pattern that stands out from surrounding chaos. This is probably yet another evolutionary matter: we evolved an ability not only to pick out the fruit from the leaves, the snake from the grass, and the flower from the brush but also to enjoy the search and the recognition (Gombrich 1984). So our foraging career may be the foundation of our love for geometric patterns, just as music is based on

Tomatoes for sale, Istanbul. This Mexican crop came to the Mediterranean in the sixteenth century, but did not spread until the seventeenth and eighteenth centuries. Along with other New World foods, notably chile peppers and maize, it has been wildly successful in Turkey. *Photo by E. N. Anderson, 2000*

recurrent themes and rhythms, which must have something to do with heartbeat, breathing, and sex (*pace* Robert Jourdain's [1997] claim to the contrary).

In all these patterns, we like subtle surprises. We want the pattern to be varied just a bit, in systematic but exciting ways. Simple mindless repetition is all very well, but complex, understated variations on the theme are much preferred. This is why "keyboard" and "synthesizer" music set to produce an automatically repeated sequence sounds so dull and boring.

So familiar tastes and familiar combinations are reassuring and become inherently lovable, but the exact same meal, over and over again, becomes deadly. Good home-baked or at least human-baked bread is never dull, because it not only has a complex and rich taste, but the taste is also never quite the same from bite to bite. By contrast, nothing is duller than factory bread, because it is the same simple stuff time after time.

A good meal is like a symphony: familiar and exotic tastes are combined in constantly varying and intricate ways, but the whole should add up to a unified creation. This explains the worldwide importance of rules for service (appetizers, soup, main dish, dessert) and for canonical combinations (meat with green beans and potatoes for some cultures, chicken with apricots and cinnamon for others.)

Food is often made visually beautiful. Preferences in food spectacle range from the wildly lush table sculptures of the Baroque to the wondrously *shibui*—subtle and low-key—art of Japanese Zen cooking (Ishige 2001; Yoneda 1982). Obviously, wider cultural aesthetic rules lie behind these differences.

Feasting is often accompanied by music in virtually all cultures that make the slightest claim to elegance. The music may range from trumpets to didjeridoos, from plainchant to rap; the point is that a great meal is not just an appeal to taste but an appeal to all the senses.[1]

Yet we expect uniformity in apple juice, peanut butter, and many other everyday foods, and are disturbed if there is even the least variation. Here, the appeal appears not to be so much an aesthetic one as a matter of familiarity and reliability. We drink fine wines to savor their subtle variations, but we drink apple juice to put something familiar and sugary in our stomachs. Wine is beloved of adults; children, more innocent and more well supplied with taste buds (and therefore more easily overstimulated), prefer the apple juice.

The effects of alcohol on the psyche obviously have much to do with its popularity; even bad booze can be enjoyed. But good booze is better. Therefore, around the world, cults of wine and beer have arisen, and superb-tasting brews have developed. Not only Europeans make a fetish of alcohol. The Chinese adored their *jiu* (a general term for all alcoholic drinks), as shown in this poem about a Taoist adept:

> . . . The Master . . .
> Holds up his jar
> And goes on with his wine,
> Cherishing his cup
> To the last lees.
>
> With ruffled whiskers he sits,
> Legs spread indecently apart;

The yeast becomes his pillow,
The sediments his mat.
(Kohn 1993:301; her translation from an early medieval poem)

2

Everything can be made acceptable if you know how to prepare it, and it
is not yet twenty years since a famous caterer served to some gentlemen
(for the lack of other meats) an old pair of water-buffalo leather gloves,
shredded and stewed, with onions, mustard, and vinegar, which they
found excellent as long as they did not know what they were eating
—François Marin, mid-eighteenth century

In New York and Los Angeles, there is considerable snob value to trying
exotic new restaurants. One learns to cultivate a wide taste because it is
often necessary if one wishes to keep up with one's peer group. In the
Midwest, in contrast, cultural pressures are diverted toward everyone
eating the same familiar dishes day after day and year after year.

Throughout history, elites and merchants have found it expedient to
cultivate varied and rich tastes. They have to entertain. Lavish feasts have
been based on dull food, especially in simple cultures, but usually the
pressure of competitive feasting forces elites to cultivate variety as well as
quantity. This is most true in the great old courtly traditions, from China
and India to the Aztec and Maya courts. However, it is true also among
the traditional native peoples of the Northwest Coast. The famous potlatches and feasts of that region led to a spectacularly varied and wonderfully subtle cuisine.

The pleasures of the table have been celebrated in all lands and time
periods; they are already well known and well attested in the earliest historical documents, from Mesopotamia and ancient Egypt. Fancy recipes
occur among the Babylonic cuneiform texts (Bottéro 1995). Ancient texts
in these areas and in ancient China tell of delicacies, royal feast foods, and
choice grades of beer (usually mistranslated "wine" in the Chinese case).
In Mexico, the Aztec kings had elaborate gourmet fare at their feasts, including frogs, lake salamanders, and "Mexican caviar"—eggs of water
bugs (Coe 1994; Duran 1994; Sahagun 1950–1982).

Connoisseurship often reaches slightly surreal levels. Wine experts can
tell from one sip the origin of the wine, often down to a fraction of a vine-

Fruit vendor artistically sculpturing a pineapple, Jamaica. Fruits are critically important to nutrition in much of the world. Mangoes, visible here with other fruit, are a particularly valuable source of vitamin A in many regions otherwise short of that essential nutrient. *Photo by Barbara Anderson, 1989*

yard. (There is a vineyard in northern California that produces three different wines, because it has three different soil types, and each soil imparts a different flavor to the wine; Howell and Swinchatt 2000.) In the Pacific Northwest, I have encountered many salmon connoisseurs, most of them Native Americans, who could tell what river a salmon came from and even which month it ran up the stream. Melons from Green River, Utah, and Hami, China, are deservedly famous (the hot, dry days and cool, dry nights seem magical). Similar levels of expertise exist locally for coffee, tea, ducks, apples, and other luxuries and indulgents.

Later chapters of this book will consider these matters in detail. Class, rank, and status are particularly influential. The identification of quality and variety with the elite usually produces middle-class emulation, and often creative adaptation; often it is the middle class that produces the best cuisine (Goody 1982).

However, also possible is a middle-class reaction in the form of puritanism or reverse snobbism. Dull food is idealized as "simple and plain," while the luxuries of the fortunate are viewed as alien and evil. (The poor rarely share in this attitude; they are too worried about getting any food at all. They are abstemious, but not by choice.) Reverse snobbism is perhaps especially common in island and frontier societies, where obtaining a varied, high-quality diet is particularly difficult and thus particularly prone to separate the rich from the middle class. Long-established, well-off farming regions allow everyone but the poorest to have some variety and quality, and are thus the natural home of cuisine that is varied and tasty even among the relatively poor. (These generalizations emerge from my research; full documentation must await another occasion.)

In the Midwest of my childhood, strange or different food was feared and hated, both because it was "foreign" and because it was an indulgence. This was not so much religious puritanism as a wider attitude, related to Calvinist Christianity but probably more related to the realities of life on what had been, until very recently, a hard-scrabble frontier where good food was identified with the idle rich. When pizza came to Lincoln, Nebraska, where I was raised, there were letters to the papers denouncing it as "foreign" and therefore "Communist." One person proposed banning it. The Midwest's puritanical society distrusted anything "of the flesh": sex, dancing, booze, good food, and even nonerotic massages. Sex and dancing flourished anyway (how could they not?), but good food was effectively banished. Indeed, the failure of the puritans to stop sex and dancing made many people all the more eager to do penance at the table. The sinners felt redeemed and the puritans felt triumphant. My Calvinist father and my lenient, worldly mother disagreed on this issue, which made me very conscious of it all. (Raised on my mother's cooking, I made the obvious choice.)

Food puritanism—the idea that enjoying good food is sinful—flourishes in many cultures around the world. It failed in China, in spite of much early support. The reason was social: elders and ancestors could not be insulted by being served bad food (Anderson 1988). This idea spread to ritual sacrifices, which fed even higher beings. Chinese religion produced food fit for gods. Even Buddhism, inherently puritanical, has not stopped gourmetship in Asia. Zen temple cuisine is one of the highlights of Japanese fare. This Buddhist cuisine is simple and rigidly vegetarian, but exquisite in its refined and subtle flavors, and no bargain economically. Rather than celebrating the abstemious, it celebrates the full, rich flavor of ingredients that purport to be simple and straightforward but are actually exceedingly expensive and difficult to obtain. This would seem to be rather a mockery of puritanism.

Puritanism has had a very up-and-down course in Islam, where the war between spoilsports and gourmets has been a self-conscious and hotly debated battle since Muhammad (van Gelder 2000). Muhammad's own words, preserved as *hadith*, reveal him as a basically abstemious man, but one able to enjoy good, solid cooking—so he can be, and is, quoted by both sides. His favorite food was said to be *tharid*—meat stock thickened with bread. His followers naturally imitated his taste (not least because it really is good stuff). The *migas* ("crumbs"—soups thickened with bread) dishes so popular in the formerly Moorish parts of Spain, and their equivalents in formerly Moorish parts of Italy, have been influenced by *tharid*. Later Muslim society often adored good food, and immortalized it in fine poetry. Whole books of Arab poetry about food exist. The famous Persian quatrain that begins "a book of verses underneath the bough . . ." (in Edward Fitzgerald's translation) has a variant in which the book is forthrightly replaced by a leg of mutton (Arberry 1959:121). Both versions of this verse, along with literally millions of other Muslim poems, also pay homage to wine—in spite of the Quranic prohibition.

Judaism has a similar mixed heritage, but the consensus of rabbis seems to be that one should not be ostentatious but should enjoy (Cooper 1993; Rosner 1997). Life is something to celebrate, not to deny. One recalls that a married man has an obligation under Jewish law to provide sexual pleasure to his wife. This worthy religious charge is implied in Islamic tradition as well (misrepresentation of Islam by the likes of the Taliban notwithstanding), but absent from Christian tradition.

In Christianity, food puritanism has had a field day. Jesus, good Jew that he was, fed the multitudes well, and made wine for them. His example has been neglected in this, as in much else. By about 200 AD, Clement of Alexandria was writing, "For neither is food our business, nor is pleasure our aim. . . . Food . . . must be plain, truly simple . . . ministering to life not to luxury" (quoted in Clifton and Spencer 1993:194). Since the days of Clement and the desert fathers, the more dour of Christians have hated and distrusted good food.

This attitude did not prevent said desert fathers from eating much better than they said they did; recent excavations have revealed a rich and varied diet, with plenty of spices and choice vegetables, in the very monasteries where the monks claimed to live on dry bread (Harlow and Smith 2001). It did not prevent the monasteries and nunneries of the Middle Ages and Renaissance from being homes of good living and laboratories for the development of culinary arts. The "fat abbot" remains proverbial.

However, abstemiousness to the point of "holy anorexia" (Bell 1985; St. Catherine of Siena provides a good example) was valued then and later, as was self-mortification in all things. The saints piously refrained from good food, as well as from bathing. (As recently as the sixteenth century, bathing was enough to get one in trouble with the Inquisition on suspicion of infidelism; see e.g. Weckmann 1992:456–57. Part of the reason was the promiscuity associated with public baths in the Middle Ages.)

The Reformation and Counter-Reformation brought (to some quarters, at least) a new and even more extreme hatred of all things aesthetic. The extreme-puritan tradition has mercifully become attenuated in Europe, but one recalls that Charles Dickens's "Christmas Carol" was written to *revive* Christmas and the Christmas feast in England. Christmas had been virtually eliminated by the Puritans, who regarded it as a pagan holiday. (It does, of course, have pagan roots.) Dickens's contention—that puritanism was a hypocritical cover for selfish greed—seemed accurate to the people of his time, and seems accurate today.

Ebenezer Scrooge has left a legacy in the continued opposition to feeding the hungry worldwide. Selfish cruelty, masquerading as opposition to "giveaways," remains very much with us.

In short, puritanism nests in religion, but it is a wider social phenomenon; religions can take it up or not, and not all puritanical traditions are really religious in origin.

7

Food Classification
and Communication

If you learn to be honest with food, it spills over into your whole life.

—Liane Kuony (chef)

1

We are all aware of the value of food as a mark or badge of ethnicity, religion, class, and other social groupings. The baid statement of this obvious fact is fairly banal. In fact, there is more to food talk.

I did a small bit of field work in Tahiti, decades ago. People would often greet me by wordlessly offering a piece of fruit or a sip of a drink. I learned that this substituted for a verbal greeting. One could say "*ia orana*" ("hello"), or one could offer a piece of food. I went on to learn that constant exchanges of food, from a chance sharing of fruit to a major feast, were the social threads that bound Tahitian society.

Communication often provides the fine-tuning — the actual specification—of foodways. Biology and economics set limits, and personal preferences and tastes matter, but cultural foodways are specified largely by the needs of communication.

One can read food as a text and decode what people were saying, or trying to say, when they managed food. Claude Lévi-Strauss and Mary Douglas have written magisterial works on the subject (see e.g. Levi-Strauss 1964–72; Douglas 1966, 1970) and a generation of interpretive writers has followed (see e.g. Counihan and van Esterik 1997).

Lévi-Strauss attempted to analyze foodways in terms of grammar. This was a major part of his life project: finding the deep structures of all cultural activities. He held that foodways would have such structures, just as grammar does, and that one could isolate rules just as one can state rules for changing an English verb into past, future, or perfect tense forms.

Up to a point, this worked well. Douglas, following up the idea, pointed out that the English formal dinner is sentencelike in its exact order: appetizers, soup, fish, and so on to dessert. One can point also to the equivalence of ingredients and phonemes (meaningful linguistic sound units), and the similarity of a complex dish to a word made up of phonemes. A dinner made up of such dishes is rather like a sentence; a feast is a paragraph; an individual's whole food system might be likened to a book; and so on.

Clearly, this analogy can be pushed too far. Sometimes Lévi-Strauss's own application of linguistics was purely metaphoric, as when he rather cuttingly described French food as "marked" and English food as "nonmarked." The parallel is with the linguists' distinction between the "unmarked" form of a word (in English, forms like "go" and "run," which can be used as "general" forms of the verb) and the "marked" forms ("went," "gone," "ran," "was running"—words that specify a time or other definite conditions). Obviously, the parallel isn't a good one, as English anthropologists immediately pointed out.

Food is, indeed, rather like language, but one can be more free with food. It is not so tightly structured as the elements of language are. Consider the simplest case: the similarity of combining phonemes into a word and ingredients into a dish. "Tree" has three phonemes: /t/, /r/, and /i/ (/i/ is used to write the "ee" sound in standard linguistic transcriptions). A minimal sort of Texas chile might have three ingredients: beans, chile, and meat. (No, I don't make it that way either, but bear with me.) With the word, if you mispronounce it (dree), drag out one sound (treeee), write it, yell it, or otherwise mangle it, it is still "the same word" to an English speaker. With the food, tripling the chile, or using a different type of bean, changes the dish materially and provides a quite different experience. To that extent, food is less tightly structured. One does not automatically reduce a range of different experiences to "the same thing."

A meal is even more variable. If it is like a sentence, it is like a sentence in a language much less grammatically constrained than any real language on earth.

In fact, food is more like music or painting than like language. Lévi-Strauss came to see this. His magnum opus, *Mythologiques* (in four huge volumes, 1964–1972), analyzes myths and myth making in terms of language, food, and music. Interested always in structures, he sought for common structures in all the four realms, and pushed as hard as he could to find in food, music, and myth the tight, formal rules that characterize linguistic analysis. To do this, he had to infer "deep structures," unstated patterns underlying these arts. The intuition of the anthropologist was needed to discover such structures.

Naturally, this approach produced a reaction. Poststructuralists not only doubted the validity of deep-structure analysis of myth and food; they challenged formal analysis itself. Practice theories, such as those of Pierre Bourdieu (a Lévi-Straussian at first; see Bourdieu 1977, 1990) and Jean Lave, privileged the flexible, improvised quality of practice and action over the formal structures inferred by analysis. Even language itself was analyzed from a "practice" standpoint, as in the brilliant work of William Hanks (1990).

The dust has somewhat cleared from the battlefield, and one can now take a rather dispassionate view. Practice is everywhere important, but rules exist. They can be very strict, or they can be mere vague guidelines.

Some communities—orthodox Jews, caste Hindus, and devout Seventh-Day Adventists, for instance—do structure their foodways tightly enough to make them easy to analyze in a formal, Lévi-Straussian way. Others, however, are riotously improvisational. Just try to set structural rules for the foodways of typical Los Angelenos or San Franciscans.

Anthropologists describing foodways are usually seeking for rules, generalizations, and guiding principles, rather than trying to cover the whole kaleidoscope of practice. This makes anthropological accounts read far more like formal linguistics than the reality warrants. One cannot really escape this—anthropologists, like ordinary cookbook writers, are in the business of giving general accounts. Such accounts tell people what to expect if they go to live and eat among the X People. Novelists and chefs are, usually, the ones who write individual practice. The chef can write down her unique recipe for truffled lobster; the anthropologist's job is to describe daily bread.

This tendency has rather obscured the fact that cultures manage food as art, not as (ordinary) language. Food is closer to visual art or to music than to poetry, for poetry must depend on the strict rules of language, while food, like painting, can play practice games at all levels.

Yet, cultural foodways have to be predictable and comprehensible if they are to have any communicative value.

Moreover, foodways are under technological and biological constraints. Pie crusts can differ only so much; there are functional constraints on them. Mayonnaise, Chinese stir-fry, and Japanese sushi have to be made just right to be recognizable. A practice theorist who sets out to make mayonnaise by slowly stirring up some oil, egg, and water will not make anything even remotely recognizable as a mayonnaise relative.

The conscientious describer of foodways, then, gives all the rules possible, in the most clear and concise way. After that, said describer can specify "rules for breaking rules"—acceptable variants of a dish, acceptable shortcuts in making it, acceptable substitutions of ingredients, and so on.

Cooks learn this sort of thing just as children learn their language: by inferring guidelines from practice. A cook soon learns what can be varied in making a dish, and what cannot. A normal chile recipe must (by definition) be a stew of meat and chile, normally with salt and pepper. Typical additions include beans, cumin, and oregano. Improvisers routinely add beer or even whiskey, various spices and herbs, and various kinds of chile pepper. Adding maple sugar produces something that might raise the hair of a purist, but I know chile cooks who have done it. Using fish instead of meat would seem to push the dish beyond the limit; no one (I think) would call it "chile" any more. (One might get away—barely—with calling it "fish chile.")

Cooks also learn when they can use shortcuts and when they cannot. Many a dish is ruined in the process, but that is the price of learning.

Eating has its own rules; politeness and etiquette are concepts everywhere, though the "polite" thing to do can vary from throwing bones to the dogs under the table to knowing when to use which of four or five forks. Renaissance Europe had a vast set of rules, deserving a modern book (Albala 2002). Naturally, most of them are different from those of, say, highland New Guinea—or from those of modern Europe.

Therefore, food, like every other art, can convey subtle and complex messages. Many of these are emotional—matters of mood, feeling, and tone—rather than precise and specific. Language is often about being exact, but food is usually about being warm, homey, religious—anything broad and deep, but little that is narrow and defined.

Even when religion or custom enforces a peculiar discipline, there are countless variations; Jewish cooking has hardly become monotonous! Most American Jewish food, in my childhood, was structured not only by religion but also by nostalgia for East Europe. Lox and bagels, knishes, potato latkes, pastrami sandwiches, and many other characteristic foods were universal in Jewish delicatessens and were pretty much the same everywhere. With the passing of the generation that remembers the pre-Holocaust world, this cuisine is dying out. It is being replaced by a cuisine that is recognizably a descendent, but that has been influenced by recent Sephardic immigration from the Mediterranean and Israel; by American gourmet trends; by French restaurant cuisine; and much else. One now enters a deli with little idea what to expect. Knishes stuffed with chop suey are not unthinkable.

This means that a whole set of messages that American Jewish food used to carry—messages of ethnic identity, of bonds with the *shtetl,* of memory and home and family—are gone. It now carries messages of sophistication, experiment, cosmopolitan living, and openness to the new. If one feels nostalgic, one can seek out the last few traditional delis (if there are any—in Los Angeles, even the historic Junior's and Cantor's are not as they once were). If one is feeling cosmopolitan, one can try the newer places.

Where once the old-fashioned deli communicated familiar messages of home and ethnicity, it now communicates powerful nostalgia. It is now a voice from a vanished world.

2

Humans classify their world in order to simplify it. Treating each new stimulus as a totally new, unprecedented event would make life impossible. We thus rely on the simple rules noted by Immanuel Kant long ago (Kant 1978 [orig. pub. 1796]): the principle of aggregation and the principle of differentiation. We lump together things we find it convenient to think similar. We separate, very sharply, things we find it convenient to think different.

The world thus gets classified into food and nonfood.

This is not merely a cognitive matter. We now realize that cognition and emotion are inextricably intertwined (Anderson 1996; Damasio 1994). Nothing we know is emotionally neutral; we are involved, as living and feeling persons, with all our knowledge.

Often, one culture's choicest delicacy is another culture's abomination. The ancient Israelites loathed shellfish, but recognized grasshoppers and locusts as excellent eating (see Leviticus 11:10, 21–22); Anglo-Americans have the opposite reaction. Conversely, the same ancient Israelites loathed the pig, as do modern Jews and Muslims. Yet the pig is favored to the point of culinary adoration in America and most of Europe. The "Islamic Center of America" is in my wife's home town of

Plainfield, Indiana. My wife's comment, as we passed the Center after eating in Plainfield's wonderful, popular, and thoroughly pork-centered Kristy's Café, was, "They won't make many converts here."

Things that violate neat pigeonholes—especially pigeonholes sanctioned by sacred writ—are often regarded as uncanny (Douglas 1966, 1970; Lévi-Strauss 1962, 1964). Thus, items that are obviously food, but are not *our* food, get seen as horrifying, disgusting, or unclean.

Ideas of disgust change. Fifty years ago, organ meats were prized in the United States. Liver was universal on menus. Kidneys, tongue, and sweetbreads were commonly eaten. Chitlins—intestines—were locally popular, as were tripes (cows' stomachs). Today, these have been banished from stores and menus, except where recent immigrants from organ-eating cultures are concentrated. Vegetarianism, animal rights, health findings (liver is high in cholesterol), and other factors played into this change, but it remains poorly understood. Marshall Sahlins (1976) theorized that anything called by its right name is avoided: tongue, liver, and tail are out, but pork, beef, and steak are in. Presumably, if we called pork "pig meat" and beef "steer meat," nobody would eat them. However, this theory does not work; we use honest and forthright terms for rump roast, lamb, chicken, and turkey. Conversely, squeamishness is not much diluted by using special food-market terms for chitlins, tripe (ruminant stomachs), and sweetbreads (thymus gland). The prohibition is one of identifiable innards (whatever they are called) versus undifferentiated skeletal muscles. Even things like chicken necks are now being avoided by some hypersqueamish eaters.

A similar change in foodways occurred in Tasmania long ago. When European settlers reached Tasmania, they were surprised to find that the Tasmanian aborigines had no concept of eating fish. The native Tasmanians were surprised and intrigued to see the newcomers catch and eat such creatures. Archeology has since revealed that this state of affairs was the result of a sudden, dramatic change about four thousand years ago. The only possible explanation is a massive, long-continued outbreak of poisoning by fish that had been eating toxic organisms. Small outbreaks of this type are common in the Pacific world. No such massive outbreak is known in recent history, but recent environmental degradation is causing larger outbreaks, and some strange environmental change probably caused a big, ancient one.

Paul Rozin and his students have demonstrated that squeamishness and disgust are learned (see chapter 4). Young children eat anything; they

Food to some, not to others, Cambodia. Deep-fried tarantulas are sold on the roadside. *Photo by E. N. Anderson, 1998*

learn from their parents and peers what to like and dislike. Rozin may overstate the general case, but clearly the dislike of organ meats is learned. These foods are prime delicacies in other cultures. The Plains Indians ate the tongue and liver of the buffalo even if they had to leave all the rest.

Insects are widely eaten in Mexico, but the Yucatec Maya are almost as limited as Americans in their dietary choices. Unlike other Mexican indigenous peoples, they eat few insects, though they relish wasp and bee larvae. They do not eat mushrooms, which they find disgusting. They avoid reptiles and all small animals. They do, however, consume all parts of the animals they eat. Brains, blood sausage, and liver are notably popular.

Much ink has been spilled on why pigs, dogs, and the like are tabooed as food in many cultures. Such items are seen as edible but inedible, and thus strange. Most taboo animals seem to be similarly anomalous in other ways: they are both human and inhuman, or they are hoofed but do not chew the cud, or they chew the cud but are not truly hoofed. Dogs appear to be both human and nonhuman—they live with us, but they are four-footed and don't talk. Thus they are uncanny (Douglas 1966, 1970;

Leach 1964). They are even considered poisonous in some cultures. Where they are just another outdoor livestock animal, as in much of China and Korea, they are just another food. (We will pick up this subject again in chapter 11.)

Of course, to vegetarians, all animals are out of the food category. The Jains of India sometimes go on to avoid even milk (taking it might starve the calf) and seeds (they are living plant propagules). Very strict Jain priests may live entirely on fruit, since fruit is clearly offered by the plant as food, for the purpose of getting the seed distributed. *Very* devout Jains, in fact, may feel called upon to plant the seeds after eating the fruit—a good idea in this age of global warming.

One does not usually see moral attitudes toward plant foods. Almost everyone, except the strictest Jains, eats any and all plant foods. Mushrooms and algae—not really plants in the strict biological sense—are, however, often avoided. The reasons why some plants are eaten in one culture and avoided in another must then be buried in history. Americans, disliking strong flavors in vegetable foods, avoid many greens that are greatly relished by Greeks, who love bitter herbs such as wild lettuce, wild fennel, wild radish, and other acrid greens (Gray 1997). The French use chervil and marjoram, the Mediterranean countries use coriander greens and oregano; this has much to do with climate—chervil does not grow in hot, dry zones.

In my wanderings I have noticed that the tender young leaves of manioc (tapioca, cassava) are prized delicacies in parts of Indonesia and Africa, seen as famine food or inferior food in other areas, and viewed as inedible in other parts of Africa and in most of Latin America. This is a matter of sheer habit (though urban Indonesia's serious problem with availability of vitamin-rich vegetables clearly has something to do with the use of the leaves there).

Why did the Spanish enthusiastically adopt maize, tomatoes, and vanilla in Mexico, but not chia sage seeds, tomatillos (green tomatolike fruit), or the large, anise-flavored leaves of *Piper auritum*? At least we know why the Spanish suppressed the cultivation of that excellent food, amaranth seeds: these were used to make cakes with the blood of sacrificed captives, and Spanish Catholics saw in this a satanic parody of the communion host.

More complex than taboos are the detailed classifications of how the things that are fit to eat manage to fit together. Some cultures view sweets as natural accompaniments to meat; Morocco and Algeria, for instance, cook chicken, lamb, and even fish with honey, sugar, and fruit. Others, including most Anglo-Americans, would never think of such a combination. The English traditionally found the combination of meat and sweet repellent in general, but made exceptions for lamb with mint jelly, game with Cumberland sauce, and roast pork with applesauce. In medieval times, fish with mustard and rose petals was popular in Europe; it would be a virtually unthinkable combination now (though the medieval recipe is, in fact, very good).

Food habits usually make sense, but many are simply the fossilized record of past fads or historical accidents. One cannot hope to explain everything. But one can try, and the attempt is always amusing.

People often classify foods in hierarchies, much as botanists classify plants. The "sandwich" category includes turkey sandwiches, Denver sandwiches, and so on. At one level, "sandwich" includes hamburgers, but at another level it contrasts: "Do you want a hamburger or a sandwich?" (Frake 1980:5–8). The "fish" category can include shellfish (as in the "fish" section of menus) or exclude them (as in "fish and shellfish" cookbooks). When whale meat was served in restaurants, it posed a problem: was it a fish dish or a meat dish?

Most English speakers know that the folk and botanical definitions of "vegetable" and "fruit" differ. To the botanist, all plants are "vegetable" productions, and all structures that enclose a seed in a flower-derived covering are "fruits." To the folk, "vegetables" are edible nonsweet plant tissues, and "fruits" are sweet ones. Thus, many items are vegetables to the folk but fruits to the expert: eggplants, tomatoes, red and green peppers, and so on. Conversely, some items that are fruits to the folk are not fruits to the biologist. The "fruit" of the cashew plant, for instance, is a swollen stem. (The nut grows at the tip of it, not inside it.) Many "fruits" are actually aggregations of many tiny fruits grown together: pineapples, blackberries, and the like. We think of a pineapple as a single fruit, but it is actually a whole cluster of fruits that grow together into a single mass.

"Berry" in folk English refers to any small, seedy fruit, but in botany it refers only to single soft fruits with many seeds per fruit. Thus, botanically, the category does not include such familiar "berries" as strawberries (small, hard, true fruits on the outside of a swollen stem base) or blackberries (lots of little one-seeded fruits stuck together). Conversely, tomatoes and eggplants are berries to the botanist but not to the diner.

Similar problems occur in other languages. In parts of Mexico, *fruta* even includes sugar cane and sweet potatoes—because they are eaten as snacks and are sweet. In Chinese, no distinction is made between fruits and nuts, both being *guo*, but fresh soft fruits are separated off in a sub-category: *shui guo*, "juicy fruits." Squash and melons are combined in a quite different category, *gua*; Chinese realize that these are "fruits" of a sort, but do not think of them as *guo*.

Virtually all cultures differentiate between animal and vegetable foods. Probably all differentiate fish from land flesh. Most distinguish leaves from root foods. Beyond these obvious distinctions, classification and terminology can be confusing. One need only recall the Norman French food terms in English: "beef," "pork," "venison," and "mutton" for the meat of cattle, pigs, deer, and sheep, respectively (yet "lamb" remains recalcitrant).

Or consider "herb"—from the Latin *herba*, meaning any small plant. In English we now use it to mean fresh or dried flavoring-plant leaves used in very small quantities, like spices. In French, *herbe* is usually used this way, too, especially in the combination *fines herbes*. Chinese has no equivalent to this, because Chinese don't usually use plants this way. Maya, too, lacks any comparable category. "Herb" took on its modern English use quite late, as the spices of medieval cooking were supplemented and then replaced by these aromatic plants, in the sixteenth and seventeenth centuries. The usage crystallized slowly. It has still not lost its medicinal applications. Until the nineteenth century, "herb" in English carried strong medical overtones. Today its prime focus is culinary, but "herbal medicine" is making a comeback, and "herb" may be regaining its earlier reference.

"Spices" are normally differentiated from "herb" by being seeds, hard, dry fruits, or bark rather than leaves. As usual, we should not expect comparable terms in other languages. Most European languages have an equivalent, dating from spice-trade centuries. But Chinese does not; the nearest equivalent means "flavoring things" or "aromatics."

Terms thus change as uses of foodstuffs change. Of course, they do not always perfectly mirror changing foodways. A term may get stuck, frozen in the language long after its world has changed. "Sweetmeat" recalls a day when "meat" in English meant any food, not animal meat per se. "Steak" was once the cut of meat that was broiled on a stake, like a large kabob; the name persists, under an odd spelling, long after the cooking method has changed. Changes sometimes begin and never progress; "tart" has replaced "pie" for some specialized usages, but "pie" remains the standard.

The negotiation of meanings can involve negotiation about class, about locality, about specialization. Prized foods like caviar, Camembert, Stilton, and burgundy are subject to militant name defense when imitated. The last three are now legally protected (to varying degrees in different countries). Caviar remains vulnerable; lumpfish and salmon eggs pass under the name, the edible eggs of insects breeding on the lakes of central Mexico have been called "Mexican caviar," and, at the extreme, a Turkish and Armenian eggplant dish is known in some quarters as "eggplant caviar."

Huge battles over the right to use a prized name are routine in the courts and legislatures of Europe. Thousands of pages of legal codes list and describe, precisely, the exact regions and exact artisanal processes that produce true Roquefort, champagne, and so forth. The French (of course!) developed this system of *appellations controlées,* and (of course!) first used it for wines, but over time the system spread to other foods and other lands. The Japanese independently developed something similar. The idea of *appellations controlées* has spread to other countries recently, especially in wine labeling but also—increasingly—for cheeses and other local foods.

Serious conflict developed in the 1990s over the attempt to patent the name "basmati," a word used heretofore as a general description for aromatic rice varieties of northwest India and neighboring Pakistan. An American firm attempted (unsuccessfully, in the end) to patent the word as a name for a rice variety they grew. Ironically, it was not, in fact, a basmati. This became an international scandal and has led to intense investigation of the whole issue (Shiva 1997).

In short, food classification and nomenclature are not obscure and irrelevant issues. Food names can be fighting words. Nomenclatural food fights can be serious courtroom battles that go on for years.

Nomenclature for particular dishes and recipes is far too complex to discuss in a general book. Everyone has a favorite list of odd dish names: bubble-and-squeak, toad-in-a-hole . . . The Chinese dish "Buddha jumped over the wall" is a slow-cooked dish of mixed meats, which smells so good in cooking that the most religious vegetarian would leap a wall to get to it.

More serious is the tendency of humans to consider anything classed together to be truly, deeply similar. We expect "vegetables" to be uniformly good nutrition sources, and are surprised to find that some are incomparably better than others. We see a logic to the use of the term "pepper" for various unrelated plants; they are alike in that all of them are piquant, "peppery."

But words grow organically, like plants, and similar words can cover very dissimilar things. In addition to the miscellaneous "peppers," we have a range of "potatoes," from white to sweet to air (the "air potato" is a yam that bears small tubers on its aerial vines). "Lettuce" extends to lamb's lettuce, which is not much like lettuce but can be used in salad, and even to sea lettuce, an alga with a superficially lettucelike appearance. "Spinach" has become a general term for a boiled green-leaf vegetable; Malabar spinach and New Zealand spinach are not much like the familiar species, though they cook up similarly. From the days when every land creature was believed to have its sea-creature equivalent, we have dogfish, catfish, rabbitfish, sea cucumbers (which are animals), sea urchins (an "urchin" was a hedgehog—originally), and so on.

In short, words extend from an original focus. The way a word extends is not always predictable. Words also get misapplied over time, shifting their meaning. Nobody knows what the original "cardamom" (Greek *kardamon*) and "cinnamon" (*kinnamon*) were. The Greeks used them for local Mediterranean spices. The terms were misapplied at some point early in the spice trade (Crone 1987). Similarly, *kaktos*, a Greek word for a kind of thistle, was misapplied to a group of New World plants that the ancient Greeks never saw.

"Corn" is a familiar example of name use and misuse. In England, it means any grain, or even any seed ("acorn" is really "oak corn," "aik" being a local variant of "oak"). When the English settled America, they naturally referred to maize as "Indian corn." But maize soon became so familiar that the "Indian" was usually left off, producing monumental confusion to this day. In some specialized usages, it was the "corn" that was left off. "Rye an' Injun" was rye-and-maize-meal bread. "Indian pudding" is made of Indian corn meal, but is a thoroughly English recipe—not a Native American one.

Other languages change in similar ways. Most American crops, when they came to China, were called "barbarian X" or "western X," X being the name of whatever Chinese plant looked like the new one. Thus, tomatoes became "barbarian eggplants." Winter squash is "barbarian melon." Pineapple is "barbarian jakfruit." Pomegranate came to China from the west in medieval times (Laufer 1919) and was called "seedy willow"; then, when guavas came, their fruits looked enough like pomegranates to earn them the name of "barbarian seedy willow." Maize was lumped with millet, asparagus with a native grass eaten as shoots. Spinach is called "Persian vegetable," leaving us in no doubt as to its origin point. Over time, the "barbarian" or "foreign" component is apt to drop, leaving people confused over whether (for example) guavas or pomegranates are being mentioned.

The white potato received various local Chinese names: "Dutch yam," "horse bell yam" (Chinese horse bells are round and small-potato sized), and so forth. Sweet potatoes, when not "barbarian yams," are "sweet yams" or "golden yams."

Maya expanded the name of the native mamey fruit to cover the introduced banana. Native Americans everywhere called the horse the "big dog" or "white man's dog," knowing no other domestic animal. The Maya, however, called it a "tapir," recognizing the close relationship of these animals. Today, in Yucatec Maya, the word has lost its original meaning, and means only the horse; the Maya have had to borrow the word "tapir" for their native animal! Several North American native languages use the word for the native plum to label introduced peaches or apples; whichever fruit was most familiar got the name "white man's plum" (Brown 1996).

In Indonesia, a rabbit is a "Dutch cat," a turkey a "Dutch chicken," both names commemorating the people who introduced these edible animals to Southeast Asia.

Such coined names are often wildly wrong. White potatoes, which come from Peru and Chile, are "Irish potatoes" to many English speakers—leading to geographical confusion about the plant's origin. We call a Mexican bird a "turkey." In Turkey, it is called a "chicken of India." (Presumably they heard it came "from the Indies." The Chinese name, "fire chicken," seems much better—at least it is creative.) Maize, another Mexican plant, used to be called "Turkey corn" in Europe; in Turkey it is "Egyptian corn." The Jerusalem artichoke is only somewhat like an artichoke and has nothing to do with Jerusalem. (The geographic label is said, not very believably, to be a corruption of *girasole*, the Italian for "sunflower," but the etymology of the name remains controversial; see Heiser 1976:183–84.) And how the Peruvian cavy became a "guinea pig," when it is neither African nor piglike, remains a mystery.

Word usage grows like a vine. It starts from a root, but then takes its own way, according to the lay of the land and the opportunities for climbing and extending. The principles of aggregation and differentiation are applied ad hoc, often according to historical accident.

On the other hand, there is method in the madness. No one lumps dogs and apples, or potatoes and wheat. No one even goes so far as to lump blackberries and strawberries, except that both are "berries" (in folk naming if not in botany). Things must seem truly basically similar in *some* important way to be lumped under one name.

The most extreme extensions are metaphoric ones. Calling a yam with an aerial tuber an "air potato" is one thing; calling a lazy TV addict a "couch potato" is quite another. "Corn" can refer not to grain but to bad art—the sort of stuff that appeals only to eaters of America's most rustic grain food.

Most widespread (and outrageous) of all are the sexual metaphors. Every cultural group revels in teasing out parallels between humanity's two favorite realms of experience. From the blues singer's "candy stick" and "jelly roll" to the Chinese poet's "brown pepper" and the indigenous Mexican's "chile," the male genitalia find comparisons with similar-looking local edibles—mostly sweet or spicy ones. Nor does the female escape. South Mexico seems downright obsessed with such matters. The relevant item of female anatomy is variously referred to as "cheese," "meat," "tripe," "papaya," "brown sugar," and a dozen other edibles, providing enough material for a legion of Freudian interpreters. Nor are food preparation vessels neglected. A South Chinese equivalent is "wok," as in "large frying pan." In the southern United States, in my childhood, semen was "sugar"; thus sex in general was "sugar." The red-light district of town was Sugar Hill.

Poets from Shakespeare to the Delta bluesmen constantly draw on such metaphoric language.

Classification is, at base, an attempt to simplify and make sense of the world. Metaphor plays against this. It is the art of using classification to make the world more unpredictable and striking, and therefore more interesting. It is the art of playing with language so as to bring out pointed, unusual, or funny comparisons. It uses the principles of aggregation and differentiation not as tools to get a handle on the world and render it manageable, but as tools to play with the world and make it more entertaining and exciting.

I distinguish between true metaphor and mere extension of a term, contra Lakoff and Johnson in *Philosophy in the Flesh* (1999). I do not agree with their claims that humans routinely think via metaphor, and I do not agree with their "metaphoric" extension of the word. Metaphor deserves to be retained in its original meaning: a striking parallel between two dissimilar things that can be seen, with the eye of a poet, as having something in common. A mountain lion is not really a lion, but neither is it a metaphoric lion. A social lion is.

We classify to understand, but we humans can never let anything rest. Once we understand something, we feel a compulsion to make it mysterious. A world of clearly labeled foods becomes a world of mysterious poetic symbols.

8

Me, Myself, and the Others
Food as Social Marker

I love to eat fish, and I also love to eat bears' paws, but if I can't
have both, I will leave the fish and take the bears' paws. I love life,
and I love doing right; but if I can't have both, I will give up life to
do what's right. . . .
  Here's a basket of grain and a plate of soup. Getting them means
life, lacking them means death. But if you offer them with a harsh
insulting voice, even a traveler won't accept them, and if you step
on them, even a starving beggar won't accept them. Here is a salary
of ten thousand, but offered without concern for the right. What is
that ten thousand to me?

—*Mencius* (Book 6, passage 10, my translation. In this passage, the
great Chinese social thinker Mengzi [Mencius to the western world]
is in desperate straits but is turning down a compromised appoint-
ment. Bears' paws remain a Chinese delicacy—which is now a
problem for endangered bear species. "Right" undertranslates *yi*,
which, here, means acting with absolute honor and probity.)

1

Food as communication finds most of its applications in the process of
defining one's individuality and one's place in society. Food communicates class, ethnic group, lifestyle affiliation, and other social positions.
Eating is usually a social matter, and people eat every day. Thus, food is
available for management as a way of showing the world many things
about the eater. It naturally takes on much of the role of communicating
everything. Indeed, it may be second only to language as a social communication system.
  Elaborate social messages are carried in feast behavior. In Chinese formal hospitality, honor and respect are showed by the host using his own

chopsticks to serve the guest; by hosts serving chicken and wine rather than salt fish and boiled water; or by literally thousands of other gestures. Weddings are supposed to include shark-fin soup. Lotus rhizomes may be served at a wedding, too, because when you break a cooked lotus rhizome the starch forms long strings that hold the two pieces together no matter how far apart they are pulled. The symbolism is obvious. At birthday parties, long noodles mean "may you live long." More generally, food has its own meanings. Everywhere, food is associated with home, family, and security.

At a deeper level, food may become a real part of one's identity. Rice is so important in Japanese culture that Emiko Ohnuki-Tierney wrote a brilliant study of Japanese character and food with the significant title *Rice as Self* (1993). This book explains in detail the cultural reasons behind our poetic guide Ryokan's use of a phrase like "everyone eats rice." Ryokan was indeed speaking not only of food but also of self—that interpersonal construction that is regarded by Buddhists as an illusion.

One main message of food, everywhere, is *solidarity*. Eating together means sharing and participating. The word "companion" means "bread sharer" (Latin *cum panis*). Buying dinner, or otherwise feeding a prospect, is so universal in courtship, business, and politics that it is almost certainly grounded in inborn tendencies; we evolved as food sharers and feel a natural link between sharing food and being personally close and involved. Such venues as cafés, coffee shops, coffee houses, cafeterias, bars, neighborhood restaurants, and other eateries are vital to social life. Ray Oldenburg, in a very important book, showed that such "third places" were almost as important as home and work (the other two places) in people's lives (Oldenburg 1989). Note that several of these types of eateries have names based on coffee; caffeine has been the stimulant of sociability for centuries, more so even than alcohol (Anderson 2003; Hattox 1985).

The other main message is *separation*. Food marks social class, ethnicity, and so on. Food transactions define families, networks, friendship groups, religions, and virtually every other socially institutionalized group. Naturally, one group can try to use food to separate itself, while another is trying to use food to eliminate that separation.

Clearly, humans are social feeders. There are some obvious benefits, such as the creation of social alliances, or the possibility of combining to defend the food. However, the immediate reason for most social feeding is that people simply like to eat with others. A big feed almost inevitably

Local tastes, Venice. Fresh mushrooms—six out of a good dozen local species for sale. Mushrooms were feared and avoided as "toadstools" in the English-speaking world through much of history, but in Italy they are a veritable cult, and one can see bankers and lawyers on their lunch hours foraging for mushrooms in public parks. *Photo by E. N. Anderson, 2002*

becomes a party, and a party almost always involves food—and drink. The importance of family mealtime continues to be recognized, even in the contemporary United States, where the average nuclear family sits down together for only three meals a week. Major holidays are occasions for family reunions, inevitably defined and structured by food.

In cultural contexts that require polite formulas rather than honest words, language may lose almost all its communicative function, and here food often takes over the role. In formal dinners around the world, for instance, it is not usually appropriate to send the important social messages verbally. Words are bland and carefully chosen. More information about the actual social transactions going on at the dinner is transmitted by food choice and distribution. The most valued guest gets the choicest portion, and so on down. Other aspects of the ritual may communicate even more. Everyone carefully observes who sits next to the host, who sits at the host's table, who is the first one to be greeted, who is served first, who gets the best piece of meat, who is urged to have seconds, and so on (and on and on).

The whole purpose of a feast is usually to bring people together and affirm their solidarity. Alliances are formed, deals are struck. Visiting dignitaries are feted. In Chinese society, no important deal can be concluded without food and drink. A major contract signed necessitates a lunch or dinner. The more important the contract, the larger and more expensive the meal.

Often a feast has the purpose of affirming the host's generosity. From the feasts of ancient Ireland (*The Tain* 1983) to the potlatches of the Northwest Coast, a leader earned the loyalty of his followers by feasting them and giving them lavish gifts at or after the feast. This was a life-or-death matter. A leader who was ungenerous lost his followers, and was soon conquered and almost certainly killed by rivals. Thus, a reputation for generosity was life, and the opposite was death. This is the most important reason for the extreme power of the bards of old Ireland and the *griots* (bards) of west Africa. They can literally destroy a man by publicizing his stinginess.

Dinnertime, India. The family gathers round to cook dinner. *Photo by Barbara Anderson, 1996*

We say someone is "below the salt" because in medieval and Renaissance Europe the salt was set in the middle of the table, separating the higher-ranked people near the table's head from the lower ones near the foot (Scully 1995). According to scurrilous (but dubious) history-student folklore, at a family dinner the legitimate children would sit above the salt, the bastards below it.

2

When you sit at the table with others, sit long, for it is a time that is not counted against you as part of [the ordained span of] your lives.
—Ja'far al-Sadiq (medieval Shi'a Muslim leader)

So socialized food is always structured along particular lines. Perhaps most frequently, it conveys messages about group identification. Regions are defined by preferred staple: rice, bread, potatoes. Religions are defined by food taboos (see following chapter). Some religions have entire food cultures of their own; the Hindus (Khare 1976a, 1976b, 1992) and Seventh-Day Adventists are notable among these. Foods can convey a rich symbolic mix of religion, philosophy, lifestyle, and identity in a complex, shifting, exquisitely fine-tuned pattern (Curtin and Heldke 1992). The phenomenology of food and eating would require many volumes to survey.

Even political ideologies have their food cultures. Conservative Americans cling to beefsteak, baked potatoes, and presliced white bread. The eastern Midwest has a heart disease rate far higher than that of the rest of the nation, partly because of obesity and high cholesterol levels. Poor eating, lack of exercise, and above all smoking combine to produce a deadly combination, with heart-disease death rates over two hundred per one hundred thousand people per year (data from an untitled note on pages A8–A9 of the May 11, 2001, edition of the *Los Angeles Times*). People know the lifestyle is unhealthy, and the food is not usually good-tasting either, but it is *their* lifestyle, and people are loyal to it unto death. Their identity is caught up in it; they will sacrifice themselves for it. By contrast, liberal urban sophisticates seek out the trendiest Europeanoid restaurant. They maintain a zealous commitment to "fitness," but the commitment is not infrequently misguided; being "with it" takes precedence over actual research into the issue. Vegetarian cuisine defines yet other political factions. Health devotees express political as well as medical conviction when they seek out greens and tofu.

Lifestyle—that most protean and most important of concepts—results from political identity, from regional identity, from association with friends, from status, and from other factors. It defines individuals and their foodways.

Kin and family structure food in important ways. This has been the focus of much food research, especially since Audrey Richards's pioneering studies in Africa in the 1930s (Richards 1939, 1948). Every family has its traditions. These get passed on indefinitely. There is an old joke or urban folktale of a girl who was learning how to cook a roast. Her mother was teaching her to cut the ends off the roast. The girl asked why. Answered the mother, "That's the way my mother did it." The girl then sought out her grandmother and got the same answer. Fortunately, the great-grandmother was still alive, and revealed that when she was first married she had a small pan, and had to trim the ends off the large roasts of those days to get them to fit! This story appears to be purely legendary, but, as the Italians say, *si non e vero, e ben trovato* (loosely: if it isn't true, well, it's a good story).

3

Food studies have followed other research into the forests and thickets of identity, gender, and ethnicity. These are the three classic topics of cultural anthropology—now important to all social sciences. It is transparently obvious that foodways are powerfully structured by considerations of personal and group identity. Identity is often constructed and communicated with regard to foods: "I'm a dry martini person, myself."

Vegetarians make up a special food subculture in the United States. Devout Seventh-Day Adventists make up a special subset within the vegetarian world. Devout Buddhists form another subset. More loosely defined are the groups of vegetarians who abstain from meat simply because they hate the thought of killing animals, or because they simply don't like meat. Vegetarians can be quite militant, zealously propagating their cause, often to the acute discomfort of meat eaters.[1]

Similarly, food fights have erupted over the frenetic huckstering of junk food that passes for "modernization" in the modern world. Some of my European friends are active in the Slow Food movement, a political cause that started in Italy and has spread widely. It has not really caught on in the United States, though it does have transatlantic members. More widespread is a general opposition to foods transformed by modern technology: processed, genetically engineered, additive laden, and so on. We have learned from bitter experience to distrust such foods. The additives and processing are rarely tested. Currently, giant corporations assure us that genetically engineered foods are safe but refuse to allow them to be tested. Said untested foods now make up 70 percent of America's grain and soybean supply, but are banned in much of Europe.

People identify themselves in terms of locality, also. American regional cooking is less developed than European or Chinese, but Americans still stereotype "Boston" baked beans, Kansas City barbecue, and New Orleans gumbo. In France, every village or rural region has (or used to have) its own distinctive cheese, wine, baked goods, and—often—sausage and other preserved meat specialties (cf. Root 1958). Italy seems to have a truly different cuisine in each town (Root 1971). China has regional specialties ranging from the melons of the far west to the vinegar of Jiankang in the east.

These mark identity; people from the place in question often make a point of eating their specialty. Even if they do not, their "sense of place" (Feld and Basso 1996) is very much involved with the sense of taste. We are "consuming geographies," as food geographers David Bell and Gill Valentine put it (1997). As we all know, nothing brings back a place, time, or occasion more powerfully than a scent or taste. To eat the familiar home food is to be at home, at least in the heart—as well as the stomach.

In China and especially in Japan a traveler visiting a place has to bring back samples of its specialty foods for his family and friends. The Chinese phrase is *xianpin,* "local products." This social rule explains the Japanese-labeled, extremely overpriced packages of smoked salmon one sees in Northwest Coast airports; the similarly overpriced steaks in Denver airports; and so on around the world. Japanese travelers who have put off buying the "local products" till the last minute are held hostage; they have to buy something, at any price, for the folks they are returning to.

Gourmets and foodies do not form true subcultures but are still defined by their tastes. Some cannot rest till they have sought out every pit barbecue in any city they visit. Others become absorbed with finding the perfect paté or taco or french fries. Individual taste has something to do with all this, but much of it is driven by the need of individuals to communicate something special, distinctive, and personal about themselves.

Food as communication, rural China near Loyang. Hospitality by production brigade head, serving superb fried pasta she made. *Photo by E. N. Anderson, 1978*

4

> One might recall . . . an anecdote of Darius. When he was king of Persia, he summoned the Greeks who happened to be present at his court, and asked them what they would take to eat the dead bodies of their fathers. They replied that they would not do it for any money in the world. Later, in the presence of the Greeks, and through an interpreter, so that they could understand what was said, he asked some Indians, of the tribe called Callatiae, who do in fact eat their parents' dead bodies, what they would take to burn them [the Greeks cremated their dead]. They uttered a cry of horror and forbade him to mention such a dreadful thing. One can see by this what custom can do. . . ."
>
> —Herodotus, *The Histories*

Darius was making a point: "Custom is king." He was making it to confound the Greek claim that there is a natural law grounded in human sentiment—a human ethical sense. His story is also interesting to nutritional anthropology. One way that people define group identity is through cannibalism. There are endocannibals who eat their own dead as a means of burial, and exocannibals who eat their enemies, almost always as an act of revenge. (Lurid travelers' tales to the contrary notwithstanding, no one eats people just as food, except in cases of extreme starvation.) Claude Lévi-Strauss (1964) suggested that endocannibals should boil their relatives, since this transforms the food more than roasting does— exocannibals should roast. This turns out to be untrue; cannibals boil or roast indifferently (Shankman 1969).

Everybody loves a good cannibal story. Thus, travelers being what they are, cannibal tales are vastly exaggerated. William Arens subjected cannibal stories to a devastating critique (Arens 1979), showing that almost all of them were clearly travelers' fabrications. Arens argued that cannibalism occurs only when people are desperate for food (as in the cases of the Donner party, or the soccer team marooned in the Andes). Arens was partly correct. Cannibalism usually happens because of famine (as in China; Chong 1990). Other forms of cannibalism are rare, and most of the lurid claims in the popular literature are exaggerated or fabricated. However, Arens was overstating the facts; cannibalism often does occur for purely cultural reasons (Brown and Tuzin 1983). Burial of loved ones by endocannibalism used to be common in New Guinea, and exocannibalism was widespread. Consuming parts of war captives was a well-nigh universal practice in many parts of the New World before contact, rising to a peak among the Aztecs. Among them it was definitely done for religious reasons (associated with warfare), not for protein (contra the incorrect theory of Harner 1977; see Ortiz de Montellano 1990). Arens (and others) did establish that the scale of cannibalism was vastly exaggerated by European accounts, particularly after the Pope banned enslavement of New World indigenes *unless they were cannibals*—a clause that guaranteed endless attempts by conquistadors to label everyone they met as sure-enough man-eaters.

Herodotus's story is well taken, but natural law does seem to surface in the human tendency to eat *either* one's own or one's enemies, and to do it as an act of ritual, in spite of felt disgust.

5

Individuals fit into the social structure in terms of status and role. Role is perhaps the less important of the two. Particular roles (father, fisherman, homemaker, teenager) may be signaled by food, but this is usually a minor part of a culture's foodways. Fishermen have their own foods, because of their occupation—it makes mixed seafood readily available while making land products harder to get. Often, they develop a gourmet-ship based on the small and less saleable products of their catch. The result may taste better than the "good" products, and thus wind up commanding a higher price in the end; San Francisco *cioppino* is an example (or was, before it became debased for the tourist trade).

Similarly, Hispanic cowboys in Texas made fajitas from the less saleable cuts of beef (specifically, the skirt steak), and wound up making fajitas a more popular dish than anything created from the expensive cuts. Chop suey, created by southeast Chinese vegetable growers as a way to use up small, unsaleable shoots, has had a more mixed fate. On its home turf, it is an excellent dish. Unfortunately, in California, it was debased by oil, flour, and canned vegetables. It became synonymous with "bad Chinese food," and even spawned several urban legends about its origin; according to these, it was invented by a restaurateur forced to prepare food when he had nothing left but the day's scraps. The fact that the name means "miscellaneous leftovers" (in Cantonese) did nothing to disprove the myths.

Many other role identities are stated through food. Police are identified with doughnut shops (ideal places to gather information on a neighborhood). Still, most occupations and stations are less clearly labeled. There seems to be no signature dish for computer scientists or astronomers or sales clerks.

By contrast, status, class, and prestige comprise probably the most important area signaled by food. Jack Goody (1982) has shown systematically and in detail what many of us had more or less suspected: fancy cuisine is a product of social differentiation. Societies divided up into elites and commoners have a corresponding division of food. Really elaborate cuisine, such as that of modern France, Italy, or China, apparently depends on the rise of a middle class and of *regional* elites and middle classes. The interaction between class and region, and between central and regional societies, gives us fancy cooking.

In the modern world—and for centuries before—we all know the social roles of fancy restaurants, champagne, etc. Taking one's date to Chez Snob not only shows off wealth; it also shows off personal power and authority—particularly if one addresses the maitre d' by first name, know the fanciest wine to order, and so forth. Cross-cultural comparison shows that women almost everywhere are particularly impressed by male ability to feed them. (This is true not only of other cultures, but even of other animals, ranging from storks to wolves.) Human females respond especially to high-status food. Bringing home large amounts of meat made sense in the days of hunting and gathering; a girl really needed to know her boyfriend could do that. Today, it may be little more than an evolutionary relic for most of us—but taking one's enamored out for dinner remains the commonest and most successful type of date. And it still has the old meaning in a few places. The Ache of Paraguay still live by hunting, and a man who brings home a large game animal has many an opportunity (see chapter 2).

Traditionally, men are impressed by women feeding them home-cooked meals. This may have a more recent, historic origin, being subsequent to the consignment of women to home and kitchen—a relatively new thing in human history. Traditionally, women were told that "the way to a man's heart is through his stomach." But women cook less today than they used to and many men have also learned to cook, which tells us something.

This is not the only way in which gender structures food. Anna Meigs (1997) has described the complex rules for men and women in New Guinea. A whole series of foods is reserved for men; another whole series is strictly women's share. This is all grounded in an elaborate belief system about the inner reality of gender, bodily strength, and sexuality. (To the cynical outsider, though, it looks suspiciously as if the men hogged all the goodies and then came up with a justification.) When I first talked to Dr. Meigs about all this, many years ago, I commented that the same thing existed in my childhood in the midwestern United States. She was most surprised; she had no idea that such a thing existed in America (she is German). But, when I was young, men were regarded as more like brute beasts, and ate and drank accordingly. Barbecue, rare steak, beer, whiskey, and the like were purely men's foods. Women were refined and cultured and ate jellied salads, creamed chicken, yogurt, and other pale, bland, soft foods. Needless to say, no proper man would eat such things, any more than a "decent" woman would gnaw on a barbecued rib. Lévi-Strauss (1962) pointed out that such equations of respective genders with nature and culture are common in the world. In the Midwest, men were "nature" and women were "culture." In New Guinea and many other places, men are seen as the cultured ones, women as the "nature"-like. Take your choice.

A common experiment (beloved of introductory anthropology and sociology classes) is to get a student couple, male and female, to go into a restaurant, and have the woman order a double whiskey and the man a glass of white wine, or for the woman to order steak and the man fish. The waiters almost always get it wrong.

Children are assigned special foodways everywhere. (The whole question of food in the life cycle requires an entire book; see Goody 1982). Children throughout the world were breastfed until recently. Breastfeeding is supplemented with some sort of weaning food, usually a soft, tasteless mush, at around six to nine months. Solid foods are gradually increased, and nursing tapers off. Children tend to stop nursing, spontaneously, at around two to three years. Some go on indefinitely, especially in societies whose food is uncertain and scarce. Nursing till the age of five or six is not uncommon in many societies. Weaning age, and the foods considered acceptable, are thus highly subject to cultural manipulation.

Much has changed with the coming of baby formula. Cow's milk is so poor as a human food that it never could substitute for breast milk; infants nursed or died, until the last six or seven decades. Cow's milk has too little vitamin C, iron, and other nutrients. It also lacks the stimuli to the infant's immune system that human colostrum and breast milk have. Even now, formula is a rather poor substitute for breast milk. Every year, new substances critical to development are found in breast milk. Formula-fed babies are sicklier. This is especially true when formula is mixed with not-very-clean water, as is usually the case in the Third World and often even in the United States. Also, poor families are tempted to dilute the formula too much, slowly starving the baby (Van Esterik 1997).

Foods suitable for children have changed a great deal over the last century. In the early days thereof, when infant mortality was still high, there was a genuine fear of giving children food that was "hard to digest." Nursery foods in much of the world were extremely soft and bland: rice pudding or gruel, soft grain gruel, custard, boiled eggs, and the like. Some of these—things like rice gruel—did not offer much in the way of vitamins and minerals, but most cultures had ways to compensate for this. For instance, in China, jujubes and other fruits with at least some vitamin and mineral value are now added to the rice gruel—though in the 1960s I heard a Chinese doctor say that rice gruel was a perfectly adequate food by itself, and that "Chinese babies don't need vitamins, they eat rice."

Vegetables and fruits are now far more prevalent. Yet the old ways persist, widely.

Dr. John Ho of Queen Elizabeth Hospital, whose specialty is cancer epidemiology, found that the risk of nasopharyngeal cancer was greatly increased by infant malnutrition, especially lack of vitamin C, a common problem at the time (early 1970s). One problem was that Chinese parents believed fruits and vegetables were cooling to the baby, and could be dangerous; the baby could get chills (see below). Dr. Ho was able to transform Hong Kong childrearing patterns, persuading doctors all over the region to make sure that babies got their orange juice (this story is based on my work with Dr. Ho, Anderson et al. 1978).

6

Elite groups *always* try to mark themselves off by consumption of special-status or prestige foods (caviar, champagne, goat cheese, etc.), and upwardly mobile people try to rise in respect by being seen eating those foods (Goody 1982; Mintz 1985). Food snobbism is perhaps the most widely remarked bit of pop food sociology; the ancient Greeks, Romans, and Chinese all held forth at length on it.

Status emulation leads, inevitably, to an endless progression. The foods and restaurants of the "in" crowd are quickly discovered and patronized by people who yearn to be "in." Of course, when there are too many of these "outs," the "in" people go somewhere else—and the cycle starts again. Los Angeles restaurant guides even specifically mention the "celebrity-watching" potential of restaurants, sometimes listing "stars" to be seen there. This is apt to become a self-unfulfilling prophecy, when celebrities—knowing that they are being stared at—change watering holes. However, the guide writers persist, knowing that many celebrities *like* being stared at (in fact, that often seems to be their only real qualification for stardom), while others will tolerate staring if the food is good.

Foods as class markers are so important that elites have often resorted to "sumptuary laws" to protect themselves from status emulation. Such laws ban the "lower orders" from eating elite foods, wearing elite clothes, riding elite horses, and so on. This was intended to stop the vulgar masses from buying status by imitating the elite lifestyle.

Of course, such laws rarely work well. There is just too much pressure. Not only do people naturally want to imitate the high; they also derive benefit from doing so, because people tend to treat anyone who acts elite as a real elite.

One of the original duties of the coroner, in medieval England, was to see that ordinary people did not eat porpoises or sturgeons they caught—those fish were reserved for the court. No doubt many a peasant ate the sturgeon he caught, and the coroner claimed he never heard a word about it . . . even if (*especially* if) the coroner was there at the dinner.

Even without sumptuary laws, status associations of foods can be strong. There is a traditional blues verse:

> I asked for water and she gave me gasoline,
> I asked for cabbage and she gave me turnip greens.

The low-status turnip greens are just as disgusting as the gasoline, evidently.

Many other blues verses (and the Black Muslims) denigrate the lowly turnip greens, though they are not really very different from cabbage (except in being more nutritious). Such is status. There is one old song glorifying "greasy greens" (turnip or collard greens cooked with bacon), but it is suspected of using the phrase with an obscene double entendre.

However, the status of foods can change for symbolic reasons. Collards and turnip greens saw their status rise spectacularly with the Black Power movement of the 1960s and 1970s. Black Power activists consciously sought to reevaluate the symbols of African American culture, notably including "soul food": the old-time food of the impoverished rural South. Collard greens, chitlins (chitterlings: hog intestines), barbecued pork, corn pone, sweet potato pie, and other such foods suddenly became the food of the African-American elite. White elites tried them and usually loved them—except for the chitlins. This trend leveled off, but African-American restaurants still often serve these wonderful and nutritious foods.

So, with the self-conscious revitalization of Black identity and the revalorization of Black culture by African Americans, soul food took on great prestige, and was served in the best restaurants—not just African-American ones, either. This led to a minor culture war, since southern whites and Native Americans could lay equal claim to the food; it is a joint production. Interestingly, the most clearly African of southern cuisines—Carolina rice cookery (Hess 1992)—was *not* revalorized. It had become too popular with whites.

But African Americans pointed out that they had certainly set their distinctive and creative stamp on it, and above all they were the main consumers of such food in the late twentieth century. As African-American culture has become more mainstreamed into American culture, soul food has declined—though it remains popular, and continues to be a minor but real point of ethnic identification.

Parallel phenomena occur everywhere. In Portugal *couve tronchuda*, the collardlike food of the poor, is revalued as a nostalgic ethnic marker. The traditional Portuguese "green soup" of finely chopped *couve* greens and pureed potatoes is found in virtually every Portuguese restaurant. It is gourmet fare now. Crayfish and gumbo were revalorized in Louisiana, as the Cajuns rose from a downtrodden minority to an important ethnic group. Polenta, once fare for the poorest, is now on gourmet regional menus in Italy.

Conversely, foods can fall in status. The most spectacular example is white bread. It was *the* prestige food in Europe for millennia. In the nineteenth century, the development of processing machinery made it cheap. After that, its low nutritional value and lack of taste caused it to fall farther and farther, while brown breads rose. At last, in the late twentieth century, "artisanal" white breads came back into fashion—but the everyday loaf sank to very lowly status.

Foods can fall in and out of popularity, and pepper and saffron did in west Europe: they were popular in the Renaissance, banished in the Baroque, rehabilitated (only locally for saffron) in the twentieth century.

Whole cuisines can be local fads. In Los Angeles in the 1980s and 1990s, there were jokes about the "cuisine of the year." Thai, Cajun, North Italian, and other cuisines went in and out of fashion with dizzying speed. The wise restaurateur would reinvest his windfall profits in a new line of dishes after a year or so. This sort of fad chasing is characteristic of societies in which economic dynamism has created a situation in which a rich "in" group feels itself "threatened" by a vast number of newly rich "outs" trying to break in. The "ins" have to show their superiority by public eating, as elites do everywhere. But, wherever they go, they are chased by the "outs"—often with the enthusiastic collaboration of the local newspaper.

The definitive study of food fads and wild changes is Claude Fischler's *L'homnivore* (1990); this book seems to be untranslated into English—possibly because it depends on a series of horrible and untranslatable puns, starting with the title. My favorite Fischler word is *gastro-anomie*—punning off "gastronomy" and "anomie."

Climbing the social pyramid with one's mouth is no new phenomenon. It was the subject of hilarious remark in Sung and Ming China—periods of economic dynamism. The rich merchants of the Yangzi Delta, in particular, were considered mere vulgar upstarts by the old landed power structure, and were consequently desperate to establish themselves as sophisticates. Fad chasing and restaurant roulette inevitably resulted. The same thing happened in London in the eighteenth century and Paris in the nineteenth and early twentieth.

All these social matters can be discussed in a remote, clinical way, but they are desperately important to the individuals who do the eating. Food study requires a phenomenology, a study of how individuals perceive and experience their world. It is easy to speak in clinical terms of the ability of all mammals to form an instant aversion to a food that has made them sick, and to comment learnedly on the rarity of such one-trial learning. It is quite another thing for me to experience nausea, almost sixty years later, at the very thought of ill-fated Christmas candies. There is a vast difference between my learning that caffeine acts by preempting adenosine receptors in the brain and thus interfering with the body's innate sleepiness mechanism, and experiencing the indescribably heavenly bliss of my first sip of morning coffee. My wife lives in a world of tomato gourmetship that I can barely imagine. Tomatoes taste alike to me, as long as they are better than the supermarket's low-end ones (which appear to be red golf balls rather than tomatoes). She, however, discerns differences comparable to those I find between a superb wine and a dollar-a-gallon product.

Social scientists are only beginning to investigate such matters (see e.g. Counihan 1999); there is a great field to explore. Of course, novelists, food writers, and poets have been there long before, recording the shifting tides of snobbism, convenience, economics, custom, and worry—often with an ironic or sarcastic vision.

9

Food and Traditional Medicine

1

One very important area for meaning and significance is medical use of food. Diet therapy is performed everywhere in the world.

I have been especially interested in the very widespread belief that some foods are "heating," others "cooling" to the body, while still others are "balanced" or "neutral" (Anderson 1987, 1988, 1996; Foster 1994; Laderman 1981). This has nothing to do with actual food temperature. The belief can be traced back to Hippocrates, and he says he got it from earlier sources (see Hippocrates [ascribed] 1978; see also Dalby 1997).

His later disciple, Galen, is the one who really popularized it (Galen 2000, 2003). Galen was a born salesman and promoter. Scathing in his denunciation of other systems, he tirelessly advocated his own. He was bright enough to provide value for money; his elaboration of Hippocrates is sensible, orderly, well worked out, and thorough. If it does not always accord with modern diet therapy, it at least comes close to following Hippocrates' wisest cautionary note: "First, do no harm."

The full system, as worked out by Galen, involves four conditions: hot, cold, wet, and dry. Each is associated with the four elements of classic Greek science: fire, air, water, and earth.

Their interaction produces four body fluids, called "humors." The hot and dry humor is blood. Hot and wet make phlegm. Cold and wet make bile. Cold and dry make black bile. There is no such thing as black bile, which was thought to cause melancholy, but early accounts make it clear that the term refers to the breakdown products of blood that clog the bile duct, liver, and sometimes intestines in cases of malaria and liver disease.

These humors were thought to influence personality. We still refer to sanguine (*sanguinis*, "of blood"), phlegmatic, bilious or choleric, and melancholy people. Modern psychology has partially confirmed Galen; people do fall into a few broad personality types that seem to be innate.

Sanguine people are much like the extraverts of modern psychology—in fact, Carl Jung developed the concept of "extraversion" by modernizing the old humoral category in the light of modern clinical knowledge. Excessively melancholic people are now called "depressed," "paranoid," or "schizophrenic" (cf. Robert Burton's classic *Anatomy of Melancholy*; Burton 1932 [orig. pub. 1638]). Food was much used in treating these conditions.

Foods can heat, cool, dry, or wet the body. Spicy and oily foods are heating. Water is cooling—not wetting, because if you fall into water you get chilled but your internal organs don't get any wetter. Wetting foods are those that cause retention of fluids. Later writers established a system of degrees, from first degree (very mild) to third or fourth degree (fatal). A food could be heating to the third degree and drying to the first degree.

For Hippocrates, thin barley broth was the great cure-all. Sick people were usually put on a regimen—a lifestyle or routine—of barley broth and bed rest. The worldwide use of pearl barley in healthful soups owes its origin to this. Pearl barley seems to be losing its spell now, but when I was young it was universal in both Euro-American and Chinese healing soups.

Galen wrote much about different sorts of breads, beans, waters, meats, and other foods. He had extremely sharp and penetrating comments on these, though he was prone to exaggerate their medical importance.

More complex systems developed. The great Arab, Persian, and Jewish physicians of the Near East and Muslim Spain added their contributions, of which more later. A popular class of work was the *Taqwim* (Arabic: "disposition, arrangement"; Serventi and Sabban 2002:57). This class of work became wildly popular in Europe, when it was translated into Latin; the Salerno school's *Tacuinum Sanitatis* went through countless editions. The highly prestigious medical school in Salerno, Italy, drew almost entirely on Near Eastern Galenism. The *Tacuinum* is *still* in print, in fact—in several translations (that of Luisa Arano, 1976, being notable among the English versions). Today, it sells more copies to historians and lovers of its artistic illustrations than to suffering patients. This is rather a pity, for, however much more we now know about specific foods, the book's more general advice is actually quite good.

In fact, the quality of Galenic practice always ran ahead of the theory. Galen's theory was good as a first approximation, but its long reign of eighteen hundred years is a sorry commentary on the progress of nutritional science. Even Hippocrates and Galen seem to have practiced better than they theorized. By the Middle Ages, after dozens of brilliant Near Eastern scholars had worked on the system, the theory was a miserable and threadbare net holding together a rich collection of more or less accurate and reasonable clinical observations on foods and nutrition. Much of the knowledge was wrong, mostly when it was deduced from the theory. But much was right and useful.

Many modern foods were evolved along Galenic lines. In Europe, salads balance cooling greens with salt and oil, pork is balanced by mustard, and heavy foods for workers balance light foods for the nonactive (Albala 2000:206). In China, the influence is far greater, and almost all self-consciously health-related food combinations are influenced by hot/cold theories (Anderson 1988).

The Galenic system spread throughout Europe and the Middle East. It influenced medicine throughout South, Southeast and East Asia. With European expansion it spread around the world. By the mid-twentieth century it was unquestionably the most widespread belief system on earth, far outrunning any single religion.

In Europe, it continued to be state-of-the-art until replaced by modern nutritional science in the late nineteenth and early twentieth centuries. It was believed by educated biologists well into the twentieth century. It survives robustly throughout the Middle East and in much of Latin America.

Several different cultures seem to have come up with rather similar theories: yin and yang in China, hot and cold in native America (Ortiz de Montellano 1990), and an independent heating/cooling system in Malaysia (Laderman 1981). It is a fairly obvious thing to think. We all know that a person who is too hot (feverish) is sick, and a person who is too cold (hypothermic) is in trouble. We all know that a characteristic syndrome of fever, pain, and diarrhea follows consumption of poorly kept food. We know that a feast with much alcohol produces headache and indigestion later. We know that chronic poor nutrition leads to pallor, weakness, and low body temperature; the modern nutritionist calls this "anemia." Nothing could be more natural and easy than to assume that food affects all of health.

Humoral medicine spread to China along with Buddhism around 400 AD and fused with the Chinese yin-yang theory. In modern Chinese medicine, high-calorie foods are regarded as heating, low-calorie foods as cooling. This is indeed a way of expressing a truth that the Chinese know perfectly well: you get more metabolic heat out of the former. The Chinese have had enough experience with hunger and famine to know which foods maintain body heat in cold weather.

The perfectly balanced and temperate food is cooked grain, around five hundred calories per pound. (Everywhere in the world, the balanced food is the local staple: cooked rice in China, bread in the Near East, tortillas in Mexico.)

Foods that feel burning are, of course, heating: ginger, alcohol, chile, black pepper. Foods that are bitter tend to be heating; sour, cooling. Foods that are "hot" colors (red, bright yellow, etc.) are heating; foods that are pallid and greenish are cooling. Foods that cause a burnlike reaction (reddening, swelling, irritation) are heating; thus if you are allergic to a "cold" food and get a rash from it, it's "heating" for you, even though "cooling" to most people.

Foods that treat such burnlike conditions are cooling, while foods that treat "cold" conditions are heating. Herein lies the real value of the system. Lacks of vitamins A and C are classic "hot" conditions (reddening, sores, dry skin, etc.), and vegetables are the cure. It works. Anemia is the classic "cold" condition (pallor, weakness, etc.), and gently warming meat, especially organ meats and blood, is the standard cure. It works. So the system is validated in the eyes of those who use it.

In short, the Chinese observed cause and effect quite accurately. But they then inferred an incorrect or overgeneralized intervening variable—a mystic internal "heat" or "coolness" in this case. They then logically extended the system in inaccurate ways, as when red-bean soup is used to "heat" and dried-green-bean soup to "cool" people, just because the former has a hot color, the latter a cool color. Nutritionally they are identical.

This is exactly the way scientists develop theories. The Chinese were even aware of the need to test theories, and developed the case/control experiment more than two thousand years ago (but in agricultural, not dietary, research; see Anderson 1988). They had a superb nutritional establishment. The court nutritionist was the leading medical officer in China in the Zhou Dynasty (ca. 1000 to 221 BCE) and remained so in most subsequent dynasties.

However, China did not have an adequate research-and-publication system. Nor did the Chinese have an advanced chemical science that

Food and religion, Hong Kong. Dividing up sacrificial pigs at a temple fair. The god has consumed the spiritual essence of the food; the worshipers now get the material remains. A group of women banded together to provide these pigs, so the meat is now divided among group members. *Photo by E. N. Anderson, 1966*

could isolate vitamins and mineral nutrients. They did not have journals that made new findings widely available. Thus, though Chinese nutritional science remained the best in the world well into the nineteenth century, it was supplanted by international biomedicine.

Still, Asia remained a leader even in the latter field—which is why I do not refer to "western" medicine here. The first vitamin (B1) was discovered in what is now Indonesia (around 1900). Chinese and other East Asian scientists were involved in modern nutritional science from the beginning. The old hot/cold theory, which lasted in both China and the west well into the twentieth century, was soon supplanted by newer concepts that stood up better under experimental testing. Yet, China and Chinese scientists remain in the forefront, continuing a tradition that has lasted for twenty-five hundred years.

In China, rising knowledge of wheat agriculture, and rising yields of wheat varieties, caused wheat to displace millet during the period from 1000 BC to 1000 AD. Wheat was preferred, being more versatile and storable. Thus more people worked to grow it more successfully.

Most cultures have belief systems of this sort concerning their foods. China, in addition to the Galenic system, has a whole series of beliefs connected with cleanness, dangerous food combinations, poison-potentiating foods, tonic foods, strengthening foods, energy foods, and so on (Anderson 1988). This has led to the extermination or near-extermination of hundreds of species of plants and animals; believed to be tonic foods, they have been hunted into extinction. India has a quite different but equally rich and complex system of beliefs (Achaya 1994). The taboos of Leviticus and Deuteronomy seem often related to health beliefs, now obscure. Ancient Egypt had a complex and intricate series of beliefs about food, known today only from a few medical papyri (Darby et al. 1977; Nunn 1996). Most western traditions—European or Islamic—are based on the Galenic tradition, but they added a great deal from their own experiences, modifying and changing; the results are often very different from each other. Nutritional beliefs of smaller societies are less well known, but they exist and deserve further attention.

Health, status, and pricing all influence each other. Today, formerly very expensive foods like white bread and white sugar are very cheap, thanks to industrial processing techniques. But, on the other hand, formerly very cheap foods are now very expensive or totally unavailable, because of environmental devastation. Not only are game and caviar depleted; we are also now facing the loss of ordinary vegetables, which require good soil and a lot of work and fertilizer. They are getting rapidly more expensive in the First World and are often completely unavailable in Third World cities. Similarly, local staple starches are losing out to processed grains. Fruits, ever more expensive, are losing out to white sugar.

In former times, when white bread and rice were more expensive and thus were markers of higher status, they were believed to be the healthy foods. Today, with the brown forms more expensive, the nutritional beliefs have shifted; brown is good. In fact, white is less rich in nutrients but is more digestible. When white was expensive, digestibility counted for much (see e.g. Galen 2000). Today, with brown more expensive, vitamin content gets featured.

There is a strong tendency in China and Europe, and I believe elsewhere too (but no one has looked), to ascribe great tonic and aphrodisiac value to rare and obscure foods—at least if they have any nutritional worth. Price, again, affects perception of nutritional value.

2

Today, health and food interact in other ways. Starting around the end of the eighteenth century, western Europeans began to react against processed foods. The movement reached the United States in the early nineteenth century, and found its natural home. Americans disturbed by rapid urbanization and immigration were especially prone to adopt the gospel of whole grains and simple country foods.

Sylvester Graham, inventor of the graham cracker, was the first preacher of this gospel to win fame (Nissenbaum 1980). He inveighed against white sugar, white flour, and other processed foods. They were not only poor in nutrition (which is true enough); they were signs of the degenerate life associated with the cities. He taught that people should live largely on Graham flour: the whole wheat grain, bran and all, ground into meal. This and pure water were close to an adequate diet. His disciples were desperately short of vitamins. Ironically, the graham cracker is now mostly sugar and white flour—the very things he hated.

Health foods achieved religious status with the Seventh-Day Adventists. Sister Ellen White, founder of the sect, was, as we have seen, close to the health food movement. The Mormons, less extreme, taught abstinence from alcohol and caffeine, and advocated a generally healthful diet. Utah, today, has one of the lowest death rates of any state, and is particularly low in heart disease and similar food-related problems. Anti-alcohol sentiments became widespread, leading to the brief experiment with near-absolute prohibition in the twentieth century.

Yogurt abounds today thanks to one man: Nobel Prize winner Elie Metchnikoff, who worked out the dynamics of the immune response system (Gardner 1957). He wondered why people in rural parts of his native Bulgaria were extremely long-lived in spite of their poverty and poor health care. The most obvious difference between them and other Euro-

pean peasants was that they ate great quantities of yogurt, a food unknown in most of the world at the time. He settled on yogurt as the only
reasonable explanation for the longevity. We now know that, although
yogurt does indeed have many virtues, the Bulgarians owe more to the
fruits, vegetables, herbs, and vegetable oils in their diet. Brown bread,
breakfast cereal, and many other foods owe their initial popularity to
health concerns. In China, countless foods are eaten for this reason, from
wild duck to wolfthorn berries. Medicinal value is the only real reason for
the cultivation of the wolfthorn, whose leaves and fruits are nearly tasteless but incredibly rich in vitamins and minerals. The nutritional value
was known long before vitamins were discovered.

By the mid-twentieth century, the "health food" movement remained
largely committed to whole grains and vegetarianism. Unprocessed nuts,
fruits, and vegetables were advocated. From Graham onward, the concept of "naturalness" was critically important—hard to define, to be
sure, but always valued (as it still is).

The resulting diet was not, however, either very natural or very healthy
(Deutsch 1977; Gardner 1957). Far too much highly processed brown
sugar, oil, and starch got into it. Lack of full understanding of the role of
iron and of vitamins A, C, E, and the minor B vitamins led to far too little advocacy of fresh vegetables. Health-food eaters tended to be elderly,
and either strongly religious Seventh-Day Adventists or strongly conservative white Americans in the old anti-urban, anti-immigrant tradition.

Clearly, what defined "health food" was more a matter of opposition
than of health. The category was established long before vitamins and
minerals were known to be nutritionally significant; vitamins were not
even discovered until almost eighty years after Graham's first work. Instead, the issue was unprocessed versus processed: whole grain versus
white flour, brown sugar versus white sugar, and so on. Also, such urban
or imported items as alcohol, tea, and coffee were anathema.

Whole grain is indeed a nutritionally valuable commodity, but brown
sugar and even honey are not significantly different from regular sugar.
(Blackstrap molasses has much iron—but it comes from the processing
machinery!) Vegetarianism has its points, but only if one is very careful
about vitamins B12, B6, and so on. Opposition to change is not always a
perfect way to pick a diet. As of mid-century, health food users tended to
get their vitamins from pills (if at all). Both health-conscious and health-
unconscious Americans, even those who knew about vitamins and minerals, did not often take them very seriously as dietary concerns.

Into this mix came, quite suddenly, two dramatic new factors. First, Ancel Keys's findings on heart disease implicated animal fats and gave the vegetarians a new lease on life (see Keys 1980). Keys's findings unleashed a whole new field in nutrition studies.

Second, the hippies took up the cause of health food with a vengeance—but they were far more concerned with fruits and vegetables, and they consumed a number of plant substances that were far from acceptable to the older health food consumers! The result could be most entertaining. I well remember the expressions of small-town health-store owners—solid far-rightists, often members of extremist patriot groups—when their stores were invaded by hordes of flower children.

Over the rest of the century, concerns with healthy eating grew rapidly. Fads grew and died; alfalfa sprouts were considered magically potent, but eventually faded. Tofu became a trademark of the urban healthy eater, and then of Californians in general. Far more nutritious foods like chiles and turnip greens were notably absent from the roster. Chiles were associated not only with pain but also with Mexicans. Turnip greens, similarly, were associated with African Americans. Even in the liberal and hippie days, health foods remained white folks' foods, and the foods of the minorities were almost by definition unhealthy.

Soon the far-right-wing eaters had totally changed their ways. Propaganda from food-processing companies told them that real Americans ate processed foods, and that these were the healthy foods. Meanwhile, it was clear that "healthy eating" was becoming a trademark of hippies, yuppies, and other enemies. The defining marks of the American Right became white bread, beef, barbecue, mass-produced beer, and hamburgers. The very phrase "white bread" was used in the late twentieth century as a disparaging way to refer to conservative Americans. Predictably enough, many of the new "health" foods were not particularly healthy, though the level of sophistication of the new consumers was high enough to guarantee some awareness of ongoing scientific progress.

Vegetarianism received added impetus from other liberal causes, from animal rights concerns to fears that too much grain was going to animals rather than humans. (See e.g. *Diet for a Small Planet* by Frances Moore Lappé, 1971; *Beyond Beef,* by Jeremy Rifkin, 1992. Most grazing animals worldwide are raised on grass that humans can't eat, not on grain, but facts did not slow the movement down.)

Meanwhile, even the most unaware could not remain totally ignorant of new findings. Beef and whole-fat dairy products suffered a massive decline in popularity. Consumption of beef and of full-fat milk declined by about a third in the period from 1960 to 1990. Yet, gourmet ice cream bucked the trend, becoming popular to the point of near universality just as full-fat milk and cream were becoming rare commodities in many markets. Organ meats almost disappeared, being considered disgusting as well as unhealthy—in spite of the fact that they are the best of all sources of vitamins and minerals. Fish, considered healthy in spite of its frequently high levels of toxins and mercury, became far more abundant and expensive.

Similar changes, meanwhile, were taking place in Europe and elsewhere. Animal-rights activists made vegetarianism especially common in England. Germany began to slide away from beer, its historic drink. By the turn of the century, beer production was up but consumption was down (untitled note on beer, pages A8–A9 of the May 11, 2001, edition of the *Los Angeles Times*). This had much to do with image: beer was linked to the same sort of stodgy, conservative world that was identified with white bread—and mass-produced beer—in the United States. However, as in the United States, microbrewery beer became more popular.

In all these cases, the common theme is clear: "healthy" eating often has as much to do with image as with health. What is unhealthy turns out to be what is associated with those whom one does not like. Health foods are defined in opposition: they are the opposite of what The Enemy eats. Anti-alcohol agitators claimed that alcohol produced nothing but violent drunks. Vegetarians have often condemned meat for making people act wild, savage, and vicious, like carnivorous animals. (This is a slander against wolves and big cats, but that is another story.) Liberals and conservatives structure their foodways to insult each other.

By the turn of the century, the health-food movement had fragmented into many streams. Some people depended heavily on pills ("dietary supplements"). Others had taken up the Mediterranean diet, known to be associated with longevity. Others were still devouring sprout-and-avocado sandwiches on whole-grain bread. Most simply tried to abstain from high-fat foods, especially animal fats. Salad and yogurt had exploded in popularity—in spite of the exceedingly high-fat dressings on the one and the heavy sweetening usually found in the other.

Much of this really is healthy, but sellers of fads know how to manipulate images, and tend to get the ears of Hollywood stars and other highly visible beings. They thus sometimes sell their messages more successfully than real nutritionists do.

Health concerns inevitably lead us to chicken soup, traditionally the health food of the Jewish world, but equally popular as a health stew in China, India, and most other old civilizations. It conveys messages far beyond mere disease control. It is associated with family, with caring, with love and tenderness. The scent of a good chicken soup is intensely evocative to a very large share of humanity.

Foodways hallowed by tradition and by family are inseparably bound with love, with feeling, and with life itself. Philosophers have spent much time discoursing on the phenomenology of food (Heldtke 1988). Poets have sung of it. Writers have concentrated on it; few indeed are the novels that do not draw on the symbolism of food and drink. For all of us, food is about much more than nourishing the body. It is nourishment for the soul.

3

Throughout the world, there is today a rise of foodways based on white flour, white sugar, and oil. Particularly prominent are mass-produced sweet and salty snacks; white bread and white-flour, mass-produced baked goods; hamburgers and fried chicken; and various processed potato products such as french fries. The rise of such food, sometimes (at its worst) called "junk food,"[1] was originally due to two factors. First, it is seen as American (in spite of the fact that french fries are explicitly labeled with their real origin), and it is indeed the lowest common denominator of traditional American cuisine. It thus partakes of the cachet that America's wealth and power give. Second, it is cheap to make and store. (This food is, of course, also high in those things people crave: sweetness, salt, fat. This may "taste better" to some, but in areas I have studied and interviewed, notably Hong Kong and Mexico, such food is popular in spite of—not because of—its taste; people prefer their own foods.)

The healthiest-eating areas of the world have begun to fall from medical grace. The "Mediterranean diet" has been held up as a model of health. As Serventi and Sabban point out (2002:162), we may really be speaking of "the . . . invention of the Mediterranean diet by the Americans"; there are countless Mediterranean diets. However, many of them are based on complex carbohydrates supplemented by olive oil, herbs, vegetables, fruits, and small amounts of dairy products—a healthy diet indeed. In Cyprus and other modernizing areas of the Mediterranean world, a massive shift away from this diet and toward the international processed-food diet has sent rates of degenerative diseases skyrocketing, according to recent studies (Matalas et al. 2001; an anonymous reader of my manuscript noted that rural Cyprus clings to its older foodways, and I have seen the same thing in many Mediterranean areas, but Matalas's figures speak for themselves, and one sees much to worry about in the urban Mediterranean today). Similar trends are reported from east Asia (Watson 1997). I see the same thing happening in Mexico, even in the remote villages where I work.

The rise of fast food and highly processed food has a long and complex history, involving a great deal of political manipulation. This story has been so well told by Marion Nestle (2002) and Eric Schlosser (2001) that it would be superfluous to discuss it here. Suffice it to say that the giant food corporations—who are often also giant tobacco corporations—have lobbied industriously to get their products blessed rather than banned by local and national governments. Many "food experts" writing on food health were simply public relations agents for the corporations. "Revolving doors" between government regulatory agencies and food corporation directorates have also been noted: today's food corporate manager sometimes reappears as tomorrow's regulatory agency director, and vice-versa. Food corporations tend to be fairly closely tied to agriculture, and farmers vote in large numbers, making their interests paramount to many a government around the world. Developed countries give them huge subsidies, making "free market" a hollow phrase.

Industrial and chain-outlet food is here to stay, because of economics, work and family changes, prestige, and other factors. Getting people to change will require attention to all of these. Fortunately, this is coming to pass; among other things, some international chains have recently responded to criticism by upgrading the nutritional quality of their offerings.

Peanut butter is a case of a successful health food. Invented by John Harvey Kellogg (the original Kellogg's Cereals man), it was propagated by people such as Ellen White, his associate, who founded the Seventh-Day Adventist Church and dedicated it to healthy eating (Smith 2002). Popular with children, cheap, and easy to use, peanut butter succeeded with little difficulty, though it too has sometimes suffered from adulteration with sugar and cheap oil.

In Guatemala, the famine relief agency INCAP developed a nutritional supplement for the desperately malnourished poor, in the late 1940s. This

"Incaparina" was sold or given away as a food for the poor. Of course, no one would touch it. Anthropologically sophisticated nutritionists Nevin and Mary Scrimshaw took over the program. Immediately, they promoted Incaparina as an elite food. They persuaded Guatemalan stars and celebrities to consume it with (apparent) relish and delight on public media. Incaparina succeeded brilliantly.

By contrast, any number of campaigns for healthy eating and against "junk" food have failed dismally. I have seen many of them rise, flutter, and fall (and see Schlosser 2001).

The most common problems are four. First, such campaigns are usually preachy. Young people everywhere hate to be preached to, yet young people are the ones who most need the message. Second, such campaigns are usually phrased strictly in terms of health—especially the health of old people. They do not address the fact that people choose foods for many other reasons. Third, the campaigns tend to nest in health and social-welfare agencies, not in food markets or shopping areas. Fourth, the campaigns are rarely very visible in the schools. Even if they are taught in the classrooms, they do not affect the actual foodways of the school. As parents know, school lunches and other foods found in schools are often among the lowest in nutritional terms. Also, corporations have placed vending machines selling candy, cakes, chips, and soft drinks in many schools, often providing some of the profits to the school for band uniforms, sports facilities, and the like; this makes it hard for the schools to control the machines.

What should be done instead—what is, in fact, being done by many successful campaigns?

- Nutritional educators should target their campaigns toward active people between ten and forty, unless they are specifically concerned with older folk.
- They should do everything possible to make good food and nutrition the prestigious, stylish, with-it option.
- They should brand junk food as the choice of fools—people who are neither with it nor health conscious, people who are gullible and out of date.
- They should talk about health in positive terms: this will improve your looks, your performance, your sex life, your whole body. People at the age and stage when they are forming their lifelong food habits

are far more concerned with these positive matters than with dark thoughts about the far future.

- However, scare stories about heart disease, cancer, and diabetes are also appropriate. These problems can start early, and lifelong food habits are laid down early. On the other hand, heavy-duty campaigns *focused* on these issues should be directed mainly at people old enough to be directly and immediately concerned with those conditions.
- Especially in the Third World, campaigns should make *some* effort to be adapted to local conditions. In Chunhuhub, my Maya town, the nutrition posters at the local clinic are excellent, except for one thing: Mexico being a highly centralized country, the posters are composed in Mexico City. They reflect Mexico City realities. Most of the fruits and vegetables they recommend cannot be found in Chunhuhub. Conversely, Chunhuhub's superb and unfailing workhorse producers of vitamins and minerals, the chaya plant (a green vegetable) and the mamey (a fruit), are not listed on the posters. Such lack of attention to local reality is almost universal. I have seen similarly ill-adapted posters in small towns from rural America to China and Malaysia.
- Campaigns about infant nutrition should, again, be directed at real-life mothers: young, often confused, concerned about everything from survival to maintaining their looks. In the Third World, they are usually poorly educated, impoverished, and forced to work twelve- to sixteen-hour days to survive. Even in the First World, the luxury of staying at home with the baby is simply not possible in many cases. Yet nutrition campaigns still often talk as if there is a full-time mother and homemaker on the receiving end. Long, difficult routines are recommended. Shortcuts are not suggested.
- Above all, all nutritional campaigns should be based as much as possible on direct word of mouth. This is not to say there should be any cutback on media use. Media are wonderful things. However, people rely—still—on what they hear from their friends and from trusted health providers in their communities. This is especially true of the Third World people and impoverished First World people that we most want to reach.

10

Food and Religion

> Not very long ago, belief in the supper natural was quite common-
> place.
>
> —from a less-than-stellar student paper

1

Foodways are perhaps at their most complex when they become involved
in religion. Some religions order the eating of meat, when sacrifices are
shared out (Smith 1894). Others ban the eating of meat, at least for holy
devotees; meat is seen as involving the killing of animals, a violent and an-
tispiritual thing. The religions based in India—Hinduism, Buddhism, and
Jainism—share this commitment to what is called in Sanskrit *ahimsa,*
"nonviolence." As noted above, the most devout Jains eat only fruit (see
Chapple 1998).

Robertson Smith's studies (see Smith 1894) of food sharing as the classic, basic religious act among ancient and modern Near Eastern peoples
were among the earliest works to discuss this in scientific detail (Mintz
2002).

His work led, in part, to Emile Durkheim's studies of religion as "collective representation" of the social group (Durkheim 1995 [1912]).
Durkheim showed that—whatever truth, awe, reverence, or mystical experience individuals may find in religion—the real basis of religion is society. Religion was, for Durkheim, the way a society could hold itself together and "sell" its ethics and standards to the rising generation. To accomplish its goals, a social group embraces everyone in the powerfully
emotional activities of ritual, ceremony, and celebration. Inevitably, such
intense and all-involving action involves food. Food is a basic and universal human concern. It is central to religion—as symbol, as subject of
prayers, as marker of sharing and unsharing, and as communion.

It is all very well for religious studies professors to speak of awe, of abstruse theology, and of transcendent experience. It is all very well for agnostics to see religion as failed science—as a set of foolish guesses about how the world began and how humans wound up where they are. But in the real world, virtually everybody comes into his or her faith as a young child learning it from parents, or as an older child and young adult learning it from peers. The social-emotional bonds come first. Philosophy, mythology, and mystical experiences follow later, if at all. For the vast majority of human beings, religion remains a matter of sociability, festivals, and personal faith rather than formal theological speculation. Even for those who care about subtleties of doctrine, interaction and communitas remain basic.

Food is a daily reverence. The child, the hard-headed worker, and the mystic theologian all join for the ritual repast—whether they kneel to take communion together, join to eat the Sikh ritual food that is shared by all, or come together in the temple for Buddhist vegetarian food. It is food sharing, not solely dogma and creed, that unites them all. We are reminded of Glynn Isaac's argument that food sharing made us human (chapter 2). Isaac's "origin myth" may be the deepest and most religiously powerful of them all—and it is probably the sober truth.

Readers will recall that, in the first important book that was explicitly about "anthropology," Immanuel Kant (1978 [1796]) spoke of the principles of aggregation and differentiation; we have already seen the relationship of these classification devices to tabooed foods. People, when they classify the world, tend to treat "similar" things as if they were the same (aggregation) and to treat things perceived as even slightly "different" as though they were utterly separate (differentiation). Religion usually does this: one is a member of the Holy Faith or one is not. Typically, aggregation and differentiation are stronger and more emotionally intense in religion than in other human activities (though political ideology and ethnicity have sometimes taken pride of place in the last century or so). Food is almost always a marker. The sharers eat together at ritual meals. Often, they go farther, and define their congregation by shared rules. All must eat certain foods, often in a certain way; all must avoid certain other foods.

The group that prays together stays together—especially if its members share religious feasts. Holy Communion in Christian churches is a form of this sharing. Sikh temples insist that the worshippers share a sweet food, made of substances acceptable to all the Indian religions. The worshippers have to eat together, thus publicly renouncing the widespread Indian restrictions on dining with members of other occupations and groups. More impressive feasts that bring people together around religious themes include Thanksgiving and Christmas in standard American Christian traditions; Passover and Hanukkah in Judaism; Buddhist temple feasts throughout East and Southeast Asia; and the countless sacrificial or hunting-related feasts of indigenous peoples.

In thinking about American religion, which is often highly individualistic, we tend to forget how very social religion usually is. Working in another culture can be a very dramatic experience; one learns that social rituals that involve entire communities (or even nations) are frequent and vitally important.

The general theme is that religions almost always use food to mark and symbolize matters of communion and theology. The mainstream Protestant American churches stand at one extreme, managing food very little (unless to prohibit alcohol). At the other extreme are the Orthodox Jewish rules and the complex food rules of Hinduism (Khare 1976a, 1976b, 1992). Of the 613 rules in Leviticus and Deuteronomy, the biggest chunk consists of rules related to food. Some of these rules are related to sanitation, some to kindness to animals (Feeley-Harnik 1994), some to symbolism and logic (see below), and some simply forbid usages typical of the religions of enemy tribes. For instance, "thou shalt not seethe a kid in its mother's milk" is traditionally (and almost certainly correctly) explained as a prohibition against a sacred dish of an opponent group (Moses Maimonides, quoted in Rosner 1997:243); "kid boiled in its mother's milk" seems to have been a sacrificial dish of enemy peoples. The term continues in use today, in the Middle East, as a rather morbid name for meat cooked with milk.

2

This rule introduces us to the favorite subject for speculation in nutritional anthropology: taboo. Taboos are found in most societies. Technically, we distinguish *taboo* (a *religious* law) from simple *avoidance*. American Christians have no real taboos, except in some sects (such as the Seventh-Day Adventists) that observe Old Testament rules. But Americans have many avoidances, including insects, dogs, and horses.

Our avoidance of horsemeat (Harris 1985) is, in fact, a religious taboo, but we have forgotten that. The horse sacrifice was the greatest and most important sacrificial rite in ancient European religion, and recent converts tended to backslide, so Pope Gregory the Great explicitly banned horse eating by Catholics in the early Middle Ages. The modern eating of horses by the French is a new custom, arising from desperation during sieges in the nineteenth century (Gade 1976). In the United States, the Harvard College faculty club serves horse meat, because of urging by anthropologists during World War II when food security was looking dicey (at least this is what I was told at the club). The custom persisted long after the war, as a slightly macabre bit of fun.

Our avoidance of insects has not even that excuse, since certain insects are explicitly said to be good food, in the Bible (see above). Countless modern nutritionists have counseled eating them. They are an excellent, cheap source of nutrients, widely eaten around the world (see Ramos-Elorduy de Conconi 1991; Ramos-Elorduy 1998; Ramos-Elorduy and Pino 1989; Schwabe 1979; Sutton 1988; there is even a *Food Insects Newsletter*, started by entomologist Gene DeFoliart). Yet, most English-language books on food insects concentrate on the shock value rather than the nutritional value (see e.g. Hopkins 1999; Menzel and D'Aluisio 1998). Anthropologists hate these exoticism-as-shock books. They appear to ridicule behavior that is actually much more sensible and intelligent than that of the intended readership. However, I have to confess a soft spot for Peter Menzel's book, because the cover shows a Cambodian eating a fried tarantula; she was, I believe, the girl who sold me a tarantula I ate when in Cambodia.

Avoidances remain very difficult to explain. It has been argued that insects are not worth the bother (Harris 1985), but this is clearly not the case; edible insects abound in vast quantities in many areas (Ramos-Elorduy de Conconi 1991; Sutton 1988). Americans seem squeamish about an increasing number of things (cf. Sahlins 1976).

Taboos seem much more straightforward, though still confusing.

Taboos are often used as rules for sharing. Among the Inuit and many other hunters, adult women get one part of the game animal, girls get another part, the hunter gets yet another, other adult males get still another (details are exceedingly complicated; see Boas 1888; Rasmussen 1927, 1931). In Polynesia, chiefs impose sacred taboos to prevent overfishing (a fish species is tabooed till its population recovers from heavy fishing), protect fruit so that it may ripen, and save leaf crops from destructive overharvesting (see e.g. Firth 1936, 1959). In many places, scarce but well-liked food is "sacred" to the people who make the rules! Chickens and eggs go to the senior men in much of East Africa (Simoons 1994). Sometimes there is symbolism here: the top of a fish's head is sacred to the chief in some Pacific Northwest groups, and in southeast Asia the head of the sacrificial buffalo goes to the local headman (these examples are from my own field experience). Sometimes purity is a factor. The highest, most sacred Hindu castes and Buddhist religious devotees must avoid all bloodshed, and thus all meat (Simoons 1994; Doniger and Smith 1991). Eating meat necessarily involves bloodshed, even if one does not do one's own butchering, and is thus contaminating and violent.

Most ink has been spilled on the pig taboo in Judaism, Islam, Hinduism, and several minor religions (particularly good reviews of Jewish rules are found in Cooper 1993; Feeley-Harnik 1994). It is known that the pig was *not* banned because it carries diseases (e.g. trichinosis), contrary to the myth still occasionally found in the popular press (on this and other issues see Simoons 1994). A theory started by Carleton Coon (1958:24) and recently upheld by Marvin Harris (1985, 1987) maintains that the pig was banned because it is a bad long-term economic risk in the Middle East. For one thing, it is not an "all-purpose animal" (Coon 1958:24); it is not a source of milk, wool, or traction power. But, less believably, it is said to do poorly under conditions there, and is hard to herd. This is untrue; wild pigs abound in the less desert parts of the Middle East, and pig keeping was a common and very successful occupation of other religious groups, e.g. Christians. Paul Diener and Eugene Robkin (1978) proposed a theory that the state wished to divert grain from pig feeding to state coffers; this is unlikely, since pigs were fed on acorns and garbage rather than grain. Mary Douglas (1966; cf. Douglas 1970, 1975) showed that the animals tabooed in Leviticus and Deuteronomy are mostly anomalous—cloven hoofed but not cud chewing, in the pig case; anomalous animals, violating category boundaries, are taboo or sacred in most religions. Finally, Eugene Hunn (1979) showed beyond reasonable doubt that the pig is banned because it eats blood and animals and carrion. All the creatures banned in the Old Testament are carnivores or scavengers, and all the carnivores and scavengers in the Near East are banned. The animals specifically listed as clean are those that are clearly vegetarian. The Bible actually says this explicitly.

Food and medicine, Hong Kong. Medicinal food for sale by roving peddler. Such roving peddlers have long vanished. This one's wares include red jujubes (for blood), black jujubes (for flesh), lily bulb scales (to harmonize foods), ginkgo nuts (for sore throat), dried daylily buds (warming), and many other medicinal foods. *Photo by E. N. Anderson, 1966*

Other Near Eastern and south Asian religious groups share some or most of these prohibitions. The Muslims simply picked up the Jewish taboo. The Hindus, as one would expect from their nonviolent ethic, also look with disfavor on animals that eat blood and carrion. Even Hindus of "low" castes, who eat a variety of meats, avoid such flesh. The same is true of the Jains (Chapple 1998). Buddhists too are supposed to be vegetarian; in practice, only the monks usually are, but lay Buddhists usually avoid carnivorous animals (though they often eat pork).

The cow taboo in India is a different matter. The medieval Muslim al-Biruni (1971) thought the Hindus banned cow killing and cow eating because the cow was so useful alive—it is a plow animal, cart puller, source of fertilizer, source of milk, and even a source of warmth (the peasants took in the cows on cold nights). Marvin Harris (1966, 1985, 1987) has argued for a modern version of this idea. There is clearly much truth in it. However, other cultures that use the cow do not worship it or need to make it sacred as a conservation measure. We do not worship our dairy cows.

Actually, the cow was sacred before modern Indian society arose. It may even have been sacred before it was domesticated. It was at first a sacrificial animal, the most sacred of all along with the horse. When nonviolence came into Indian religion, apparently at least in part as a way of keeping people from rebelling against the state, the most sacred animals came to be protected along with people (Doniger and Smith 1991). Gradually the idea of nonviolence was extended to more and more species, but the cow remained in first place. Its utility certainly has been important, perhaps instrumental, in protecting it. Frederick Simoons has shown, however, that neither this nor most other Indian taboos and protections can be adequately explained by utilitarian arguments (Simoons 1994). Wendy Doniger and Brian Smith (1991) point out that the logic of nonviolence started from humans and extended to the most valuable animals, then outward from there; logic, practicality, and ritual (including priestly politics) were all involved.

Simoons's works set a seal on a long tradition. He has shown that using foods as religious symbols is not a mere reflex of utilitarian concerns. It cannot be predicted from nutrition or ecology, though it is often strongly influenced thereby. It has to be explained in terms of religious logic and history. Foods are perhaps the richest source of symbols. Because they are literally taken into the body, and have all the associations of life, home, family, health, and embodied being, they are the ultimate "natural symbols" (Douglas 1966, 1970, 1975).

In short, the position that all long-established foodways were not only optimal in terms of obtaining calories from the environment but also were explained solely by that factor does not stand testing (Sahlins 1976; Simoons 1994, 1998).

Marvin Harris originally defended this theory as part of a research strategy. One should—he maintained—take the materialist-ecological theory as far as it could go, then successively invoke other explanations.

Harris sometimes viewed his theory as the only one, which was unfortunate, but his arguments remain useful if they are taken as originally intended.

Ecological explanations, however, are only a beginning. History reveals too many cases in which food has been shaped by status, religion, ethnic rivalry, and other factors. Many foodways do make perfect ecological sense, but others—notably taboos and avoidances—do not. Moreover, it is not clear whether the sensible ones are the result of ecological rationality, or of a group of people deciding on a foodway and *then* finding out how to make it do its best in their environment, as seems to have happened in the Hindu cow case.

American abstention from insects, for instance, is ecologically and economically foolish. Yet this avoidance not only persists; it has been spread by missionaries to areas where it is genuinely dangerous. In Central Africa, missionaries often convinced local people that insect eating was disgusting—and thus persuaded them to abandon a valuable source of high-quality protein and mineral nutrition (as we found in Zambia, and have heard from other areas).

Religious foodways thus can be explained either on the basis of ecological sense or on the basis of religious and ritual logic. They are not blind immemorial tradition, but pragmatic adaptations to community life.

11

Change

1

Leopold Bloom, in James Joyce's *Ulysses* (1961:55), expressed a fondness for organ meats, fish roe, and, in short, what we now sometimes call "variety meats." He was especially fond of kidneys, with their "tang of faintly scented urine," and was having them for breakfast on the day commemorated in the novel. The hundredth anniversary of the original publication of the work was just celebrated in Dublin, and thousands of people ritually consumed grilled kidneys—culture history in the making.

Bloom's delights are no longer acceptable to most English-speaking eaters—a pity, for they are indeed very good.

Foodways change. We all know this, yet we sometimes talk as if foodways were conservative or even changeless. All things change, though sometimes they change very slowly.

In this chapter I use European (largely Mediterranean) food as an example, because it is the best studied; the history is well researched and the documentation is available. The only other country with this kind of documentation is China, which I have covered elsewhere (Anderson 1988) and need not detail further. (There are also excellent histories for some other regions, notably Achaya 1994 for India; Rodinson et al. 2001 for the Arab world; Ishige 2001 for Japan.)

Fernand Braudel wrote of the *longue durée*, the long term, in the Mediterranean world (Braudel 1973). Recently, a book on Mediterranean history, *The Corrupting Sea*, challenged this, bringing forth evidence that the Mediterranean world had changed very quickly (Horden and Purcell 2000). I read this book as preparation for a trip to Spain and Portugal; I was especially interested in the food history of Andalucía, so I spent a lot of time poking around that favored land.

Nothing could have been better calculated to vindicate Braudel and disprove his opponents. The food of Andalucía is about what it was in, or even before, Roman times: crusty bread, wine, olive oil, pork (especially cured as ham or sausage), cabbages, herbs, Mediterranean fruits and nuts (especially almonds), onions, garlic. The Arabs introduced a few foods: sugar, oranges, lemons, and minor items. From the New World came potatoes, tomatoes, green and red peppers, chocolate. None of these changed the basic diet, though potatoes and tomatoes have become locally common and popular. The staples are still bread, wine, oil, and meat.

The grain fields still occupy the broad plains, the grapevines the fertile slopes, and the olives the infertile hills, just as they did two thousand years ago. The olive orchards in their neat rows extend up to a neat trimline on the mountains: the level at which nature says "no more" by freezing the young trees (olives cannot stand temperatures below about minus ten degrees Celsius). Above that, the same oak woodlands, usually degraded to scrub, produce the same wild boars and partridges they did for the Romans—though now the numbers of game animals are tiny fractions of what they were then.

I know and love a medieval Spanish song about Moorish girls picking olives in the Andalucían town of Jaén. I went to see the town, and found it still a center of the olive industry. "Moors"—migrant workers from Morocco—still do the picking.

The *longue durée* is real.

At the other extreme, oregano consumption in the United States increased 5,200 percent between 1948 and 1956, tracking the explosive growth in popularity of pizza and Italian sandwiches (Norman 1972:248; see Diner 2002 for the full story of Italian food in America, including the earlier days of rejection). Oregano was virtually unused before, except in Italian and Greek ethnic strongholds. It subsequently declined again, because pizza and grinders succumbed to Americanization in taste. However, Mexican food followed Italian into the mainstream, and saved oregano from oblivion.

Probably, most change throughout time has occurred because of necessity, or at least economic pressure, not taste (Lentz 1999). Far too often, change is toward coarse, inferior, nutrition-poor rations, thanks to unfortunate political occurrences and policies (Sen 1984, 1992), economic vicissitudes (Lentz 1999), or local crop failures.

In these cases, the causes are all too obvious, and the cures also reasonably clear. The brutal force of poverty and the still more brutal one of war routinely cause whole populations to stop eating their culturally preferred and nutritionally reasonable diets, and live instead on coarse grains or, worse still, bark, weeds, husks, straw, and even the bodies of the dead. This is not really culture change; it is response to immediate environmental necessity.

Far different is cultural change—voluntary, socially constructed alteration in the tastes of whole peoples. The worldwide spread not only of hamburgers and hot dogs but also of french fries, brand-name candy bars, and all the rest of the constellation, needs no elaboration (see Schlosser 2001). Most universal of all are the sodas. The current Mexican expression for the most remote place imaginable is "where the Coca-Cola truck doesn't go." We often forget how much the healthier types of modern food have also spread. Breakfast cereal, frozen orange juice, nonfat milk, yogurt, and whole-grain products have gone worldwide along with the hamburgers.

When foodways persist unchanged, the reason is often that they are identified with the old, the traditional, the time hallowed. This does not prevent change. Frequently, a traditional food is subject to drift over time. A traditional food that is not liked much will simply fade away. If it is liked, it will often be made more sophisticated: as time goes on, and people acquire new resources, they will add spices, new techniques, and other elaborations to it. This is happening to East European Jewish food today, and it has happened many times in the past, the changes in Jewish foods tracking the economic situation of the Jewish community (Cooper 1993). The religiously valued traditional foods are made lower in fat and higher in spices and other flavorings, thanks to creative chefs like Judy Zeidler (1999).

Alternatively, a food may lose its old virtues and become a mere hollow shell of its former self. This has happened with Thanksgiving pies. The superb pumpkin and apple pies of my youth have been replaced almost everywhere by store-bought pies that have the same appearance but taste largely of hydrogenated vegetable oil and sugar. It is sometimes difficult to find slices of apple in the sugar-and-flour fillings of the "apple" pies (cf. Schlosser 2001; and on the decline of traditional American foods, Sokolov 1981).

The apple pies were, themselves, one of the last bastions of English Renaissance cookery—a brilliant, sophisticated, elaborate cuisine that is not even a memory except to dedicated food historians. Once, the English board groaned with all sorts of pies spiced with the classic cinnamon-clove-ginger-nutmeg mix that survives (or did until recently) in these pies. (This mix is now often sold as "pumpkin pie spice," and pumpkin pies certainly preserve a medieval aspect—a soft-filled pie with the characteristic spicing—but the pumpkin is a Native American squash.)

England preserves the tradition better than the United States; England even has real mince pies—made of minced meat and spiced fruit—and a few other ancient survivals. "Mince pie" in America is actually a sort of raisin-apple pie, with only some of the old flavorings.

Tamales—a ritual (and everyday) dish of the Aztecs (Sahagun 1950–1982), still ritually eaten at Christmas in the Mexican and Central American world—have been elaborated beyond belief in El Salvador, reduced to vestiges in parts of the Southwest (Peyton 1994; Pilcher 1998), and changed into a myriad of forms in the lands between. There is even a giant tamale, the *zacahuil,* in northeast Mexico; it can contain a whole turkey and weigh a hundred pounds, and it is immortalized in local folk songs.

Easter eggs have hatched so many changes in their radiation that it takes a huge book to chronicle them (Newall 1971). The meat-and-fruit stews that used to characterize all Arab-Persian cooking have survived in and around Iran, been wildly elaborated in Morocco, and died out in most of Arabia and some of North Africa. We have countless recipes for them in medieval cookbooks from all over the Arab world, but they have persisted only locally.

Consider a straightforward list of factors that affect food, and frequently change it:

Environment. Any environmental change will affect food economics, usually favoring some foods over others. Global warming will no doubt give us more hot-weather crops, fewer cold-weather ones.

Health. Some foods become too associated with dangers of contamination. More often, a food becomes accepted because it is considered healthy. We have examined the cases of yogurt and brown bread. Breakfast cereal and many other foods owe their initial popularity to health concerns. In China, countless foods are eaten for this reason, from wild duck to wolfthorn berries. Herbs and health supplements are today sold in some countries (including the United States) as "food supplements," because the laws are less strict than those governing medicines. This exposes the public to risks that can be serious (Katan and de Roos 2003).

Economics. In addition to the brute force of poverty noted above, less dramatic price changes for inputs make huge differences. Plants that need heavy fertilizing will become more available as fertilizer does. In China, rising knowledge of wheat agriculture, and rising yields of wheat varieties, caused wheat to displace millet during the period from 1000 BC to 1000 AD. Wheat was preferred, being more versatile and storable. Thus more people worked to grow it more successfully.

Today, formerly very expensive foods like white bread and white sugar are very cheap, thanks to industrial processing techniques. But, on the other hand, formerly very cheap foods are now very expensive or totally unavailable, because of environmental devastation. Not only are game and caviar depleted; we are now also facing the loss of ordinary vegetables, which require good soil and a lot of work and fertilizer. They are getting rapidly more expensive in the First World and are often completely unavailable in Third World cities. Similarly, local staple starches are losing out to processed grains. Fruits, ever more expensive, have lost out to white sugar as its price has plummeted. Now white sugar is losing out in turn to high-fructose corn syrup, an industrial product that is now the cheapest sweetener of all.

Even brown rice and white rice have changed pricing. Brown rice was once cheaper, because it required less processing. White rice is now cheaper, because it is more storable—being less nutritious and thus less desirable to bugs and bacteria and less prone to spoil through rancidification of oils.

Work dynamics. Coffee and tea came in with alarm clocks and time clocks. The rise of fast-food chains correlates with the rise in work hours and work "discipline" (Anderson 2003).

Family and family/work dynamics. Fast foods also came in because no one is home to cook. This is only the latest stage in a long process. The breakdown of the extended family and its replacement by the nuclear family, a process typical of the last few centuries in much of the world, forced many changes in a similar direction. Food became simpler, and more often prepared by full-time experts such as bakers, brewers, and caterers.

Politics. Chinese avoid dairy products partly because of the association thereof with "barbarian invaders" such as the Mongols. Americans drink coffee partly because of hatred for the colonial British tax on tea, made infamous in the Boston Tea Party. The tax was slight—not enough to be an economic barrier. Today, nationalism often shows itself at the dinner table, throughout the world. This is especially true in new nations (Hungary in the early twentieth century, for instance) and would-be nations (Cataluña). In Hungary, Karoly Gundel created a gourmet Hungarian cuisine partly out of sheer national pride (Gundel 1964; Lang 1971).

Somewhere at the intersection of family and politics is the epidemic of eating disorders that has struck women in the developed world in recent decades. Anorexia and bulimia are, at least in large part, responses to social pressures to be thin, and family pressures to be successful in all manner of demanding activities. There is also a copycat effect; stories about movie-star eating disorders are said to lead to increases in same among teenage women, though I have not actually seen good studies demonstrating this.

Religion. Religion is, notoriously, a force for stasis. It makes people eat certain hallowed foods and follow hallowed traditions. When religion changes, foodways must often change. The spread of Islam through southeast Asia, especially Indonesia, led to a progressive disappearance of pigs. The pig was the major animal protein source in many areas. Religious conversion had unfortunate nutritional consequences in some of those areas.

Status, role, class, prestige. (See chapter 9.)

Fad and style. Fads for particular ethnic cuisines sweep the United States almost annually. Some beget permanent changes in foodways, as did the pizza fad. Others disappear, as did the Cajun food craze of the 1990s.

Permanent taste change. The rise of pizza in the United States was only the most obvious symptom of a major taste change, from the bland, puritanical tastes of the early twentieth century to the exciting, potent ones of later times. It is no accident that the rise of pizza correlates perfectly with the rise of "sex, drugs, and rock 'n' roll." Rock rose at the expense of crooners and lullabylike popular music. Stimulant drugs rose at the expense of tranquilizers like tobacco and alcohol. On a more elite plane, abstract expressionism, political demonstrations, and other indications of a lively scene appeared about the same time. The reason, I believe, is that the horrible events of the Great Depression and World War II had thoroughly traumatized the preceding generation, driving them to lullaby music and bland, soothing food and art. They raised their children in sheltered, low-stimulus homes. Breaking out into adolescence, these children were hungry for intense experiences of all kinds.

Another rapid but (so far) permanent change was the sudden disappearance of the highly spiced Renaissance cuisine from England and France as the Baroque waned (see below). England went toward blandness, France toward fresh vegetables and herbs. The change was rapid and permanent (at least so far).

Such taste changes are the hardest of all to explain. I am firmly convinced that the change in American culture in the middle 1950s is real and took place for the reasons stated; I was there and experienced it. I can see why France got bored with Renaissance food and wanted something fresher and more local. But why did England renounce a superb, varied, exciting cuisine for dismal stodge?

2

With all these forces of change, it is clear that we have to explain persistence. It is not the norm. It is not the null or unmarked case. It occurs only under special circumstances.

Consider the Andalucían case (most of what follows is my own research, but see also Grove and Rackham 2001). Wheat, olives, and grapevines are among the rather few things that grow well in Andalucía's hot, dry, Mediterranean climate. Most of the possible competitor crops—maize, potatoes, most vegetables, and so on—do not do well. Pigs flourish on the acorns produced in the oak scrub and forests that cover all uncultivated areas. Add to this a conservative social body. Almost everyone was desperately poor until recently, and the land is still far, far behind the rest of Spain in wealth. Poverty forced people to live on those few easiest things to grow, and also made them afraid of change—especially in light of the fact that change, in Andalucía, has usually been of a less than pleasant sort. From the Vandals (who gave their name to a whole concept) to Franco's fascists, the conquerors of Andalucía have been such as would scare anyone away from change. The few changes that have occurred, most significantly, follow from Andalucía's two golden ages. The first of these was the peak centuries of Arab rule in the early Middle Ages. The second was the sixteenth century, the days of Spain's conquest and empire, when gold and silver as well as potatoes and tomatoes flowed in through Cadiz and Sevilla.

South China, too, has not changed much in a long time. Rice is simply too far ahead of any other staple, in productivity and nutritional value. The local vegetables too have been developed and perfected for millennia, and outyield any competition. Once again, New World food crops came in to revolutionize the economy, but otherwise no important additions have been made to South China's foodways in two thousand years—since the days when north Chinese, and their foods such as wheat, invaded and genuinely transformed the region. A few plants from West Asia and Southeast Asia trickled in, but are not common or important.

Personal conservatism is not a factor here, since the south Chinese are arguably the world's fastest people when it comes to taking up a challenge or pressing an advantage. And foodways have changed, quickly, in the last few decades. What mattered was the solid "lock-in" of ecology and the economy, caused by the creation of the paddy system. It is too good, and too tightly integrated, to change easily. China does change—for reasons of taste, class, and ethnic rivalry (Anderson 1988; Chang 1977) as well as ecology (Marks 1997). The "changeless China" stereotype must be rejected. However, it has its kernel of truth; changes are slow, and basic patterns endure.

A final example of persistence is the victory of Mexican indigenous food over Spanish culinary culture. This was partly due to Spanish policy; the crown discouraged cultivation of our old friends wheat, grapes, and olives in Mexico, so that Spain could make money selling them there. However, wheat and olives did not do well in Mexico anyway. Maize far outproduced wheat. Moreover, chiles were cheaper than imported spices. New World vegetables tasted better and produced better than Spanish ones. New World squashes were so superior to Old World equivalents that they replaced the latter rapidly even back in the Mediterranean world. Add to this the fact that most New World cooks were "Indians," and all is explained.

The basis of Mexican food thus continued to be tortillas, tamales, chiles, Mexican frijol beans, squash, agaves, tomatoes, avocados, and other native foods, until the recent spread of junk food.

However, in this case, we are looking at stasis only in the most basic staples. Spanish cooking did not fail to establish itself; the fancy dishes, the stews, the breads, the ritual foods, and the feast foods were Spanish or were the wonderful Spanish-Arab-Mexican fusions that are now usually regarded as the highest achievements of Mexican food. Change was incremental, and often from the top down, but it was real, and it profoundly transformed Mexico over the centuries.

3

Foodway change is an age-old concern. Moses persuaded the Israelites to follow their hundreds of dietary rules. Muhammad simplified and changed these, and succeeded in developing a dietary code that now affects a billion people. More secular concerns of political economy moved crowned heads of Europe to popularize the potato by novel means; Catherine the Great supposedly wore wreaths of potato flowers. Parmentier, according to legend, had soldiers guard royal potato patches to "prevent" peasants from stealing the potatoes; this, of course, got the peasants interested, and they stole all the plants—for the soldiers were instructed to look the other way (Lang 2001; Salaman 1985). By such means, stubborn, reactionary farmers came to grow potatoes all over Europe. Chinese are more amenable to adopting the new, but even China had its militant developers, popularizing sweet potatoes and maize (Anderson 1988).

More recently, countless development agencies around the world are propagating staples and luxuries. Much is made, today, of sustainability. In the contemporary world, soil, water, forests, and crop nutrients are precious commodities that cannot be wasted. A new crop or farming system must not be too demanding. The reckless days of forest clearing and steppe plowing are over. Foolish schemes have desertified vast tracts in most continents, and the end is not yet.

The search for stability has led to some strange schemes. People in remote areas are growing apples, vegetable seeds, opium (not always with state cooperation), ducks, llamas. Others are working to bring back the taste for wild foods. Started by the legendary Euell Gibbons (1962), this movement has taken on a life of its own. Leaders like Christopher Nyerges (1995) in my home area and John Kallas (2002) in Oregon live by teaching wilderness skills and wild food uses. A similar rehabilitation of Mediterranean gathering was spearheaded especially by Patience Gray in the mid- to late twentieth century (Gray 1997). Her enthusiasm was infectious, and led to aristocratic European gourmets rubbing shoulders (metaphorically, at least) with destitute peasants in the gathering fields of Cyprus and Crete. In fact, at least in parts of south and east Europe, aristocratic gourmets were doing it long before; one can see men in expensive suits and ties hunting mushrooms in the woods along with local subsistence farmers. Hunting and gathering is fun! More seriously, though, in a world where resource limitations are ever more real, we can no longer afford to neglect anything. The foods of our hunter-gatherer and peasant ancestors are back in style.

Even wilder development schemes exist. While my wife was in Tibet teaching midwives safer procedures, another member of her team, cheesemaker Jonathan White, was teaching Tibetans to make quality cheese from yak milk; there is hope that this will be a commercial success as well as a nutritional supplement.

4

Perhaps the best-known and longest-running case study of change is provided by the case of bread. Bread remains one of the greatest inventions of the human species.

People were grinding seeds by forty thousand years ago, as indicated by milling stones. These, originally, were flat rocks on which seeds were ground with a smaller, rounded rock. Such rocks are called "saddle querns" in England. Here in southwestern North America, we call these metates and manos—metate from the Nahuatl ("Aztec") word *metlatl,* and mano from Spanish *piedra de mano,* "handstone." The Native American peoples all used them. The typical metate is a big flat slab, around a foot or two square. It weighs a great deal, but a good metate would often be carried for tens of miles. Often, seeds were ground on a convenient boulder, producing a "bedrock metate." Manos can be flat-bottomed, circular stones or longer, thinner cylinders. They weigh a pound or more.

As with everything else, there is art and skill in metate making. The most important consideration is the rock. One hopes for a rock with largish or uneven-sized crystals that fall out under heavy pressure; such a metate is self-renewing. Rock that grinds down to a glassy polish, like fine-grained granite, is not useful for long; the glassy surface does not make grinding very feasible. Sandstone or rough volcanic stone is preferable. Bedrock metates on granite become smooth soon, but the rain eventually renews them. Rain is slightly acid (it picks up carbon dioxide as it falls, producing carbonic acid in the raindrops), and standing rainwater eats away the bonds between crystals, which gradually fall out, reroughening the surface. In a pinch, one can always reroughen the surface by pounding with a rock.

Mortars and pestles are useful for mashing seeds, but they do not produce fine flour; they produce a coarser grade.

Once one has flour, all one has to do is mix it with some water, cover it with ashes at the edge of the campfire, and let it bake an hour or so in the hot ashes. The ashes can be brushed off; a few of them on the bread add flavor and nutritive value. This makes the choice of firewood important, since some woods produce better-tasting ash. Alternatively, the bread can be wrapped in tough leaves and baked. Then it is the choice of leaf that affects the flavor.

The original bread was of this sort, and so things remained for thousands of years. Eventually, agriculture began, at first in the Near East. Grains were cultivated. Bread presumably became more elaborate.

Yeast, growing naturally on grain and fruit, came into the home. At some point, it was domesticated—turned from a wild contaminant into a domestic servant. Nothing in all history so thoroughly combines momentous importance and total obscurity as this event. Perhaps it was first used for brewing. The classic "just so story," repeated thousands of times, is as good as any: someone left grape juice, or perhaps watery grain gruel, standing around for a few days. The result looked spoiled, but tasted surprisingly good. A few minutes later, much more substantial virtues made themselves known; the drinker became expansive, cheerful, and outgoing.

The origin in spoiled grape juice is likely, because the natural habitat of *Saccharomyces cerevisiae* (now both bakers' and brewers' yeast, as well as wine yeast) is the smooth skin of the grape.

The native rice beer (*tapai* or *tapeh*) of southeast Asia is a rice porridge inoculated with a batch from the last brewing; it looks like the proposed ancestral beer. Often it is so thick that one eats it with a spoon.

It is hard to imagine yeast finding its first use in bread making. First, wild grains and primitive domesticated grains do not leaven well. Second, people do not leave bread dough standing around. If they make dough, it is for baking, and they duly bake it. Abandoned bread dough is unlikely enough in itself, but if dough were abandoned, it would dry out or spoil instead of fermenting. Third, yeasts don't like flour. Even if they are on the grain, they will probably be discarded when it is winnowed, husked, cleaned, and ground. Yeast has to be deliberately added, somehow, to dough.

Thus, it seems reasonable to suppose that wine making and brewing came before leavening. (Baking of ashcakes and flat breads or cakes was, of course, already ancient.) Grapes have been cultivated for at least six thousand and probably more like eight thousand years, and wine was almost certainly part of the picture right from the start (see McGovern et al. 1996). I would suspect that wine technology quickly spread to grain gruel when wine yeasts filled the air with spores and contaminated watery gruel left about. Beer was born. Thrifty people probably soon began to use beer lees to make bread.

Against this scenario, one can argue that early beer in ancient Egypt and Mesopotamia was made by crumbling up bread in water, and adding a starter from the previous batch. (Russian *kvas* is still made this way.) So perhaps the bread came first, and beer arose when someone's dinner of bread and water sat too long. I find this theory less credible, but it remains possible. It leaves us still wondering how the yeasts got into the bread. Use of wine lees in baking has been suggested.

The separation of "bread yeasts" and "beer yeasts" is a very new thing. They are artificially selected forms of *Saccharomyces cerevisiae*. Today countless subvarieties occur, especially in the brewing trade. Before the development of such selected strains, the same starters were often used for both bread and beer.

In the evolution of bread, another momentous discovery followed almost immediately. Some eight thousand years ago, just southwest of the Caspian Sea, one of those unsung geniuses who have shaped human history noticed that some odd wheat from the edges of the fields was producing astonishingly superior bread. Instead of making the familiar flat and solid loaf, this bread rose like a pregnant woman's belly, and became marvelously fluffy and soft. The discoverer—very probably a woman—must have become locally known for her special bread. Others tried to imitate, and learned in the process that its qualities depended on seeking out that odd-looking wheat.

We do not know the names or even the ethnic identity of these women, or how long it actually took them to develop leavened loaves from flat breads, but we know where they were: in northwest Iran and Azerbaijan, roughly between Tabriz and Baku. We know this because that is the range of the subspecies of goat-face grass, *Aegilops squarrosa*, that was actually responsible.

Baking bread, Turkey. Woman using a long peelboard to take her bread loaf out of the village oven. Wheat was first domesticated not far from where we took this picture. *Photo by Barbara Anderson, 2000*

Goat-face grass is a common weed in Near Eastern fields, a wild plant whose seeds in their husks look like tiny goats' heads. It hybridizes with wheat; hence my assumption that the first bread wheat came from around the edges of the fields, near the stands of wild grass. But perhaps the goat-face grass grew in among the cultivated stems, and whole fields may have become crossed.

Bread depends on gluten to hold it together. Leavened bread depends on gluten to trap the carbon dioxide particles that allow it to rise. Our familiar fluffy loaf is born when dough full of very strong, tough, elastic gluten is kneaded for twenty-five minutes or so. The combination of water, gluten, and constant stretching and pulling creates a sticky mass that traps carbon dioxide particles evolved by yeast. Yeast grows incredibly quickly, doubling in size every few minutes. It grows by converting carbohydrates into yeast tissue and energy. Carbon dioxide and alcohol are given off by this process. (Chemical leavening, with complex carbonates that break down under heating to release CO_2, came much later in history.) The amount of alcohol in bread is insignificant; it is the CO_2 we want. In brewing, of course, the alcohol is the target.

The gluten that is best for bread dough does not occur in ancestral wheat. Try making bread with semolina, which is made from durum wheat. Durum is a direct descendent of wild emmer wheat, genetically labeled AABB. The necessary gluten was introduced to wheat through hybridization with goat-face grass. Genetic studies have recently shown that the "D genome," the goat-face genes in wheat, come from the subspecies found in the range above noted (Giles Waines, personal communication, 1995; see McCorriston 2000; Smartt and Simmonds 1995:184–91). Of all cultivated grains, only bread wheat—hexaploid wheat, AABBDD—makes the now-familiar leavened loaf. Rye, barley, and other bread ingredients produce hard, heavy loaves unless bread wheat flour is added. Corn bread can be made light by other means, but does not leaven well.

Modern works tend to sound very superior about discoveries such as the D genome. These "primitive" people discovered everything "by accident" or "by trial and error." They did no such thing. The development of bread is far too complex and specific a process to have taken place without conscious thought, planning, discussion, testing, evaluation, and trial. Every baker knows this; even with the technology totally routinized, years of self-conscious practice are required to learn baking. Think of figuring it out with no prior instruction. Villagers and traditional cultivators are no less intelligent and self-conscious than modern people; they have their brilliant scientists and their tireless experimenters. I have known and worked with many such. Surely, many great minds devoted countless years to the perfection of bread.

The origin of bread wheat in the Iran-Azerbaijan lands has had an odd and significant effect on history.

Durum wheat loves relatively warm, moist conditions. Like other wheats, it is usually sown in the fall, to come up in spring. Durum flourishes as a summer crop in Canada and the Dakotas, but otherwise has not spread much beyond its ancestral Mediterranean lands, because these have the mild winters and early springs that winter-sown durum prefers. Cold-tolerant forms exist, but durum still loves hot days and moist climates.

Bread wheat is hardier, preferring continental conditions. (After all, it originated in a cold upland.) Though it tolerates Mediterranean climates, it prefers to overwinter in conditions of more intense cold. Good bread wheats tolerant of warm climates have only recently been developed, after long and difficult breeding work. The truly favored homes of bread wheat have always been the montane Near East, north China, and the plains of Europe. With the expansion of European settlement, it succeeded in interior North America and Australia, and the pampas of Argentina. Until the recent breeding efforts, southerly bread wheats were often soft, better for cake than bread. The finest bread flour came from hard grains grown under truly horrific conditions, in such places as the northern Great Plains, mountain Afghanistan, and remote interior North China.

On the northern grasslands of China and America, even bread wheat kernels cannot overwinter, but conditions are ideal for summer production of both hard red bread wheats and durum. Superior, cold-tolerant, fungus-resistant wheats were introduced from Russia and the Ukraine by Mennonite farmers in the late nineteenth century to the northern Plains of North America, making them the world's breadbasket.

To return to the origins of bread. (Most of what follows comes from, or is influenced by, Jacob's great classic work, *Six Thousand Years of Bread* [1944]; most of what is not in Jacob is from my own research.) Long before civilization began, bread was perfected. One step was the invention of sourdough. Until recently, all leavening depended on saving a batch of dough from the last baking, or on using beer lees. Chemical leavening, cake yeast, and dried yeast now supply almost all our needs, but some bread—sourdough—still depends on saving a bit of the last batch to serve as a sourdough culture.

By definition, such cultures are not just yeast. The souring is contributed by *Lactobacillus* bacteria. These metabolize lactose into lactic acid. They may have originally wandered in from yogurt; perhaps they were just in the air, or perhaps ancient bakers made up dough with yogurt. In any case, sourdough keeps reinventing itself, as people deprived of familiar leavening develop cultures from whatever is in their local environment. In Alaska, the prospectors quickly fixed on a yeast-*Lacto-*

bacillus combination that flourished in frigid climates. In San Francisco, Italian immigrants, making bread in bakeries full of cold fog, wound up with the peerless sourdough bread now so widespread in California restaurants. It depends on *Lactobacillus sanfrancisco,* a bacterium confined to the near-changeless temperatures and perpetual cold fog of the California coast. This bread cannot be made more than a few blocks from the ocean. Elsewhere, the sourdough culture changes in disappointing ways unless kept under special temperature and humidity controls. The proper bacterium is gradually replaced by wild, unpleasant-flavored ones. (Of course, under industrially controlled conditions, one now can make the bread inland—but the good bakeries are still coastal, as of this writing.)

Other lactobacilli produce other sourdough breads in other climates. The famous Alaska sourdough uses a starter mix that loves very cold, rather dry conditions. There are mountain sourdoughs around the world. The best breads I have ever had were in the remote mountains of Afghanistan and in a Zuni Indian hamlet in New Mexico. The Zuni learned breadmaking from the Spanish colonists in the seventeenth century, and still use Mediterranean-style beehive ovens; presumably they got their sourdough starter from the Spanish, as well.

Such, then, was the origin of the world's most widespread and familiar food. The hybridization of bread wheat and the domestication of yeast and *Lactobacillus* stand among the greatest accomplishments of all time. It is typical, and sad, that we know nothing of the women and (few) men who created this first and most valuable of all technically and chemically sophisticated industries.

The progress of milling from metate to hand-turned millstones, then to water and windmills, and finally to huge metal rollers came next, and is somewhat outside the scope of the present book. The development of millstones turned by water and wind was a major industrial breakthrough, critical in the progress of civilization. This took place in the Near East; its history and spread remains controversial. These large millstones, like simple metates, have to be made of special hard, rough stone, and have to be resharpened—usually grooved, rather than pecked—periodically.

Long before this, ancient civilizations saw the development of specialty breads and the rise of professional bakers. Regional breads arose, and chemical leavenings were discovered. Ancient Egyptian and Mesopotamian texts record many kinds of bread, and some of these have been preserved in tombs. Ancient Mesopotamia had huge state-run bread operations, involving integrated factories—*harhar* in Sumerian—where hundreds of people toiled to grind grain on metates, mix the dough, and bake the bread (Gregoire 1998). These industrial operations were staffed largely by slaves and impressed laborers, and working conditions were not of the best.

At the beginning of civilization, the great Old World centers used a great deal of bread wheat, but irrigation led to buildup of salts in the soil, and thus to a gradual shift toward barley. Wheat is extremely intolerant of salt, while barley is the most salt tolerant of major crops. This was particularly true in Mesopotamia, whose agriculture was dependent on irrigation by canals; by the end of the third millennium BCE, barley made up 80 percent of the cereal crop (Gregoire 1998:224). Similar events took place later in what is now Pakistan. (For that matter, the same thing took place five thousand years later in California, whose dry, low-lying valleys now produce barley where they once produced far more valuable vegetable crops. Humans are not always quick learners.) Egypt, irrigated by the Nile flood, was not prone to serious salinization, but even there barley became dominant. China and most of India have enough rainfall to wash the salts out of the soil, thus eliminating the problem.

In Mesopotamia and Egypt, the link between bread and beer was clear and direct. Bread was often made into beer; in any case, the same starters were often used. In the former area, Sumerian was supplanted by Babylonian (a Semitic language) around 2500–2000 BCE. Sumerian survived as a learned language, like Latin in medieval Europe. This led to the production of many dictionaries, fragments of which survive on cuneiform tablets. From these we know the terms for such esoterica as "beer of emmer, excellent ulushin-beer, reddish beer, . . . beer with a 'head,' beer without a 'head,'" beer for various offerings, and so forth. The same tablet refers to "beer-bread which has been crumbled, beer-bread which has been set out . . . flour for *siki*-bread, . . . flour of crushed barley," and various other flours and doughs (Hartman and Oppenheim 1950:23–29). Other tablets list countless kinds of bread. Beer had its goddess, Ninkasi, "she who sates the desires," who according to one myth was born to cure the pain of the mouth (Kramer 1955:11).

Mesopotamian society saw the world as a set of auras, like the halos one's eye constructs around stars (Gregoire 1998:224). Each centered on a city. The city was the center of a little world. Around it was a ring of gardens and orchards. Around this was a wider ring of grainfields.

Around that, in turn, was the steppe and desert land where shepherds herded their flocks.

Inevitably, then as now, there was not always peace between the grain farmers and the shepherds. The latter, for one thing, might occasionally let their flocks wander into the standing grain. Anyway, mountaineers and desert dwellers are a rough lot—satirized in *The Epic of Gilgamesh* in the figure of the wild and hairy Enkidu, who has to be tamed with wine, women, and song (literally; see translation by Kovacs 1985).

A revealing document tells of the rivalry of the farmer-god Enkimdu and the shepherd-god Dumuzi for the love of the great goddess Inanna (Kramer 1955). Inanna at first naturally prefers the higher-status farmer, but Dumuzi matches wits and genealogies with him and wins in the end. Among other things, they compare their products; Dumuzi matches his cheeses and yogurt against Enkimdu's bread and beer. This dialogue reflects patterns of trade and exchange as well as patterns of rivalry:

> The farmer more than I, the farmer more than I, the farmer
> what has he more than I? . . .
> Should he pour me his prime date wine
> I would pour him, the farmer, my yellow milk for it,
> [then several other kinds of wine follow, and then]
> Should he give me his good bread,
> I would give him, the farmer, my honey-cheese for it,
> Should he give me his small beans,
> I would give him, the farmer, my small cheeses for them.
> (Kramer 1955:13).

On the basis of these fair trades, Enkimdu and Dumuzi work out a mutually profitable friendship—not letting their rivalry for Inanna stand in their way. This, of course, is a religiously constructed reference to the real and the ideal in Sumerian society: farmer and shepherd depended on each other, and ideally recognized it and dealt fairly and in friendship, in spite of the differences that all too often intruded. The need for such ideals is shown by some hard realities: the Babylonians (of steppe origin) conquered the Sumerians, just as, later, the nomadic herding Israelites conquered the farming Canaanites.

Grain and bread have provided us with many symbols. The wheat seed falls and is buried; after a winter in the earth, it grows in spring. Then the head of grain forms and is harvested. The grains are crushed and made into dough. The leavening is added, and then comes that most mysterious and wonderful of all processes: The swelling of the loaf, so unmistakably similar to the swelling of pregnancy. After decades of baking (I bake all my own bread) I still feel wonder and strangeness when I contemplate a rising loaf.

Ancient peoples naturally came to see the planting and growth of the seed as symbolic of—or consubstantial with—the death and rebirth of the vegetation god, or the grain goddess, or the divine spirit of food. This was especially true where grain is planted in fall, lies dormant in winter, and germinates in spring—the standard pattern in the Near East and Mediterranean. Their gods of grain and vegetation typically died and were reborn; Tammuz and Osiris are examples. Ceres, Roman goddess of grain, has to spend six months—the cold ones, of course—in the under-world, the other six in this world.

The mythic view was appropriated by Christianity in a symbolic sense: Jesus, dying and being resurrected, was following the pattern of the grain. Easter, the old pagan festival of the rebirth of vegetation in spring, be-came incorporated into Christianity. No one knows when Jesus was ac-tually crucified—probably some time in late winter; Easter today is not set to a specific date, but takes place on the first Sunday after the first full moon in spring, following ancient pagan patterns.

In the Bible, and in other early texts from the Near East, "bread" is equated with "food." It is the Bread of Life. In the New Testament, it is equated with Jesus, the Bread of Heaven. Bread remains a divine sub-stance to many Christians, Muslims, and others, throughout Europe and the Near East. Until very recently, people from traditional parts of this vast realm regarded bread with genuine reverence. Children were trained from the very beginning to sweep up crumbs of bread from floor or table, and dispose of them properly. This was sometimes done by burning: the old pagan idea of the sacred purifying fire. In other areas, the crumbs were fed to the wild birds, a wonderfully life-affirming way to send the bread to the heavens. Children were warned that if they stepped on crumbs of bread the crumbs might sink with them into hell. At the very least, bad luck was sure to follow.[1]

Christianity, more than other Near Eastern religions, has preserved the sacredness of bread. Communion bread was once baked by the fam-ilies of a parish, in rotation. This custom survived until recently among the Basques, and was fascinating to observe. Sandra Ott, in her won-derful book *The Circle of Mountains* (1981), tells of the central importance to the community of this custom. The whole community was tightly and vitally integrated into church life by this activity. The stamp of the Cross was passed from family to family, in a set rotation, so that they could make the bread into the Host. This was good, solid, peasant bread, too, not the anemic wafer that has replaced it in modern churches.

Throughout recorded history, bread has always been the staple food of Europe. Its importance to ancient Greece and Rome needs no elaboration. What is perhaps needed is a corrective in the other direction. Bread's religious overtones made it featured even beyond its very real importance. From ancient Greece onward throughout history, bread shared the table with porridges and gruels of various kinds. These were less visible: they were foods of the poor, or breakfast and quick-lunch foods, or minor accompaniments to other dishes. These could be made of any grain, or of grains mixed with pulses. Thin barley porridge and barley water were the cure-alls of ancient Greek medical dietetics. The ancient Romans depended heavily on gruels such as *pulmentum* (whence modern Italian *polenta,* now made from maize, a crop unknown to the Romans). Russians came to rely heavily on *kasha,* thick porridge made from millet, buckwheat, or other minor seed crops.

Our English word "bread" is cognate with "brewed," and refers to leavening. The old English word was *hlaf,* which gives us "loaf." A "loaf" could theoretically be unleavened, but "bread" obviously implies leavening.

Hlaf, in turn, gave us our original words for the elite. The "lord" was the bread keeper, the *hlafweard* ("loaf-ward," "loaf-guard"). The "lady" was the *hlafdige,* "bread-kneader" (*Oxford English Dictionary*; cf. Jacob 1944). She baked for the laborers, her husband doled it out. By the time lords and ladies enter history, they already had servants to do that, but etymology makes it clear that they once did the work themselves.

Most of Europe is not ideal wheat country. Wheat is native to the dry Mediterranean lands; it likes hot, dry weather. Bread wheat, with its home in the high Iranian plateaus, prefers continental conditions, and is now raised in the American plains and Argentine pampas as well as the Near East and Central Asia. Most of Europe is too cold and wet for optimum wheat production, or was until modern plant breeding developed strains adapted to cool, wet summers. Thus, in the old days, Europeans outside of the more favored Mediterranean lands had to eke out the wheat with rye, barley, oats, peas, beans, and even bark and chaff. Wheat was a luxury; the rich got it, and even they were often reduced to wheat/rye blends for daily fare, saving wheat for special occasions.

The poor—the vast majority—had no wheat at all, and lived on rye, pulses, and the like. Even the pulses got into bread; pea bread is rocklike, but was a staple. East Europeans have made a cult of black bread and rye bread, but those were "breads of affliction" in the old days. Scots lived on oatmeal and oat cake, nutritious but stodgy. Dr. Johnson's dictionary famously defines "oats" as "[a] grain, which in England is generally given to horses, but in Scotland supports the people" (Johnson 1963:268). (Scottish folklore, passed down to me from that side of my family, has it that a Scottish lady asked him, "And where else do you get such horses— and such men?" But I can't vouch for that story.)

Finally, in the nineteenth century, technology for mass production of fine white flour was developed. Notable were the Hungarian steel rollers for breaking and flattening the wheat grain. This allowed separation of the seed coats and germ from the starch. Standard flour today includes only about 70 percent of the wheat "berry" (technically, the caryopsis). Very little besides starch is left. Many of us prefer the old-fashioned stone-ground flour, with most or all of the caryopsis in it, for quality bread. But good white bread remains far more common, and overwhelmingly so in bread-loving France, Spain, Italy, and most of the Mediterranean. Sour-dough white bread remains unbeatable for flavor by any but the very finest whole-grain or rye.

In the twentieth century, more and more efficient methods have been developed to produce a more and more tasteless and textureless bread. This sold widely. At first, it had prestige value, as white bread always did in Europe. Later, it became the ordinary "daily bread," used for sand-wiches and the like; it had no taste or texture to distract the eater. Like most cultural superfoods, it was made as unobtrusive as possible. One can get tired of any marked-tasting food if one eats it three times a day, every day of the year. No fear of that with white bread—or with Chinese white rice, Irish potatoes, or most other widely eaten starch staples.

More edifying than this sorry history is the rise of quality and specialty breads in the last forty years, in both North America and Europe. Today, few cities are without at least one or two bakeries that produce hand-made, slow-rising, good-quality bread. The perceived deterioration of French bread in France, in particular, led to the rise of the Poilâne bak-eries, which have in turn spawned many imitators.[2]

All this is well known to historians. Less well known is the fate of bread as it spread across Asia.

Bread is actually more important in the Middle East than in Europe. Over the vast dry parts of the Middle East, wheat does well and the minor grains, except for barley, do not. (Maize, sorghum, and millets flourish in a few places with special conditions, but remain ill adapted in most of the region.) Therefore, from Morocco to Afghanistan, wheat and barley breads rule the home. Usually, breads are round to oval, flat but leavened so that the small, flat loaf puffs up and can be split for sandwich making. One Arabic name for this is *pita*, which is cognate with Greek *pita* ("pie") and Italian *pizza*. The Iranian form of this bread is called *nan*, which is the same as the Romance root *pan-* (as in Latin *panis*, Spanish *pan*, French *pain*); Farsi tends to change initial *p* to *n*.

Farther afield, breads take a multitude of forms. *Nan* spread to India in medieval times, but the commoner Indian bread is the flat *chapati*, made of whole-grain hard wheat flour. In south India, fermented rice or millet dough is made into large sourdough pancakes called *dosa*, into dumplings (*idli*), or into other forms. In Sri Lanka they are made into small breads called *appa*, which the English heard as "hopper" (Cockney pronunciation: "appa"). One made of strands of dough thus became known as "stringhopper." Southeast Asia reveals forms too numerous to mention.

In China, *nan* penetrated in early times (certainly by the very early Middle Ages, probably even before that). It has been miniaturized in most of China, yielding the *shaobing* ("baked cake"). However, the full huge *nan* survives, under various names, in the far west: Xinjiang and Ningxia.

More traditionally Chinese—much older than the *nan* derivatives— are various steamed buns and steamed or boiled dumplings. These occur in such an incredible variety of forms and names that it would take a book to list them (see Anderson 1988 for a brief introduction). Some are leavened with yeast, others with ammonia salts; many are unleavened. *Mo* and *momo* are solid dough (see Liu 2000 for a great discussion of them). *Bao* are stuffed with meat or sweet fillings. *Mantou* are now solid wheat dough, but were once stuffed; the word is cognate with words from stuffed dumplings used from Korea (*mantu*) to Greece (*manti*). No one seems to know where the word started. I think it's Turkic (*manty*), but it could be Chinese. *Mantou* literally means "filled heads," but it may possibly have once been "barbarian heads," implying a foreign origin. (I find no evidence for a folk explanation given to me: they were named because of a macabre resemblance to barbarians' severed heads!)

There are millions of breads in this world, and to describe them all would be out of my reach. Suffice it to recount the travels of one bread.

One of the most amazing stories in the history of bread is the saga of the traditional Easter loaf. This bread is made from the classic fertility symbols: wheat, eggs, butter, and milk. Sometimes spice seeds are added. Today, sugar is used, but in the old days it would have been sweetened (if at all) with honey or fruit syrup: more fertility symbols. The bread is kneaded three times, and rises three times. Before the last rise, it is split into three, rolled out, and braided, so the final loaf is like a triple-plait hair braid. Today these symbolize the Holy Trinity, but the bread long predates Christianity, and the figure three was of great ritual and symbolic importance long before the trinitarian dogma was imagined.

With the rise of Christianity, this bread became an Easter food. I suspect it had already been the bread of spring festivals for thousands of years. It is now found throughout the Christian world. In Scandinavia, Easter bread is eaten all year long, as an accompaniment to coffee. In Mexico, it has ceased being an Easter food and become the "Bread of the Dead," eaten on All Souls' Day. The ancient Mexicans had a fall festival very much like the Catholic feast of All Souls: the souls of the dead returned to visit the living. For the pre-Columbian Mexicans, this was a happy time, a time to celebrate life and rebirth. The old were remembered, with love and reverence, by the new, and children were brought to the family altar to meet the ancestors and to show that the torch was passed. Easter bread naturally migrated to this wonderful and life-affirming holiday.

The recipe started in the east Mediterranean: in Greece, or perhaps in Mesopotamia, where simple, early forms are still found. It seems to have spread through Syria and the Greek Near East very early. Its spread north and west is probably well within historic times, but is hardly documented. Today, it is the Easter bread throughout Europe and the Christian Near East (in traditional areas).[3]

In some areas it has changed its meaning. Most notably, it was adopted by the Jews very early, and became *challah*, used for Sabbath. For this, the dairy products had to drop out, so that the bread could be eaten with main meals that might involve meat.

In Sweden and Finland, it is a year-round specialty. The Finns, who call it *pulla*, make a veritable cult of it. A wife used to be judged by the qual-

ity of her *pulla*. In Mexico, where the ancient Aztecs and their kin celebrated the return of dead souls in the middle of fall, the bread has become
the Bread of the Dead, and eaten on All Souls' Day, November 1. (Hal-
lowe'en is part of this day—in old times, church days started at sunset, as
they still do in Jewish reckoning.) The pre-Christian European feast of the
dead was taken over by the Christians, giving us our holiday. It fused perfectly with the pre-Christian Mexican feast of the dead. But the Mexican
feast is a joyous occasion, a time to remember loved ones and celebrate
their lives, their rebirth in heaven, and their continuing "life" in their children and grandchildren. They are believed to visit their homes and
enjoy—spiritually, not physically, of course—the foods put out for them.

So the bread of resurrection, rebirth, and new life became the bread of
that day.

12

Foods and Borders
Ethnicities, Cuisines, and Boundary Crossings

1

Foodways are created by dynamic processes. We usually think of them as "ethnic," but ethnicity is not a God-given trait. It is politically defined. It changes constantly with shifting patterns of politics, conquest, and trade.

We speak of "French food," "Italian food," and "American food," but such labels are notoriously ambiguous. Does French food include Provençal? If not, where does French stop and Provençal start? Does Italian food include the Swiss-style food of the historically German-speaking valleys of the Alto Adige? American food is sometimes taken to mean all the food of the United States and Canada; sometimes to mean the Anglo-American tradition (without, for instance, Cajun or French-Canadian food); and sometimes to mean the vernacular and fast-food cooking of the United States, limited to such fare as hamburger and meatloaf.

Cuisines confined to island nations may be more or less tightly bounded; one thinks of Japanese food, and to a less precise extent of British food. (Is Scottish food separate?) Countries that border each other by land, and trade constantly, have a more difficult time keeping their cuisines separate. Cultural differences and ethnic rivalries sharpen boundaries. The United States and Mexico have not fused their cuisines, nor have France and Germany. Yet even in these cases, there is constant influence and borrowing—perhaps especially in areas that have changed hands, such as the U.S.-Mexico borderland (Velez-Ibañez 1996) or Alsace. A region that does not have its own nation-state, like Cataluña or Provence, or like the Levant under the Ottomans, has a more difficult time. Regions with fluid boundaries, frequent conquests, and constant trade, such as the Arab world, are particularly hard to bound.

Italian food is perhaps the most confusing term of them all, and so provides a good place to start. First, we have a historical question. "Roman food" changed to "Italian food" at some point. When? Roman food, as we know from Apicius's cookbook (Apicius 1958 [originally ca. sixth–seventh centuries) and other sources (Dalby 1997, 2003), was characterized by use of lovage, rue, and other herbs absent from later Italian cooking. It also used a great deal of fermented fish sauce called *garum*. This paste was ancestral to Italian anchovy paste. However, it was, from the descriptions, rather more like the modern Southeast Asian fish sauces such as *nuoc mam*. And the early Romans had no pasta. At some point, these and other tastes were transformed. We do not know even approximately when lovage and rue gave way to rosemary and oregano (the former not used in Roman times for food, the latter rather rare; Dalby 2003), or when garum evolved into modern anchovy preparations.

We do know that the fall of the Roman empire and the subsequent conquest of southern Italy by the Arabs brought about profound changes. The Arabs introduced countless new foods, including rice, sugar, oranges, and the *sharbats* that later evolved into ice cream. They may have introduced or reintroduced durum wheat, the superhard variety of emmer used for pasta in recent centuries. Galen describes durum unmistakably (Galen 2000, 2003; Dalby 2003) and separates it from ordinary emmer, which was then and is now a regular Italian crop. (It too is used for pasta, but more rarely than durum.) Perhaps Galen may have known durum only from his homeland in Asia Minor, rather than from Italy—though, at least in later times, it has been much more an Italian crop than an Asian one. Certainly we have no subsequent unequivocal records of durum from Italy until the early Middle Ages. Durum pasta was in Sicily by the eleventh or twelfth century (Wright 2000). Ancestral macaroni (not then a tubular pasta) was recorded, and lasagna too, derived from an earlier fried flat cake known to the Greeks as *laganon* (Wright 2000). Pasta evolved from Greek ancestors, especially a pastalike item called *itria*, at some point in late classical times (see Dalby 2003; Rodinson et al. 2001).

The Arabs introduced new spicing patterns, but learned also from Roman spicing (on Near Eastern food traditions, see Rodinson et al. 2001; Zubaida and Tapper 1994). Pepper, cumin, saffron, and other spices popular with the Romans joined cinnamon, cloves, cardamom, and other newly available oriental flavors.

Sicily remains something of a museum of medieval Arab cooking (LoMonte 1990; Simeti 1989; Wright 1999). Mainland Italy lost most of the Arab dishes during the Renaissance. The history has been tracked elsewhere (Sabban and Serventi 1997, 1998; Serventi and Sabban 2002) and need not concern us here. What does matter to us is the extremely late origin of the cuisine that most foreigners call to mind when they hear the words "Italian food." On the one hand, the undergirding of bread, olives, and wine is ancient. On the other hand, however, New World crops have revolutionized Italy in very recent years. To the non-Italian world, Italian food is almost synonymous with tomato sauces, but the tomato became popular in the late eighteenth century and truly prevalent only in the nineteenth (see esp. Serventi and Sabban 2002 for the history). The first tomato-sauce recipe surviving from Italy is one from 1692, which significantly calls the sauce "Spanish" (Long 2000). It is, in fact, simply a Mexican salsa recipe—so it appears that Mexico's indigenous people inspired modern Italian cuisine, via Spanish intermediaries.

Turkey did not adopt the tomato until the late nineteenth century (Faroqhi 2000:269). Other New World crops were similarly late. Through most of Italian history, polenta (Latin *pulmentum*) was a mush of wheat or other Mediterranean natives; its identification with American-style cornmeal mush is very recent. Green and red peppers, potatoes, and other New World crops became popular at about the same time as the tomato. Hard though it is to imagine such an Italian-named commodity as the zucchini as a recent introduction, it is so; it derives its name from the older, and native, *zucca,* a large melon used now for cheap candied fruit cubes. Chocolate spread somewhat earlier—it was common in the seventeenth century (Coe and Coe 1996)—but it is hardly a marker of Italian food.

Spatial borders are as confusing as temporal ones. One can even ask whether there *is* such a thing as "Italian food." The foreign stereotype noted above is derived from the foods spread by the South Italian—especially Neapolitan—diaspora of the late nineteenth and early twentieth centuries (Diner 2002). From Naples and its hinterland came such characteristic items as pizza, unknown till recently in most of Italy. North Italian food is so different that it hardly seems part of the same world. It tends to use animal fats instead of olive oil. Until recently, it lacked pizza, and was less wedded to the tomato and green pepper; Neapolitan influence in recent years has changed this (Serventi and Sabban 2002), partly via demands by American tourists who expect "Italian food" and mean the Neapolitan-derived delicacies they are familiar with. The north still uses far more rice and maize. Cheeses, pastas, sausages, and sauces are different. Only a general commitment to pasta, bread, herbs, and hard grating cheese unites the realms.

One might even consider separating Sicily as a realm unique unto itself, given its strong Arab flavors and almost wholly distinctive dishes. Sicily is to food what the Upper Amazon is to biology: a region of high diversity and high endemism. And then there is Sardinia. Waverly Root indulged in a bit of romantic exaggeration when he described Sardinian cuisine as "Stone Age" (Root 1971:655), but certainly Sardinian food is not much like downtown Rome's. Quite apart from those Neolithic survivals, we have more historically demonstrable survivals from days of Catalan rule, French influence, and Arab trade.

We thus have at least three Italian cuisines, not even counting those Germans in the Alto Adige. Militant regionalists would split off still more. Piedmontese cuisine verges on French; Genoese is distinctive in its own way, and close to the food of Provence; and so it goes.

Conversely, Italian-type food does not stop at current national borders. The traditional food of Nice is Italian-influenced Provençal, not French in any very meaningful way. Dalmatia and Albania show the effects of centuries of influence or outright rule by Italian states. To my taste, Dalmatian food is more like central Italian food than Sicilian is.

2

Can one define a cuisine?

Yes, as long as one does not strive for exactness. If one defines a style tightly, the next creative chef to come along will surely take the definition as a challenge, just as artists and musicians do when someone defines a style in the arts. Nothing stimulates artistic originality more than a chance to ruin an academic straitjacket.

This being said, there are two possibilities for providing some definition. First, one could give an extensive definition, listing all the dishes or types of dishes in a cuisine. Second, one could give a simple rule of thumb that would predict most cases and bring some clarity without necessarily being perfect.

I prefer the second approach, since the first seems a Sisyphean task. Two particularly interesting, simple ways to define cuisines have come to my attention. First is Waverly Root's subdivision of French food according to cooking fat. He defined three regions of France, characterized by predominance of butter, of animal fat (lard or poultry), and of olive oil (Root 1958). This seems a useful way to subdivide France, and Italy as well (cf. Root 1971), but is not much use in countries, like China or the United States, that use many types of oil interchangeably. I find Root's scheme locally useful and always thought provoking, but little help with the general case.

Far more satisfying is the "flavor principle" developed by Elisabeth and Paul Rozin (E. Rozin 1983). Paul Rozin is the world's expert on the sense of smell; Elisabeth is a talented cook (as I am fortunate to know from some experience). Her insight was that cuisines, like some chefs, are best defined by signature spices. The great cuisines of the world are characterized by quite characteristic and distinctive assemblages of flavorings—herbs, spices, fermented preparations, and condiments in general. Chinese cuisine, for instance, is notoriously diverse. Staples, cooking oils, meats, and dish types vary wildly from place to place, even in the same general region. Yet we all sense a certain unity to "Chinese food." The Rozins point out that this unity comes from the specific mix of soy sauce and other soy ferments, fresh ginger, garlic, rice wine, and chile with which the Chinese flavor most complex dishes. They also note regional variants (E. Rozin 1983:3–4; see also Anderson 1988). Other regions have their signatures, duly described in Elisabeth's book.

Yet, such signature flavorings can change quickly and dramatically. Nowhere is this more clearly shown than in the spectacular fall of spices and rise of herbs in French cooking in the seventeenth and eighteenth centuries (Sabban and Serventi 1998; this was only part of a full, complex history; see e.g. Wheaton 1983). France's medieval cuisine, like that of the rest of western Europe, was based on lavish use of pepper, ginger, cinnamon, cloves, and saffron, with rather less nutmeg, mace, anise seed, cumin, and others. Tastes changed rather suddenly. There were various reasons for this: changing trade routes, local nationalism, and so on. Above all, however, people simply changed their tastes. The old dishes seemed terribly overdone. Significantly, Baroque ornamentation gave way to neoclassical at about the same time. Changes in all aspects of the cuisine took place, from use of fats to the etiquette of dining arrangements. By the eighteenth century, cooking was based more on bringing out the taste of the basic ingredients; vegetables were commoner, but pepper was the only spice widely used. Brillat-Savarin's classic *Physiology of Taste* (1925 [French original 1825]), for instance, says little about spices—especially by comparison with a cookbook of the fifteenth or sixteenth cen-

Food and borders, Mexico. New World foods have reached a Sani minority village in a remote part of southwest China; the chiles and beans drying against the adobe wall reminded my Mexican field companions of home. *Photo by E. N. Anderson, 1990*

turies! Other regions were still plainer. Travel accounts, and the major histories (Flandrin and Montanari 1996, esp. pp. 491–506; Sabban and Serventi 1998; Wheaton 1983), suggest that travelers found little that was unfamiliar, and little that tasted different, on their "grand tours" or more ordinary voyages. Roast meats of many species, accompanied by simple vegetables and sweets, were the universal rule.

By the nineteenth century, the rise of *fines herbes* was underway in France. In the twentieth, the dominance of herbs was complete. The *fines herbes* mix of French haute cuisine became, classically, parsley, chervil, tarragon, and thyme, with sweet marjoram a common fifth. Provençal cooking—itself rather variable by subregion—has quite a different set: basically parsley, laurel (bay leaf), and fennel, with tarragon, basil, thyme, and other herbs occasionally used (Chanot-Bullier 1983).

The same happened in Italy, but there the herbs were rosemary, oregano, flat-leaved parsley, and basil. Change in Italy propagated from northwest to southeast, a fact obviously related to proximity to France. Sicily remains to this day a holdout of medieval spicing.

England lost the elaborate spicing (except for pepper and mustard), but, notoriously, never replaced it with anything. A very few herbs were and are used, as in the folk song "Scarborough Fair": "parsley [or "savory"], sage, rosemary, and thyme." (Presumably those were for sale at the fair. Fairs were a major channel by which scarce flavorings reached the folk.) The core medieval mix of cinnamon, ginger, nutmeg, and cloves continued in specialized uses, notably pie—America knows this mix as "pumpkin pie spice." They were also the spices of mulled ale. An English drinking song claims,

> Cinnamon and ginger, nutmeg and cloves,
> That's what gave me my jolly red nose.

Clearly, the spices were absorbed in alcoholic solution.

The parts of Spain that were near to France also abandoned most condiments, retaining, above all, garlic. Interestingly, the Arabic and medieval cooking of Spain was heavily herb oriented, using considerable amounts of parsley and cilantro (Benavides-Baraja 1996; Bolens 1990; Eléxpuru 1994); this has, on the whole, continued, though apparently with reduced intensity. As in Italy, remote areas held out. Andalucía and neighboring provinces retain Arab spicing—though only in certain dishes, many of them rare and obscure (see Casas 1996 for many of them). Andalucía is the only part of Spain in which the wandering visitor is apt to encounter full medieval spicing, and then often only in "historic revival" cooking that is delightful but not necessarily excessively authentic.

Thus, the signature spicing of a whole region changed dramatically. In the sixteenth century, the elaborate spice mix was quite uniform across nations. By the twentieth, the elaborate mix was gone, and had been replaced by a wild variety of local traditions.

In this case, it really seems fair to speak of a basically united European cooking in the Renaissance, followed by a breakup into national and regional cuisines (see Sabban and Serventi 1997, 1998). These latter did not become really distinct until after the eighteenth century, often not until late in the nineteenth. We think of them as "traditional" today, and sometimes have the vague impression that they have "always" been essentially as they are now. Such is not the case.

Using flavor principles as our main guide, supplemented by attention to cooking oils and major distinctive ingredients, we can define hierarchies of world culinary regions. Such definition must always be rough and imprecise, for reasons stated. But the awareness that, say, Chinese cuisine is not easily separable from Korean does not mean that there is no such thing as Chinese cuisine, or that we cannot separate Korean from it.

It seems possible to define, rather tentatively, seven great culinary macroregions, each including many national and regional cuisines: North Europe (including Anglophone North America), Mediterranean Europe, Latin America (excluding Mexico and Brazil) Near East (stretching from Morocco to Afghanistan), South Asia, Southeast Asia, and China. Brazil, Mexico, Ethiopia, Japan, and arguably a few other countries have sharply distinct cuisines that do not fall within any of the "greats." Small traditions, from Native American to Australian aboriginal, provide a vast number of shifting, usually poorly described traditions, outside the great regions.

We would expect some traditions to be intermediate—boundary cases—and we are not disappointed. Balkan cuisines provide a perfect series of intermediates between North Europe, Mediterranean Europe, and the Near East, and it would be ridiculous to try to classify them as one or another. Vietnam has borrowed heavily from China, especially in the north, and become as much Chinese as Southeast Asian. Guatemala and El Salvador have a unique, distinctive, isolated little cuisine, derived in great part from pre-Columbian Maya cooking. It is not quite different enough from Mexico and Latin America to be a fully independent species, but is certainly not classifiable under either of those majors.

The winds and currents of history are reflected in all these. Just as Europe's cuisines have radically shifted, so have those of the Near East. Cookbooks reveal that cooking meat with fruit (usually dried fruit) was universal and very popular in the Middle Ages (Arberry 1939; Benavides-Baraja 1996; Bolens 1990). It survives today largely in Morocco, reflecting its enormous popularity in Arab Andalucía. Some few dishes, in fact, survive in Andalucía itself (see e.g. several in Morales Rodríguez and Martínez García 1999). Iran, the Caucasus, and Afghanistan still use some fruit in cooking. This style has become rare in Turkey, Arabia, and the Levant. Raisins get into stuffed grape leaves, but that is a far cry from the elaborate fruit-meat dishes of medieval times. Conversely, pasta has entered the Near Eastern realm since the early Middle Ages; it has become popular in quite different forms. Cuscus now defines the Maghrib (northwest Africa), while noodles are especially popular in Iran.

Foods identified with the Ottoman empire and the Greek traders that originally were part of it, such as baklava, cut across macroregional boundaries, but reflect rather faithfully the old Ottoman borders. Baklava—originally a Turkish food, however much claimed by everyone else in the east Mediterranean—is popular in the old core areas of Ottoman wealth and power; rarer but well known in Ottoman marchlands (border regions); and a new, exotic introduction to the rest of the world.

Similarly, an Arab dish, still bearing the Arab name *boronía*, is universal in and around Andalucía—but it seems to have died out in Arab lands (see Arberry 1939; Benavides-Baraja 1996; Bolens 1990; Rodinson et al. 2001; Thibaut-Comelade 1995; Wright 1999). Originally a dish of eggplant cooked in savory fashion, sometimes with fruit, it now includes some or all of the New World favorites: green beans, tomato, squash, and green pepper.[1] It has evolved rather like the ratatouille of Provence, which probably shares a common ancestry in Arab vegetable cookery.

Thus, one can now break up the Near East into several large subregions, the results of recent history: the Maghrib; Egypt; Arabia; the Levant and Mesopotamia; Turkey; Iran and its areas of influence (the Caucasus and west Afghanistan). Similar games can be played with the other divisions of the earth (for China, see Anderson 1988). Each of these can be subdivided. Within the Maghrib, Tunisia, Algeria, and Morocco all differ. Within Morocco, each major city and its associated hinterland has its own variants of the basic cuscus, tajin, shorba, and other recipes (see Hanger 2000 for a useful introduction; Wright 1999 for more detail).

3

Foods, more than anything else, reveal the workings of world-systems. The concept of world-systems was developed especially by Immanuel Wallerstein in the 1970s (Wallerstein 1976). A world-system is, basically, a collection of polities that trade and interact enough to form a single network. There is a core—the rich cluster of polities that dominate trade— and a periphery, consisting of the various areas that are economically deprived or marginalized; often they are dependent or politically weak. The classic case is the "modern world-system," dominated by western Europe, and, since the late nineteenth century, by the United States as well. These constitute the core; the rest of the world is peripheral, though Japan (and to some extent Korea and Taiwan) have come close to core status.

World-systems existed from very early times. The world's first civilizations, Egypt and Mesopotamia, constituted little world-systems; the Nile valley was Egypt's core, while its periphery was the desert region. Mesopotamia's core was the city-states of what is now central and southern Iraq. Its periphery was the mountain and desert region surrounding that (cf. Chase-Dunn and Mann 1998).

Of course, one must avoid thinking pejoratively of the "periphery," or thinking of the core as somehow special. For one thing, core and periphery regularly change places. Italy was core in Roman empire days, periphery by 800, core again in the Renaissance, periphery by 1800, and core again by 2000. France and Frankish lands were a remote periphery in the Dark Ages, receiving foods and Christian foodways from the south; puritanism and wonder working flourished as local religions declined (Effros 2002). A holy man could drink poisoned wine with impunity, or cook food in a wooden vessel on an open flame without fear of burning the vessel (Effros 2002:21–23). A few centuries later, the same areas were setting the world's food tastes and secular intellectual agendas. Other Mediterranean lands, such as Turkey, Spain, and the Levant, sometimes dominated during Italy's "down" cycles. But during the Dark Ages the core was in far Baghdad, while in the capitalist era it moved to Amsterdam, London, or Paris.

Moreover, as the great African social scientist Ibn Khaldun pointed out in the fourteenth century (Ibn Khaldun 1958), the periphery is the land that guards the age-old virtues of courage, loyalty, equality, and fairness. The core is, all too often, the land of corruption, hypocrisy, and degeneration. As cores mature, the wealth of the rich becomes more important than the lives of the poor. Justice becomes a commodity, bought and sold along with the goods extorted or looted from hapless peripheries.

The very culinary sophistication of the core was, to Ibn Khaldun and many since, a mark of trouble. Caring so much about food may replace caring about people.

Even very simple stateless societies can be involved in world-systems; the Wintu and their neighbors in northern California were a very small one (Chase-Dunn and Mann 1998), and so were the Channel Chumash and neighboring Tongva (Gabrielino) in southern California. These societies all had extensive trade; the Chumash at least had whole communities supported by trading, and their trade routes went over land and water for hundreds of miles.

Maya food, Mexico. My neighbor in Chunhuhub, Doña Elsi Rodriguez, cooking. *Photo by E. N. Anderson, 1996*

Much of history can be understood more easily with this concept in mind. The Mongol empire rose from a peripheral location between two world-systems, the Near East and China. It captured both, often using the newest military arts of one to attack the other. The Mongol khans then lived on an uneasy balance, trying to rule two realms from a desolate spot in between. The empire almost immediately fell apart. The most powerful grandsons of Genghis Khan succeeded—respectively—to the Near East, Central Asia, and China. Both the success and the breakup of the Mongol world were due to their strong awareness of world-systems: of the trade routes, of the dominance of rich metropolitan areas, of the core-periphery relationships thus created.

Mongol food, in 1200, was milk, fermented milk, wild plants, and, very rarely, some meat. Mongol food, by 1300, was sophisticated and elaborate. The *Yinshan Zhengyao*, the court nutrition and cooking manual published in Beijing in 1330, contains recipes from Mesopotamia, Iran, Central Asia, and Kashmir, as well as China, Mongolia, and perhaps other areas (Buell et al. 2000). Clearly, the Mongols wanted and needed to show their rulership of the world by serving dishes from all core regions.

Wallerstein's classic example was the de-development of East Europe—in particular, the fall of the Polish-Lithuanian empire. Between 1500 and 1850, Poland fell from vast wealth and power to political nonexistence. This was caused by the rise of Germany and Russia as centers; they reduced Poland (caught in between) to a mere supplier of bulk raw materials. More generally, Poland lost its centrality in the world-system, while shifting lines of trade and commerce made its enemies central (Wallerstein 1976). The effect on Poland's cuisine was not dissimilar to the effect on its political life (Dembínska 1999). As in Dark Age Gaul, a periphery slowly entered the mainstream, foodways and all, but then was re-peripheralized, losing much of its high court tradition of feasting (Wallerstein 1976).

Food, naturally, tracks world-systems very well indeed. Chinese food has been powerfully influential on its peripheries, classically including Korea, Vietnam, and (at least sometimes) Tibet. Southeast Asia is a culi-

Doña Elsi makes a chicken pot pie. Chicken stew, colored with achiote and thickened with corn flour, is put into a small pie made of cornmeal moistened with the chicken stock. Traditional Maya cooking did not use oil; fat for shortening was in this form—stock boiled out of meat. *Photo by E. N. Anderson, 1996*

nary realm though it has never been a political unity; close trade relationships, and frequent battles, have spread ingredients and recipes. Moreover, Southeast Asia was peripheral to India in the Middle Ages, and this has left countless traces on foodways. Geography is not a sufficient explanation for the Southeast Asian food realm; ecology and geography would not predict that Bali's foodways would be far closer to distant India's than to those of New Guinea, relatively close and ecologically similar. Southeast Asia, incidentally, is a multicored world-system, or perhaps a group of small, closely related world-systems; central Burma, central Thailand, and Java were all historic cores.

Typically, the core has the most elaborate foodways; sophistication and elaboration diminish as one moves toward the periphery. Thus, China's most elaborate food is found in its long-established trading and administrative capitals; its next most elaborate is found in their immediate hinterlands; and the least elaborate Chinese-style food is seen in the remote mountains of Manchuria, Tibet, and Burma. Indian food is most elaborate in the old capitals, least so in the mountains of Assam and Nepal. Europe's most elaborate food is found in its old core lands, France and Italy, and within them sophistication is maximized in the old centers of wealth: Paris, Florence, Venice, Rome, and so on. Normally, the cores not only have the most elaborate food but also the most prestigious. Everyone wants to copy their style. It is associated with wealth and power. Even peripheries have their centers and their even-more-peripheral peripheries; Balkan cooking is more sophisticated in Croatia than in Macedonia.

However, this generalization does not always hold. England is the most spectacular exception; for reasons still not fully explained, it remained, culinarily, a remote periphery of France, even when it rose to world rule at France's expense. Less dramatic, but still thought provoking, is the failure of many Latin American countries to develop cuisines matching their world importance. Currently, elaborate and subtle cuisines exist in Mexico and Peru, reflecting (at great remove) the glories of Aztec and Inca courts, and also the fact that they were the centers of Spanish power in Central America and South America, respectively. Brazil has a different pattern: an elaborate cuisine is in the old center, Rio, and another center of elaboration and sophistication is the state of Bahia. This reflects the slave trade and sugar economy of colonial times, and the cross-fertilization of Portuguese, African, and Native American cuisines.

Once again, a vanished world-system geography is preserved in a modern culinary one.

The United States slowly developed a distinctive, sophisticated, complex culinary landscape, after it became a world-system power, but this complexity remains almost entirely confined to the great trading centers: New York, Seattle, San Francisco and the Bay Area (home of "California cuisine"), New Orleans, and so on. "American food" of world-system notoriety is the worst and least sophisticated of American cuisine. Much of this is because most of the vast central and southern reaches of the United States remain peripheral, partaking hardly at all of American centrality; like classic Third World countries, they supply raw materials to other lands—including Japan and Europe.

Thus, food follows world-systems, but may preserve a vanished world order in a "living fossil" state. Some of the imperial cuisine of the Aztecs lives on in Mexican villages. The glory of the vanished empires of Srivijaya and Mataram lives on in small Javanese cities that have long lost leadership to the upstart Dutch capital of Jakarta. Jakarta's food is elaborate, but has not eclipsed the sophistication of Jogjakarta.

Survivals of old ways can turn up in remote places. The Toba Batak of interior Sumatera still make yogurt, reflecting the dominance of India in the early medieval period. India's dairy-food culture spread throughout southeast Asia, surviving now only in such remote, isolated places. Catalan dishes in Sardinia's ports commemorate long-vanished rule.

Conversely, the cuisine of the periphery migrates to the center. Los Angeles has been called "the capital of the Third World," and Miami "the capital of Latin America," in part because of the variety of restaurants to be found. Los Angeles has no cuisine of its own, and depends on its incredible variety of imported talent. It is no less varied for that. A person on lunch break from Los Angeles City College, strolling to neighboring cafés, can choose between almost twenty different ethnic styles.

Amsterdam's restaurant scene, with its countless Indonesian and Surinamian eateries, recalls Dutch empire lost. London, similarly, is well supplied with restaurants featuring foods from India, Pakistan, Hong Kong, and other places that gave rise to the saying that "the sun never sets on the British empire." The sun set on the empire long ago, but for the food it is still high noon.

In both periphery and center, culinary ways mix, and the specific mix reflects world-system history. Surinam, since we speak of it, has a cuisine blended from Dutch, Javanese, Chinese, and Indian roots, with bits of African and Native American influence; this reflects the mix of laborers assembled there in Dutch imperial times. South Africa's cuisine is similarly blended from African, British, Dutch, Malay, and Indian roots. New Orleans's distinctive cuisine has Native American, Spanish, French, and Anglo-American ancestry, reflecting successive rulers; above all, it is heavily African, reflecting the origins of the main labor force.

Particular foodstuffs have affected history. The classic studies of this are Salaman's work on the potato (Salaman 1985) and Sidney Mintz's on sugar (Mintz 1985). Even the lowly peanut has attracted an excellent history, which, among other things, stresses the crucial importance of African Americans in popularizing and spreading it (Smith 2002). Salaman showed how the unique root, well adapted to cold climates where little else will grow, permitted explosive growth of agricultural production in Europe and elsewhere, but also led to terrible famine (see chapter 14). Mintz traced the bitter saga of sugar, associated everywhere with slavery or indentured labor, with rural poverty, with expanding colonialism, and with viciously exploitative production and trading practices in general—all for a food that does little beyond cause cavities and make diabetes more common.

This is something more than just "history." The actual dynamics of ruler and ruled, exploiter and exploited, trader and supplier are commemorated here.

The sage, and even the ordinary eater, finds much on which to reflect. Many a land had only one day of true glory—a day that has shed never-fading brilliance on its cuisine. Many a land without culinary genius has drained the rest of the world of cooks and recipes. Many a land was exploited and used by conquerors, but at least enriched by their crops and recipes. And, sadly, many a land that once had a great cuisine has fallen beneath the wheels of time. The Mongol empire is no more; the courts of Karakoram are desert, and its modern replacement, Ulan Bator, offers little to the wandering gourmet.

4

So using food to signal ethnicity has clearly grown with the rise of trade, contact, and regional interaction. It has also grown with nationalism; each ethnic group feels it must assert its identity by having a distinctive cuisine. Status and ethnicity are combined here; to mark its rise in the political system, a group revalorizes its cuisine. As we have seen in the African-American case, groups that feel discriminated against may self-consciously develop their local cooking into an ethnic cuisine. This has happened in the last few decades to Provençal and Catalan cuisine. Catalan cooking has an ancient and distinctive tradition—it was the high-status, sophisticated cooking of the early Renaissance (Scully 1995; Thibaut-Canelade 1995). Provençal cuisine seems not to have existed as a distinct entity until the nineteenth century. Early accounts suggest that the people of Provence were reduced by poverty to a diet of little more than bread, olive oil, and local fish or cheese (see e.g. Le Roy Ladurie 1971) until trade, commerce, and New World food crops combined to bring prosperity and agricultural productivity to the region. Today, by contrast, it is not only diverse and wonderful, but it has also spawned local subvariants; each city-and-hinterland has its variants of the common dishes (Chanot-Boullier 1983; Médecin 1972). It has become prestigious worldwide, while Catalan cooking is almost unknown outside Cataluña.

We are particularly aware of food as identity when we think of ethnic groups. It is a truism that ethnic groups are characterized by, and often defined by, their foodways. Food-conscious groups such as the Italians and Chinese are particularly notable in this regard. Moreover, many countries, notably Italy (Root 1971) and India (Achaya 1994), but also China (Anderson 1988) and indeed all sizable nations, have a kaleidoscopic range of local cuisines. There are sub-varieties, sub-sub-varieties, and sub-sub-sub-varieties of the major traditions. Often a locale will be popular far beyond its own hinterland for a particular ingredient or dish; Turks everywhere seek out chiles and chile-flavored food from Adana, cream from Afyon, and grape syrup from Antep.

On the other hand, some groups have attracted almost equal fame for the sheer dullness of their cooking. The British are the famous case in the west. This dullness is, of course, much exaggerated in the stereotype. Shaanxi province has the same reputation in China; based on wheat, lamb, pork, and Chinese cabbages, Shaanxi food is simple, plain, filling, and not strongly flavored. Chinese from other provinces find it lacking in flavor and variety.

Ethnic slurs are often based on foods. In the bad old days when ethnic insults were politically correct, Germans were "krauts," French were "frogs," and so on. An Irish Catholic friend of mine complained that she was called a "mackerel smacker" in her childhood in Boston. (Catholics had to eat fish on Friday, and mackerel was cheap enough for the supposedly indigent Irish.) Chinese in the early medieval period were no different; northwesterners laughed at the frog eaters on the coast, who in turn ridiculed the northwesterners for eating yogurt and mutton (Anderson 1988).

Going beyond the stereotypes, we find some amazing manipulations of ethnicity. The folklorist Robert Georges, who is Greek American, once wrote—but, alas, never published—a paper called "You Eat What Others Think You Are" (1981). Here he noted that people who could cook Greek food very well, but were not of Greek ancestry, deprived him of their cooking because he was assumed to be too harsh a judge—much to his sorrow. His elderly relatives "back East" in older immigrant neighborhoods always cooked a set Greek festival menu when he visited them. It was always the same menu. It was nothing like ordinary food in Greece, but it had become the sacred tradition.

I have seen similar phenomena in many areas. In Hong Kong, many of my friends belonged to an ethnic group, the Teochiu, which is very different in language and foodways from the Cantonese who make up most of Hong Kong's population. My Teochiu friends would cook Cantonese food most of the time. They always ate Cantonese food when they were with Cantonese. But, for special occasions, especially family celebrations, they always went to Teochiu restaurants. In such contexts, like Robert Georges's family, they ate a more or less set menu of traditional festal dishes. Thus Teochiu identity was affirmed. For most of them, this was the only important way it was *ever* affirmed. Born and raised in Hong Kong, they spoke Cantonese, but they were still "Teochiu"—if only at festal dinners.

In Hong Kong, where the Cantonese are the majority, other Chinese ethnic groups eat their own cuisines when holding their own ethnic festivals or dinners, to reassert identity. But they eat Cantonese food when with Cantonese, to affirm solidarity and avoid being labeled. They eat a mix at home, often eating Cantonese everyday foods and their own special festive foods. Immigrant groups in the United States often act similarly.

U.S. residents in East Asia often acted similarly, eating Asian food most of the time but putting on a "proper" Thanksgiving or Christmas feast for their American and Asian friends. Often, they would go to great lengths to get "traditional" Thanksgiving foods that they did not bother to eat at home.

Not all ethnic food is cooked by people of the ethnicity in question. A huge percentage of restaurant cooking in southern California is done by Mexicans, often illegal immigrants. At one time, many of these came from Zacatecas (a state with a high level of both education and cooking). These cooks produce much of the superb French and Italian food of Los Angeles's snob restaurants. They also produce Asian, Arab, Greek, and any other food one might want. One of the most difficult of Chinese cooking arts is making hand-swung noodles; Chinese chefs take years to learn it. The only expert I have seen doing it in California was a Mexican—working in a Chinese Korean restaurant!

As usual, this is nothing new. Similar phenomena are documented throughout all history. The ancient Greeks sought cooks from particular areas famous for their cuisine. Then when the Romans conquered the Greeks, Greek cooks went to Rome, just as, more recently, Greeks became diner and pizzeria operators all over the United States. Later still, Italian and Greek migrants brought haute cuisine to France. The French then brought it to England (but it did not catch on). Chinese and Korean cooks "made" Japanese cuisine, starting from at least 600–700 AD.

5

When migrants come to a new land, they gradually change their foodways. Eventually, they usually come to eat like the majority in the new home. Some groups are more resistant to change than others. Chinese and Mexicans in California are particularly tenacious of their foodways. There are good reasons. First, their cuisines are popular with almost everyone, so there is no real incentive to change. Second, their communities are constantly renewed by immigration. Third, they maintain large and dynamic ethnic enclaves. At the opposite extreme are East Europeans. They came to California in fair numbers, but immigration virtually stopped with the Depression. They did not often start restaurants, and their cuisines were not popular with Anglo-Americans. They also dispersed rapidly into the California "white" world.

I have done research on Chinese (Anderson and Wang 1987) and Finnish foodways in California. The difference in restaurant activity is striking. Chinese restaurants are everywhere in California, and many of them serve food about as good as one can find in Hong Kong or Taiwan today. They are well patronized by all ethnic communities.

By contrast, I have only once encountered a Finnish restaurant in Los Angeles. The owners (a middle-aged couple, excellent cooks) could not resist the Finnish tradition of hospitality; they refused to take money for the food, if they knew the people they were serving! Of course, the restaurant lasted only until they ran out of capital. I have heard similar reports from elsewhere in Finnish America. There have been no Finnish restaurants in California for a long time. There are, of course, more Chinese than Finns in the state, but the difference is not great enough to explain the restaurant findings. Finns were important in the settlement of the north coast, in particular, and large Finnish enclaves used to exist from the Bay Area to Oregon. California also has rather sizable numbers of Poles, Czechs, and Hungarians. There are a very few restaurants catering to them, but not as many as one would expect from the numbers of immigrants.

Chinese immigrants in California acculturate to Anglo-American foodways in a fairly set fashion (Anderson and Wang 1987). First, they adopt American sweets and snack foods. Then they pick up American drinks, if they had not already done so in their homelands. Colas, milk, and "designer water" slowly replace tea and soybean drinks. Then breakfast Americanizes; cereal and toast replace congee and dumplings. Then lunch gives way. Dinner takes much longer to change. Finally, feast foods associated with the major Chinese holidays are the last to go. Other immigrant studies have found the same pattern. It seems to be almost universal.

We found that many Chinese drove up to two hundred miles a weekend just to food shop and eat out in Chinatown. So do many other Asians. Artesia, an enclave of immigrants from India, attracts Asian Indians from all over southern California. I remember when Artesia was a Portuguese enclave that attracted Portuguese from the same wide-flung region. The Portuguese (here and throughout California) merged fairly quickly into the general Anglo population, leaving Artesia to the latest immigrant community.

Such ethnic replacements are very common. The Indians, however, are probably going to stay, because they merge less rapidly and because immigration is continuing.

Beans at the market, Ecuador. Quechua, the largest Native American group today, provide most of the food for the town. *Photo by E. N. Anderson, 1966*

In this modern world, "global village" that it is, Chinese food is everywhere (Foundation of Chinese Dietary Culture 1998; Wu and Cheung 2002; Wu and Tan 2001)—just as McDonald's is invading China (Watson 1997). The general cultural trend, worldwide, is for American culture to blanket everything. Thus, it is particularly interesting to the anthropologist to observe cases in which other cultural traditions "swim upstream": not just holding their own against the American deluge, they actually penetrate the American cultural fortress and propagate there. Italian, Mexican, and Chinese foodways have done this. Of course, ethnic food has never respected ethnic boundaries. In fact, it is their crossing boundaries that makes them "ethnic" foods—as opposed to just "local" foods. Groups learn, imitate, and borrow all the time. With the coming of "the global village" in the late twentieth century, ethnic food has exploded from its origin points.

This is nothing new. Consider the worldwide spread of spices and spice cookery, and the spread of Near Eastern foodways to China across the Silk Road (Buell et al. 2000).

Today, American fast food is everywhere, but as America was "Coca-Colanizing" the world-system, Mexico, China, and Italy (to name only the three most notable) were conquering the United States. Italy in particular: pizza has been by far the most popular food in the United States for decades now. Spaghetti, lasagna, and Italian sandwiches are not far behind. Italian restaurants run the gamut from the most humble to the most expensive and socially elite.

Such spread never occurs without changes. The Chinese and Mongols changed the spicing of Near Eastern foods, adding soy sauce, large East Asian cardamoms, and other new flavors. Chinese food in turn changed in the United States. By the 1960s, when new streams of immigrants came from eastern Asia, American Chinese food was a distinct category of its own, complete with purely Californian inventions such as fortune cookies. The new immigrants, introducing genuine Cantonese, Shanghainese, or Szechuanese food, created a whole new culinary universe—distinct not only in taste qualities but also in the architecture, ambience, and location of the restaurants.

Pizza is probably the most dramatically changed ethnic food.[2] In its native area—Naples and environs—it was simply a flat bread baked with a topping of tomato, garlic, cheese, and perhaps an anchovy and some oregano. The word is almost certainly cognate with *pita,* meaning "flat bread" in Arabic and "small pie" in Greek. Pizza is only one of a class of Mediterranean flat breads with toppings baked on. It is comparable, for example, to Middle Eastern *lahmajun* (which just means "bread and meat" in Arabic)—which has had its own, earlier radiation into Turkey, Armenia, and farther afield.

In the United States, pizza took on a strange life of its own. Various thicknesses and forms of crust developed. For lack of true Italian ovens, pizza was baked in baking dishes in some areas. Toppings were improvised, and grew more and more innovative. The standard came to include green peppers, onions, and olives as well as traditional tomato and cheese. Oregano, the basic flavoring of the early pizzas, shrank progressively in importance. Anchovies followed it into near oblivion. Meanwhile, a vast array of new pizzas arose, topped with hamburger, sausages, arugula, smoked salmon, feta cheese, or anything else imaginable. Dessert pizzas, topped with dessert cream and fruit, became briefly popular. Perhaps the strangest, to the food historian, is the "Hawaiian pizza," topped with ham and pineapple—a combination identified with pseudo-Hawaiian restaurants whose chefs were American Chinese. Neither ham nor pineapple is a native Hawaiian food. In fact, the combination owes more to midwestern America, and ultimately to the British custom of serving ham with fruit preparations. Thus does the whole world-system inhere in one dish.

Such exchanges eventually undermine the correlation of ethnicity and foodways. In the Middle East, foodways extend broadly across ethnic lines. Central Asian food is rather uniform, in spite of some significant differences, whether one is eating among Tadzhiks, Uzbeks, or Turkmens. Where Turkey, Iran, and Iraq come together, Kurds, Armenians, Arabs, Turks, and Persians trade bullets but share foodways. There are distinctions made, but they as often distinguish cities and valleys as ethnic groups per se. Or, to put it another way, the citizens of one town may constitute a slightly distinct ethnic group of their own; Mosul in Iraq, for instance, is its own little world in more ways than one, and Mosul identity and foodways cut across religious and linguistic lines. The same can be said, with some reservations, about Istanbul, and even about some particular quarters of Istanbul. The old market and the old port have distinctive dishes and food traditions of their own.

Groups may vie to disown a foodway. Los Angeles Chinese tend to claim that fortune cookies and certain other "un-Chinese" dishes were invented in San Francisco, while San Franciscan Chinese claim they were invented in Los Angeles.

The popularity of American fast food in the contemporary world owes much to a desire to be seen as identifying with the rich, powerful, hard-driving, successful Americans (see e.g. Watson 1997). Indeed, many people believe that by eating American style (and by dressing American style, and listening to American pop music) they can actually acquire those qualities, and become rich. I often heard this article of faith in eastern Asia (see, again, Watson 1997). Some of them get to America, and discover to their horror that the foodways of their emulation are the mark of the poorest and least successful of Americans—a class of people whose existence they had not imagined.

Ethnic survival of foodways is not simply a matter of ethnic conservatism or tenacity. It is influenced by ongoing interaction with the host societies. One can see this by comparing food with other arts of life. In music, for instance, the pattern has been very different. The Latin touch wins there, too, but native Andean, Celtic, and even aboriginal Australian musical traditions have proved more successful than Chinese in surviving robustly outside the homeland. This is largely because they are more appealing to the wider world. Irish food never attracted many; Irish music has millions of fans. Chinese food seems to become instantly popular with almost everyone in the world, but Chinese music tends to be regarded as "like a cellar full of fighting cats," not only by other ethnic groups but even by younger Chinese in the overseas communities. Chinese food and indigenous Andean music vie for the distinction of being the most successful arts at "swimming upstream": not only holding their own, but actually enormously expanding their appeal and popularity, at the same time as American foodways and music were sweeping the world and overwhelming thousands of local traditions.

All this does not necessarily get us closer to understanding world-systems, but it at least emphasizes two things: first, food and foodways have been internationalizing for centuries, and have been defined on a world scale; second, foodways are to a great extent the products of global trade and global empire.

13

Feeding the World

If you don't like the news, go out and make your own.
—Graffito on a Berkeley newsstand
(observed by the author in the 1960s)

1

All this understanding of foodways would be unworthy of attention if it did not help us with the world food problem.

At present, for the first time in the history of the world, there is food enough for all (Smil 2000). Yet, around a billion people are undernourished (see chapter 1). Hundreds of millions of people go to bed hungry most nights of their lives. Starvation is still one of the commonest causes of death.

Yet, ironically, an almost equal number is overnourished, suffering from obesity. The world food problem, today, is not one of absolute lack but of absurdly wrong distribution. The Green Revolution—the introduction of new crop varieties, pesticides, and fertilizers in the 1960s and after—had many problems, but it did increase the food supply (see e.g. Evans 1998). There is, in fact, plenty of food in the world; it simply is not well distributed. India, which probably has more hungry people than any other country, also has a large surplus of grain, which often threatens to rot unused for lack of storage and distribution facilities (Stone 2002). Technology has entered the twenty-first century, but social justice has gone back to the eleventh. Consider the enormous variations in food availability between, say, the United States and Haiti—or even between Silicon Valley and an isolated Indian reservation in America.

The problem of world food supply has been well discussed by a number of authors. Notable among recent authors are Lester Brown (1995, 1996), Vaclav Smil (2000), and L. T. Evans (1998; and the International Food Policy Research Institute 2002 provides a wide-ranging set of views). All three men have written excellent books, filled with technical detail. They agree, broadly, on their data. They disagree on their prognoses: Brown is generally the pessimist, Evans the optimist, Smil the balanced, rational soul in between.

Social justice is the real problem (Brown 1996; Sen 1992). This includes the politics of science: what gets studied, what gets developed. Too often, agricultural research money goes to luxury crops for the rich rather than to staples of the poor. Raising cattle in rich-nation feedlots receives more attention than raising cattle in the Sahel. Raising sturgeons for caviar has produced more research than raising the millets that feed much of Africa (cf. National Research Council 1996).

The sheer pressure of population is, of course, not something to ignore. Most authors seem to agree that the world can feed at least thirty billion people—perhaps twice that if people were willing to go back to the pre-industrial regimen of extremely penurious lives and constant threats of famine. However, feeding thirty billion would require essentially perfect government. No mistakes, miscalculations, wars, corruption, or other ordinary sins of nations could be tolerated. Moreover, current suicidal policies toward the environment would have to stop. All this being unlikely, it is correspondingly unlikely that the human population will rise above ten billion or so. This figure will be reached by about 2050, at which time either voluntary restraint or Malthusian catastrophe will level the population off.

At present, falling birth rates and the spread of family planning make most experts cautiously hopeful that voluntary action will set the limit. However, explosive population growth in Latin America and parts of Africa remains disquieting, and the opposition to serious family planning by the Catholic Church and the current United States government is even more so.

In particular, some crowded countries still have a high birth rate. Almost all countries have brought birth rates down in recent decades, but countries such as Egypt, Pakistan, Indonesia, and Nigeria still have high rates of increase and are already desperately stressed by shortages of water, fertile land, and other key inputs necessary for agriculture and food processing.

Technology is doing quite well in solving world food problems, and even the much-maligned global marketplace is at least doing what it is supposed to do—motivating production and getting the food around.

The problem is lack of political will to help the hungry and to limit population growth.

2

In former centuries, famine was a much more constant threat than it is now (see Murton 2000). China had a famine, somewhere, almost every year in recorded history (Mallory 1926). The Aztecs were also bedeviled by frequent and horrible famines (Duran 1994). Abnormal weather of any kind could produce famines anywhere. A great volcanic explosion in what is now Indonesia in the early nineteenth century produced "years without a summer" in Europe and America; the volcanic dust drifted north, and there was so much in the air that the sun was blocked. Europe starved. Many Germans blamed the Jews for somehow darkening the sun. Anti-Semitism, all too common even before, began a steady rise that led eventually—after many other episodes—to Hitler (Post 1976).

Perhaps the most famous famine in history was the potato famine in Europe in 1846–1848 (Salaman 1985; Woodham-Smith 1962). We in the English-speaking world speak of this as the "Irish" potato famine, but it affected far more people in Germany, Poland, Russia, and neighboring areas. The immediate cause was potato blight, *Phytophthora infestans* (usually described as a fungus, but actually in the brown algae group—closer to certain seaweeds than to fungi—and thus dependent on wet soil). The genus *Phytophthora* is one of humanity's worst enemies, ranking with malaria and tuberculosis as a killer—but its murders are indirect. *P. infestans* slays not only potatoes but also many other crops, and important trees such as oak. Avocados and related trees are killed by a closely related species, *P. cinnamomea,* and still other species kill still other crops.

In 1846 and 1847, cold and wet summers allowed *P. infestans* to proliferate. By this time, much of Europe had become dependent on potatoes, especially the "lumper" variety. Evolving as organisms do, *P. infestans* naturally became more and more successful at parasitizing lumper potatoes. The wet weather brought things to a head, and the potato crop was virtually wiped out from Ireland to Russia. Ironically, Ireland continued to export thousands of tons of food to England—but the food was wheat and other elite products, too expensive for the Irish poor. Social problems exacerbated (if they did not actually create) the situation; the role of land-lords and other elites is still debated (Lang 2001). The money earned by exporting crops bought some food from outside, but much of that was maize, which the Irish poor could not use; they lacked the know-how, the technology, and the fuel to prepare it. The Irish still blame the English for causing or exacerbating the famine by cold-blooded indifference, while the English still blame the Irish for laziness and ingratitude.

Millions of people died; millions more emigrated, primarily to the United States, whose culture was changed profoundly. The desperate poverty of the "hungry forties" was already severe, leading to rebellions and disorders; the famine brought desperation, and desperation produced outright revolution, from Germany to Hungary. New and uncompromis-ing ideologies, from Marxian communism to extreme nationalism, flour-ished. The world has never been the same.

Frank famine and starvation are now strictly political matters, and have been since World War II (Sen 1992). They are essentially confined to war zones like Afghanistan, or to nations in which a cruel government is starving its opposition to death, as the Sudanese government has done in its civil war with its southern peoples. The mass famines of China in 1959–1961 and Ethiopia in the 1970s were due to extremist left-wing policies. Comparable right-wing extremism led to widespread hunger and starvation in Guatemala and South Africa in the 1980s. (On these and re-lated matters see Rummel 1998.)

In most of these cases, and in countless others, the world community did rather little. The South African government was subjected to extreme and eventually successful pressure, but otherwise there was little action. Ethiopia attracted relief attention, but even after the repressive regime fell, Ethiopia's problems continue, without much international attention. Sudan, China, and Guatemala operated with relative impunity, even from mild criticism. Sudan and China had seats on the Human Rights Com-mittee of the United Nations until 2002; apparently, deliberately starving millions of one's people to death is not a human rights issue to the grave diplomats of the twenty-first century.

Serious famine is a straightforward political problem. It will be easily solved when political leaders decide that human life has value. It will con-tinue to fester until then.

Food security for the future is not assured. Brown and Smil note that there is very little food stored in the system. Moreover, only seven or eight countries are net exporters of food on a large scale. (Many others export coffee, tea, and the like, but that does not help the starving.) The problem of chronic local undernutrition is more serious and less simple. It is something of a "hidden" problem. It is well enough known to experts, but does not show itself easily.

One is left unsatisfied by the works of Brown, Smil, and the others. They talk of technical solutions: more fertilizer, less overfishing, more efficient use of water, less urban sprawl on farmland. Anthropologists with a lifetime of field experience, such as Johan Pottier in his book *The Anthropology of Food* (1999), are left saying, Yes, but everyone has known this for decades; what is *really* wrong here?

One problem is distribution of resources. According to Ismail Serageldin, "10% of the world's population subsists on less than 0.5% of the world's income" (Serageldin 2002:54). Even the more fortunate 90 percent include many sufferers from poverty. Meanwhile, the rich get richer; Bill Gates's income is more than a million times that of the average American worker, and more than the combined total gross national product of several of the poorest countries.

Only political will can bring about more reasonable distribution of food, fertilizer, agricultural research, and new food sources in a world economy that increasingly concentrates wealth in the hands of the urban, educated sector of humanity, and increasingly sucks wealth from farming and other food-producing sectors. Moreover, long experience teaches that simply handing out resources is fatal. It out-competes local industry and solves no problems. Everyone quotes the proverb, "If I give a man a fish, I feed him for a day; if I teach him to fish, I feed him for a lifetime." This works only if he can buy fishhooks or nets, and if someone makes sure that his fish aren't wiped out by pollution or uncontrolled open-access fishing. With almost all the world's fisheries now seriously overexploited or wiped out by pollution (see Brown 1995, 1996, and sources therein), this is a major problem. We have to give people the chance to produce more, but in a context of conservation. That means more efficiency is necessary. We have to do more with less. That will take careful planning.

Few First World persons appreciate just how bad life is for most of the human race. It is not enough to visit Third World countries; one has to live with the poor for months or years. The chronic hunger, disease, violence, and insecurity that are their daily lot have to be experienced to be understood.

The self-serving myth that they "do not care" or "are used to it" is, of course, incorrect. Hunger, cold, disease, and murderous brutality are hardly things that one can "get used to" or endure without pain and suffering. The death of one's child hurts as much when one is poor as when one is rich. Indeed, since the poor often depend on their families for all the security and love they have, it may hurt more.

We have no way of knowing how many people starve to death per year, especially since most are diagnosed as dying of something else. Some minor disease comes in and finishes off a weakened body that, if well fed, could easily have withstood the germs. Estimates of malnutrition deaths run as high as five hundred thousand people per year (almost one per minute). Hunger in the United States was virtually eliminated by the late 1970s, but government policies in the 1980s and since have led to massive wealth transfers from poor to rich and massive cutbacks in food-aid programs, leading to rapid decrease in food adequacy for the poor.

There are other problems. The First World has cleaned up traditional pollutants, such as animal dung and raw sewage, and has set controls on new pollutants such as toxic chemicals. In most of the Third World, the traditional pollutants are still there, worse than ever because of population growth and uncontrolled urbanization. Added to them are toxic wastes, nuclear dumps, pesticide overuse, dangerous drugs, lawless industry, and the like.

Governments very often use the full panoply of modern weapons (save only nuclear arms) against their own people, to eliminate minorities and enforce corrupt rule (Rummel 1998).

3

There is, today, a chronic malaise in the rural areas of the world. The people who should be producing food are in deep trouble. Most of the world's "hidden" food problem is, ironically, in rural food-producing areas. The hungriest people are often those who feed the rest of us.

Many rural people do not have enough land. There is barely enough farmland in the world to feed everyone, and that farmland is concentrated in relatively few hands. Giant American agribusiness firms own a very disproportionate share of it, not only in the United States but also in dozens of poor nations.

Local landlords own a great deal of the rest, especially in Latin America, and they tend to use it to produce cattle, cocaine, marijuana, palm oil, and other things that hurt more than they help. To be sure, cattle and palm oil are foods, but palm oil supplies only empty calories of heart-de-stroying saturated fat. Cattle are usually produced through the use of habitats that could produce a very great deal more of a very much more nutritious set of foodstuffs. In rich nations, cattle are fed grain that could be fed to humans. In both rich and poor nations, cattle are produced on land cleared of productive forests. Unlike some authors (e.g. Lappé and Collins 1971; Rifkin 1992), I have nothing against grazing cattle on grassland, as long as it is not overgrazed, and I have nothing against cattle fed on things people can't eat, such as cornstalks; the problem is that many cattle are not raised that way.

Concentration of land in the hands of a few is pernicious not just because it is unfair. The great landlords own far more land than they can properly oversee or care for. Inefficiency, waste, and low production are typical of huge estates. This is true even in the United States, where mechanized farming allows cultivation of vast uninhabited tracts. It is far more clear in Latin America. On the other hand, smallholders who are not only willing to work but actually desperate to work do not have enough land to occupy them. Many of my friends in the Maya villages of Mexico do not have enough money for even a hectare of land, yet they have the energy, skill, and motivation to farm many hectares. Of all the truths found by anthropologists in studying food, the clearest and best documented is that small- to medium-scale free farmers are the most efficient producers (Netting 1993). Absentee landlords are probably the least.

Land reform has a history of delivering less than it promises (Tuma 1965), but has improved the situation in some areas, from Taiwan to Honduras and Mexico. Mexico's land reforms of the 1920s and 1930s have been eroded over time, but still allow the nation to succeed far beyond most Third World countries. Some have too much land, many have too little, but the country produces most of its own food.

Unfortunately, shortage of acreage is only part of the story. More serious is the progressive degradation of the land itself.

Water is a problem that is exploding into worldwide crisis levels with unprecedented speed (Gleick 1998). Irrigation has gone about as far as it can go. Poor drainage, poor conservation, poor management, serious pollution, and overdraft of irreplaceable groundwater resources have already led to abandonment of much irrigated land. Global warming will probably exacerbate the situation in many areas.

Moreover, irrigated land is easy to urbanize and usually densely populated. From Sacramento and Fresno to Baghdad and Karachi, huge cities are rapidly expanding over the world's irrigated landscape. At current rates of urbanization, California and perhaps Mexico will have no irrigated or irrigable land in about fifty years. Iraq, Syria, Pakistan, Iran, and several other nations are in acute danger too. Even China, with its vast area of irrigation, is at major risk. I was disturbed, on my latest visit, to see how correct was Lester Brown's assessment in *Who Will Feed China?* (1995). China is copying California, building new cities, airports, freeways, factories, and parking lots indiscriminately on the best farmland. Unlike California, China had a three-thousand-year tradition of avoiding such building up of farmland, when possible. But the Communists changed all. Food production is suffering accordingly.

Soil erosion remains another major issue. The United States has largely controlled its erosion problem, thanks to incredible efforts by the Soil Conservation Service—now the Natural Resources Conservation Service—over the last seventy years. Smil (2000), in a long and very able discussion, points out that worldwide estimates of soil erosion differ considerably, because the data simply aren't there. Yet, anyone who has visited—or even flown over—densely populated parts of the world knows that erosion is often catastrophic. Simply from my own experience, I can testify that the Middle East and North Africa suffer greatly from overgrazing and consequent erosion. The Mixteca Alta of Mexico has been a horrific moonscape for years, perhaps for centuries. Much of China has gone from dense, lush, primary forest to moonscape in the last couple of generations. India is in deep trouble, and much of Africa is facing explosive increase in erosion (I have seen it especially in Ethiopia).

Deforestation is a related problem. Deforested slopes erode easily. Deforestation reduces rainfall, at least locally. Deforestation deprives rural residents of firewood, wild fruit, medicinal herbs, and other necessary resources. Even hedgerows and unused roadsides used to provide wild greens, small game like rabbits, and a few fruits. Now, land shortages force cultivation of every inch of land. Even the edible weeds that used to grow among the crops are gone, killed by herbicides.

Such damage can be reversed. In addition to the United States, my personal observation reveals that Tunisia and Turkey have made great strides in restoring their lands, through grazing control and massive reforestation. Such efforts, if carried out worldwide, would greatly reduce the danger of famine.

Pollution, deforestation, and other environmental problems cause similar losses. Chesapeake Bay once could produce enough fish and shellfish to give every American a decent level of animal protein. It now produces a tiny fraction of what it used to. At present rates of ruin, it will be producing nothing edible within a very few years. Similar damage threatens New Jersey's waters (McCay 1998), San Francisco Bay, most of Mexico's inshore waters, and so on around the world. We have ruined as much bay and river habitat as would provide more than enough protein for everyone on earth.

Traditional varieties disappear, losing more and more genetic diversity. Sometimes taste preserves them or even brings about a revival, as with flavorful apple varieties in the United States (Green 2002), where thousands of varieties have dropped out of use but many are being developed or preserved. "Slow food" movements and local loyalties preserve foods in Europe (Holley 2002). But these are situations of affluence. The vast, little-seen problem is in the poor areas of the world, where modern high-yield varieties displace hundreds of thousands of little-known, little-studied, often valuable local races of crop plants and animals.

The conditions of rural life are changing. People who could formerly support themselves by farm work are now finding that overpopulation, mechanization, loss of wild plant and animal resources, water shortage, and the spread of export-oriented and monocrop agriculture are conspiring to produce a general decline in rural areas around the world. There are no more weeds or waste grains for gleaners. The mixed farming systems that used to produce small surpluses of foods are replaced by endless rows of cotton, oil palm, rubber, or other inedibles. There is no firewood to cook what food can be found. Worst of all, as noted above, there is little work—in spite of the desperate need for human labor in erosion control, reforestation, water management, and countless other areas of enterprise. The problem lies with unenlightened governments (i.e., almost all governments); only a few, such as Tunisia's, realize that a small investment in paying people to reforest will be repaid many times over in erosion control and water retention.

Water becomes more and more scarce and polluted day by day. Two million people—almost all of them children—die each year from water-borne or foodborne diarrhea (WHO press release, 28 January 2002).

So the best and brightest move to the cities, depriving the rural areas of leadership. In the Mediterranean and in Mexico, I have encountered countless farming communities from which the best and brightest had fled. The lure of good wages in the "north," or the cities, or the factories is strong, and the incentives to stay down on the farm are few indeed. My father and uncles did exactly the same thing, so I can hardly be judgmental. And such migration reduces population pressure, and opens the world to people of talent who might otherwise never reach their potential. But, at some point, we will have to stop the flow by allowing small farmers to profit from their work.

Adding to rural woes is massive pollution by pesticides and fossil fuels. Perhaps even more serious is the spread of cheap, easily available junk foods. White flour, white sugar, and alcohol are replacing the lost wild greens, game animals, and dooryard garden crops. The same number of calories may be coming in, but vitamin and mineral levels crash.

The combination of poverty, loss of local leadership, and cheap alcohol is particularly deadly. Throughout the world—including much of the United States—regions that used to be populated by poor but stalwart, tough, and resilient farmers are now hotbeds of alcoholism. Consequences range from family violence to massive impoverishment. One can find such situations from California's Central Valley to India and Peru. I have studied the phenomenon in British Columbia and encountered it from Yucatan to Malaysia.

All this has been overlooked by most experts. Economists see incomes rising. They do not look at the loss of free goods such as firewood, wild herbs, water, and game. They do not look at the ultimate costs of "higher" incomes when much of the money goes to alcohol. Food scientists see overall improvement in the world food situation. Politicians, even the few politicians who care about the people, do not see (or do not admit to seeing) the progressive anomie, alcoholism, social breakdown, and brain drain. If they do, they blame the people themselves, or perhaps the global economy. They do not put the blame where it should be placed: on the specific patterns of resource misuse that have come to characterize modern rural life.

The combination of mechanization, fossil fuel dependence, heavy use of poisons, monocropping (often with inedible crops such as cotton, or unhealthy ones like sugar), decline of rural resources, and spread of junk food is a specific syndrome, not some sort of vague or automatic "globalization." The same can be said for the loss of small farms and the takeover of land by giant feudal estates or agribusiness corporations, shown repeatedly to be devastating to small communities (e.g. Young n.d. [1792]; Goldschmidt 1947). Much of it is driven by the global economy, but so is everything else in the modern world, including better medical care, better nutrition, and the spread of alternative agricultural techniques. We are not talking about globalization in general here, but about one very specific way of bringing globalization to the countryside.

Globalization of this sort leads to fly-by-night agricultural and fisheries developments that leave the local landscape devastated, and to perverse trade that creates or caters too much to perverse wants and creates "perverse subsidies." (See Myers 1998; case studies in point include Baer 1998; Mintz 1985; Roseberry 1996; Sheridan 1995; Stonich 1993.) The average American farm gets more than thirty-six thousand dollars in subsidies (Simon 2002). Little of that goes to the small-farm majority; most of it goes to the giant agribusiness corporations. This subsidizes a form of agriculture often accused of being wasteful and of being indifferent or hostile to conserving either the environment or genetic diversity; hence Myers's term "perverse subsidies."

Moreover, *pace* the fond hopes of the political ecologists, this pattern is not just a political matter, curable by political reform. It is sadly consistent under many different political regimes. I have seen basically the same thing in communist China, democratic America, and troubled East Africa and Mexico. Only western Europe has been fairly successful at preventing it, though one finds pockets even there. It is, of course, largely a problem of the poor nations, but it is surprisingly widespread in the richest.

Urban regions of the world are not without comparable problems. The vast slums of the rapidly growing cities of the Third World need no comment. Mexico City and Tijuana are bad; Lima and Addis Ababa are worse. In the United States, hunger in inner cities is common, especially among the very young and the very old. Only western Europe has largely eliminated genuine want, but even there one sees many a pinched face and thin frame, especially among migrant workers.

Poverty and want are not equally shared within households. In most areas, women and children suffer disproportionately; the man of the house gets the best—he is supposedly the "breadwinnner." There are ways around this (Messer 1997 gives a comprehensive review of problems and solutions). But it is a persistent, widespread problem. The future—the child-bearing potential of women, and even the children already born—is sacrificed to supposed needs of the present.

Science and education lag far behind need, and, as always, the poor nations suffer the worst. Higher education is now usual in Europe, North America, and East Asia, but as rare as ever in the poor countries (Serageldin 2002). The scientific-research establishment in the needy parts of the world is not only minute; it is shrinking fast, because of brain drain, local wars, corruption, and the rest of the catalogue of problems. Moreover, science everywhere devotes little energy to the world food problem. The Egyptian scientist Ismael Serageldin challenges "scientists to work for the benefit of the entire human family. . . . So let us start. If not us, who? If not now, when?" (Serageldin 2002:58).

4

There is no need to extend the grim roll of foolish actions. What can be done?

The technical questions of providing more food are very well covered by Smil, Evans, and others.[1] Briefly, further crop breeding, genetic modification, and use of minor and neglected crops, coupled with conservation and sustainable use of fish and wild resources, will be necessary. (The resistance to genetic modification seems due mostly to the intransigence of companies in regard to testing the products. Surely this will be resolved; we simply cannot do without genetically modified crops in the future.)

After that, we must deal with three separate (though interlocked) problems.

First, absolute want—sheer starvation. As noted, frank famine and mass starvation is a straightforward political problem. There are also pockets and even vast zones of chronic hunger throughout the world. Engaging politicians and bureaucrats to deal with such crises remains difficult or impossible.

Second, there is the problem of highly processed food: adequate calories, but decreasing availability of vitamins and minerals, as well as health problems such as diabetes that follow directly from reliance on empty calories.

Third, there is the question of overnutrition. All too often, overnutrition and undernutrition are combined in the same individual. Fat is becoming a poverty issue, as easily available snack foods become common even among the poor. Many an obese individual is deficient in vitamin and mineral nutrients.

With respect to the problems behind the problem, it is generally agreed that the great, overarching, all-encompassing problem is a single word: poverty. However, even this is not a full story. Many of the poorly nourished are indeed poor people who can afford only unbalanced diets, but usually the overnourished are affluent; they simply make very bad choices.

Like food, wealth (of any sort, by any measure) is not in short supply worldwide. The problem is one of distribution. A tiny fraction of the world's population owns most of the wealth. A quarter of the world's population exists in desperate poverty, owning essentially nothing and having no reliable or adequate income. They simply cannot buy enough good food. Even if they can buy bulk calories—cheaper all the time, relative to most goods—they face steadily rising prices for nutrient-rich foods.

Behind this overwhelming primary problem are other problems. It is obvious from what has been said above that the most immediate is loss of local resources. Rural people usually suffer most, but not always. Urbanites are buffered by their wide-flung transportation networks, but they can suffer, too, from local depletion of firewood and fresh vegetables.

Worldwide demand structures are another major part of the story. On the whole, the world market demands far too much palm oil, meat and fish, alcohol and other drugs, and wood. There is, to balance this, far too little interest in vegetables, fruits, herbs, spices—high-quality food in general. There is too much focus on a handful of crops—especially staple grains and oil seeds—and too little on the thousands of other crops that could be grown. World demand has led to a distorted rural economy, devoted to the production of a very few items. Labor-intensive, skill-intensive mixed farming used to be the rule almost everywhere. Now it is almost extinct in most of the world.

The problem of human poverty and misery rules out certain environmental strategies.

First, the cold-blooded strategy of saving the best for the rich, and letting the rest die, is ruled out by common morality. We simply can't do that. There is, also, the necessary strategic (and ethical) linking of human-rights concerns and environmental concerns. We cannot afford "social Darwinism" (which—incidentally—has nothing to do with Darwin), national triage, and the like. Not only would it be immoral; we rely too much on each other in this modern world. Globalization enforces responsibility. Neglect of the Third World comes back to haunt the affluent, as diseases, terrorism, drugs, and corruption spread across national borders (on these and many related matters see Kearney 1996).

Certain environmentalist attacks on "consumption," "greed," "development," and the like must be seen in this light. We can cut luxury consumption by the fortunate 10 percent, but that would not buy us much. For one thing, their luxury consumption is, increasingly, of services and electronic information, not of material goods. More important, though, is that most of the ecological damage in the world is caused by production of staple goods for ordinary people. More rice is grown than truffles.

Second, in spite of the need for small farms and for reviving rural communities, we cannot go back to the good old days of the family farm, the traditional community, and the romantically idealized self-sufficient lifestyle. Those times may or may not have been good, but they most certainly were less than perfect. Quite apart from the appalling toll of disease, people suffered great pollution for small benefits. Horse manure was not obviously better than car exhaust is today, and oats for horse feed took up much farmland that can now be used for human food. Children starved because the horses took the crops. Yet horses did not provide any of the speed and convenience of modern transportation methods. Pollution of water by untreated sewage was not obviously preferable to modern chemical pollution. Deforestation, animal extinctions, and general waste of the land were already serious in the Roman empire, and catastrophic in the "good old days" of the nineteenth century.

The real trouble, though, is that old-time farming was even more inefficient than the modern kind. Unproductive agriculture meant that vast areas of land were needed to achieve the same total production that we now get on tiny plots. Wheat grown with the best modern technology yields more than twenty times as much per acre as it did in ordinary fields in the nineteenth century—and does *not* need much pesticide or chemical fertilizer to do it. (Pesticides are used far beyond any real need in most of the world. In Mexico, farmers regularly use ten times the recommended amounts, which are already set very high.) Similarly, fuel use was incredibly wasteful. Most of the world depended on firewood till recently—far too much of it still does. Elsewhere, inefficiently burned coal created more fly ash and sulphurous gases than heat.

Modern technology has its problems—lots of them—but, at its best, it allows us to use land, fuel, and other resources efficiently. Automobiles improve on horses, and modern automobiles require far less energy than they did in the gas-guzzling 1950s. Computers use little in the way of raw materials, and can save vast amounts by allowing more efficient, precise use of other resources. Modern hi-tech processes use fuel so much more efficiently that the Los Angeles Basin today, with over ten million people, produces much less smog than Los Angeles did fifty years ago. This has accompanied a manifold increase in production.

However, it is unlikely that development will eliminate poverty worldwide. Effort must still be focused on increasing food supply. World population continues to grow, and world crop land is probably, on balance, shrinking. More productivity per acre must be the goal. The staple grains are already about as productive as they can get. Efforts must focus on minor crops that could extend cultivation or intensify it in areas less than optimal for staple grains. Tree crops, legumes, and dry-land crops are particularly in need of research and development.

We could make a much larger difference much faster by focusing on an area almost always neglected: waste (Smil 2000). Much of the food in the United States is thrown away; estimates run anywhere from 20 percent on up. We lose as much again during transportation and storage.

Storage losses in the Third World are far more serious. Inadequate storage facilities are the rule in India, Africa, and much of Latin America. Perhaps as much as a quarter of all the grain in the Third World goes to rats, insects, and rot. Estimates in some countries run as high as 50 percent. Smil provides an excellent discussion of the whole matter, but gives very conservative estimates for worldwide waste. In my experience, storage losses, fish thrown away by fishermen, crop losses to pests, and so on are much higher than Smil's figures. In the Malaysian fishery I studied, for instance, 90 percent of the catch was converted into fertilizer rather than being used directly for human food. Even by the most conservative estimates, we lose and waste enough food to give all the hungry people on earth a first-class living.

Most necessary of all for the future is comprehensive and worldwide environmental planning. First priority for feeding the world must go to stopping the enormous and explosively increasing problems of erosion, deforestation, pollution, urbanization of farmland, exhaustion of water and fossil fuel supplies, and loss of wild foods.

Much of the development of the last fifty years has been counterproductive from the point of view of food production.

This is obviously true when development involves urban sprawl onto prime farmland—as it usually does. However, even development sold as agricultural improvement is often counterproductive (Ascher 1999).

One example is the huge dams beloved of development agencies. Big dams, now over forty thousand worldwide, have been a disaster. I am not aware of a single case in which a big dam was a net benefit to food supply. They flood good farmland, displace farmers, create parasite and disease breeding grounds, and destroy fisheries. They are often installed more for power generation than for food production. Food supplies suffer. Even when they increase irrigation and control flooding, they usually destroy more farming capability than they create. They often enrich local landlords who grow nonfood crops, rather than helping the poor by increasing food production. By contrast, small and numerous dams, combined with careful river management and protection, can provide irrigation, flood control, fish, water, plant foods, and other benefits without massively disrupting whole regions.

The Green Revolution, much praised and much maligned, has been a less clear case. On the one hand, it has clearly saved the world from mass famine. The production gains in the last forty years have been due in large part to it. Without it, hundreds of millions of people would have starved. Yet, it increased the use of pesticides and other dangerous chemicals. In many countries these have been overused to the point of becoming major dangers to human life. It also led to a focus on staple grains at the expense of more nutritious foods.

The Green Revolution (GR) has often been blamed for increasing the gap between rich and poor. This is probably unfair, though the jury is still out. True, GR seeds and chemicals must be bought and are fairly expensive, but any government can make rural credit cheaply available, and the large payoffs easily make the small investments worthwhile—if agricultural practices are adequate. Another unfair charge is that the GR was about cash crops rather than subsistence. In fact, the GR was targeted toward food crops, beginning with the world's major ones: wheat, rice, maize, and potatoes, in that order. It went on to look at manioc and millets; research is ongoing. The boom in cash crops that came at the same time was an independent phenomenon (though it benefited from the availability of farmland released from food production by the higher yields achieved through the GR). The GR did, however, lead to farmers switching to grain (now so productive) from nutritionally better and more critically needed crops like legumes and vegetables. This led, in turn, to unbalanced diets in India and elsewhere.

The gap between rich and poor expanded where governments failed to make credit available—or, in some cases, where governments quite cynically used the opportunity provided by the GR as a way to favor their rich friends and hurt the poor and weak. Even in these cases, the poor often got better off—just not as much better off as the rich did. This latter outcome is far from ideal, but at least it helps the poor. (All these matters remain controversial. I am speaking from my own experience, which involves interviewing leading Green Revolution scientists such as John Niederhouser, as well as my rather considerable work in Third World rural development. As usual, Smil 2000 provides the most balanced view, but he is rather too optimistic, in my experience. See also Evans 1998 for serious—and optimistic—detail on future green possibilities.)

Unfortunately, the world did not heed Green Revolution scientists who warned that population control was still needed. The benefits of the GR have now been eaten up (literally) by population growth, leaving the world in danger again.

Genetically engineered crops will be part of the solution, but the technology has yet to increase production massively. It is at its best in reducing chemical use; one can engineer insecticidal properties into the plants themselves, for example. This remains controversial (the controversy is best treated by Stone 2002). The truly foolish refusal of the corporations to allow objective tests of their products has left us ignorant of the real costs and benefits of genetically modified crops. The future will be full of surprises. At present, the technology is untried, uncontrolled, and uncertain.

Genetically engineered crops are one technological complex that has suffered from hyped controversy. The United States' biotechnology establishment sees these as pure good—a bonanza. The rest of the world sees them as a threat: "Frankenstein foods." Both positions are extreme (Stone 2002). Genetic engineering merely does quickly what natural or artificial selection does slowly: it changes gene systems in a particular direction. It is not a golden gift, nor is it a monstrous interference with nature. It is just a way of speeding up a natural process. On the other hand, it is not without danger. It creates new organisms with unknown potential for risk. Their genes are already spreading into nontarget species, with unknown effects. New products have to be tested, however safe they may appear.

The blanket acceptance of genetic engineering in the United States cannot last. Unleashing such things as the "terminator gene" (that would prevent plants from seeding themselves) is unthinkable; the dangers are appalling (fortunately the gene did not, in the end, get unleashed; see Stone 2002). But Europe's blanket rejection of genetically engineered foods is not defensible either. Ironically, there is a turnabout case in the continued rejection by the United States of irradiated foods, which have been accepted virtually everywhere else and proven safe by the daily experience of literally billions of people.

What has to be done is to subject genetically engineered foods to the same checks as any other new product. They should run the gamut of tests that we routinely give to any new food or plant product. The biological and biotechnological establishment has generally taken the side of unsupervised, untested introduction of new foods. What has happened in the United States is that the foods are not tested at all, because of a legal loophole: they are traditional foods—however changed. So they are not tested.

In any case, genetically engineered crops will not solve the world food problem. Few species are involved, and those species are nearing limits, even with genetic engineering; huge increases in production are emphatically not happening. If we are to feed the starving without destroying the world in the process, modern technology has to be supplemented. The accumulated wisdom of humanity has to be brought together. We cannot afford to ignore any good ideas, any obscure plants or animals, any traditional crop varieties, any ways of managing the land.

Traditional development of minor and obscure crops, and of wild food sources that could be domesticated, will prove more and more valuable. These little-known crops and methods of traditional food production and consumption provide great hope.

The National Research Council has released several books on "lost crops," notably Lost Crops of the Incas (1989) and Lost Crops of Africa (1996). These are the tip of a very large iceberg. Every issue of the journal Economic Botany introduces us to crops that could be developed. Many of these grow in areas that now produce nothing edible or, worse, areas that produce staple foods unsustainably. Millions of acres have been ruined in attempts to grow maize, sugar, wheat, and the like under conditions where they cannot produce well. More and more land is going out of cultivation today, even as the world runs short of food, because of these experiments. All these worked-out lands could be reclaimed by the planting of locally appropriate, usually traditional, crops, or by the use of local animals.

Conversely, there is no hope for schemes to convert tropical forests and other valuable habitats into low-value monocrop agriculture such as cattle pastures, sugar plantations, or oil and rubber estates. We know that these are disasters from every point of view. They should be absolutely and permanently stopped. If valuable habitats must be sacrificed, they should be replaced only by intensive, high-yield, diversified farming!

5

One could wish for a worldwide tax system that would redirect some money from rich individuals and nations to poor ones. This is not going to happen in the foreseeable future. Worldwide opportunities for education would be more effective, and are a more realistic hope. World poverty might also be alleviated by developing ways for the poor to live better without much more money. Development efforts will have to create economic opportunities. This means more than simple expansion of economic activity. Much recent economic growth has provided opportunities only for skilled workers in affluent parts of the world. Opportunities for the poorest, in both rich and poor countries, are provided largely by local microenterprise and small-business development. The Grameen Bank and its imitators provide loans as small as one dollar to local grassroots entrepreneurs. I have seen the success of the Grameen and other programs in Bangladesh; these are really impressive programs. They work. On the other hand, they are not yet big enough to do everything. Even the loathsome sweatshops of First World multinationals have a part to play—hopefully for a very short while.

One point usually missed by developers, in my experience, is the need to keep up "value-added bootstrapping." Whether one is talking of a project, an industry, or a nation, the goal should be to keep adding to the value added to the products, and thus increasing the profitability of the enterprise. Sweatshops should be replaced as soon as possible with more profitable enterprises. This requires training the workforce (including the managers!) in more and more skilled, specialized operations.

In food production, the goal should be to replace bulk commodities with specialized, high-profit ones. In the Yucatan Peninsula, the Mexican government introduced large-scale citrus culture, but could think of nothing better to do with the fruit than to make concentrated orange juice— a bottom-end product and a drug on the market. The Maya quickly found that the profits were in selling high-quality fresh fruit in the cities, especially the new resorts such as Cancun. A single orange in Cancun brought as much as a crate of them sold to a juicer. Then the Maya learned that *fresh* juice sold on the street for many times the price that bulk juicing for concentrate would bring. Fresh orange juice, at a good, healthy price, is now a major income source in the Yucatan Peninsula. In other parts of Mexico, fresh fruit is exported to the United States, where it brings even more. Specialty fruit products could increase the profit margin even beyond that.

Something similar has happened with coffee. The government of Mexico, until recently, focused on bulk production of ordinary-quality coffee, thus trying to compete with Brazil, a hopeless task. Other Central American countries have gone for quality rather than quantity, and made a fortune doing it. Local Mexican planters—old Oaxaca families and new Maya Indian entrepreneurs in Chiapas—have bucked the trend, producing shade-grown and organic coffees of superior quality. Further effort in this direction would make Mexico's impoverished coffee countrysides much richer.

If the Mexican government would assist local entrepreneurs in developing such ideas, instead of focusing on bulk production of low-quality, noncompetitive products, rural poverty could be eliminated in Mexico. It will not be easy. (As I write, falling coffee prices have played hob with Mexico's attempts to cure its coffee problems.) But it can happen.

In fact, the most overwhelming need, worldwide, is to change rural incentives in that direction. Policies once favored small mixed-farming operations in the United States and many other countries. This was because those policies worked; they provided a stable rural economic base and lots of fresh, high-quality food. Unfortunately, huge landlords have more political power than small farmers. Landlords, later joined by agribusiness firms (the new feudal lords of the world), have been able to capture the subsidies and supports in many countries—notably including the United States (see *The Farm Fiasco* by James Bovard, 1991; Myers 1998; Pottier 1999). Virtually every study ever done finds this to be a mistake. The giant landlords, be they Latin American elites or United States–based multinationals, are inefficient, wasteful, and prone to produce only a few products—usually products that are nutritionally worthless or harmful, such as cattle and sugar. A favorite of such producers is cotton—valuable enough in its own right, perhaps, but a huge competitor with food crops for prime land and resources, and a huge polluter of the environment; a quarter to a third of all pesticides used in the world are used on cotton. Conversely, vegetables and nutritious fruits require skilled labor, and thus tend to be small-farm crops.

In fact, returning the small family farm to prominence could, at least potentially, solve most of the problems of rural decline—though one would presumably have to bring social justice and democratization to many countries as a prerequisite. Small farmers have the incentive to work hard. They are on the ground. They are prudent users of resources (Netting 1993). They can use hi-tech innovations; they need only the credit to buy these.

A necessary part of this—as every field worker in development knows but as almost no one else seems to know—is rural health care. We simply cannot feed the world, or maintain a rural workforce, if we leave rural areas to the ravages of ill health.

Of course, the United States is not going to return to the small family farms of 1900. However, few (if any) countries are so dominated by agribusiness—and even in the United States, most farms are relatively small. The immediate goal, in all nations, should be to level the playing field—to invest in small farmers and their development *as well as* in the vast plantations, estates, and agribusiness firms. At present, economic policies in many (if not most) nations favor the large operators, often because the latter provide large political contributions (see e.g. Eichenwald 2000).

Part of this agenda goes beyond agriculture itself. Rural areas everywhere (except perhaps in northwest Europe) are underserved by social services. Education, in particular, is desperately needed in rural areas. This is as true in the United States as in the Third World countries I know.

To be of any real value, the education must involve serious attention to food production and consumption and to the environment! This is as true in cities as in the country—perhaps even more true, since the rural people already know a good deal about such matters. Yet, education is all too often directed toward rote memorization of facts irrelevant to ordinary life.[2]

This raises the less serious, but more difficult question of what to do about affluent, educated people who persist in "digging their graves with their teeth." This problem cannot be solved by economics. Consider the American pattern. The Midwest persists in eating a diet of white flour, sugar, meat, and oil, with consequent high rates of heart disease. Regional tradition is stronger than life itself.

The West Coast, or at least the liberal, urban West Coast, eats and lives more healthily; it is identified with tofu and organic vegetables. But is this because of actual health considerations, or is it the same sort of conformity to local norms?

In Mexico and in East Asia, one sees a different process: the conquest of local foodways by candy, cookies, sodas, and white-flour products.

Against this, one can only keep up the pressure. Education must focus not only on health values but also—and especially with the young—on the fashionable, prestigious aspects of eating well. Yet, it should also appeal to a sense of roots. Mexicans may recall the incredible achievement, in technology and nutrition, represented by the classic Mexican tortillas, beans, chiles, and squash.

One should probably take a different approach with the midwesterners. To them, eating an old-fashioned meat-and-starch diet proves they are ordinary, traditional folk, not swayed by snobbism, fashion, or fad. One might take a different tack there, and revive the vegetable and fruit dishes that were extremely popular in the Midwest in an earlier time.[3]

So, considerations of communication, status, and identity dominate the search for solutions to this category of food problems.

6

Our wants and needs determine production. If we all want the same thing, we give enormous power to those who produce it. Inevitably, they translate this power into political advantage. This is bad even at best; it leads to market distortion through special favors and subsidies, including government-financed research. At worst (and the worst is typical), they use much of that power to divide their enemies by whipping up political and social hatreds. They thus make themselves immune to political checks and balances. A side effect is that they increase the already troublesome focus on hatred and rivalry that characterizes political systems. When the environment crashes—as it must, when there is too much focus on a few unchecked activities—the hatred may break out, as impoverished and desperate people seek for scapegoats to blame and for weaker people to rip off.

By contrast, a varied and diverse ecological system, and a political system where everyone has some recourse against special interests, is protected against both economic ruin and political violence. Genuine democracies are singularly free of famines, wars, and governmental massacres (see e.g. Rummel 1998; Sen 1992). This will last, however, only if we can tame the giant, politically powerful lobbies that have successfully put much of industry, and above all of agribusiness, logging, mining, and ranching, above the law.

Most writers on the subject seem to fall back on inadequate solutions. First is sheer technical improvement of farming. This must come, but the current problem is one of political economy, not technology.

Second is "capitalism," so beloved of conservatives and giant firms. Unfortunately, "capitalism" is a very vague and general word. There are still a few capitalist regions devoted to small-scale, owner-operated mixed farming, and even organic farming. There are many others dominated by monocrop, chemical-intensive agribusiness. There are others dominated by virtually feudal landlords, who run scrub cattle, destroy forests, and shoot workers who protest sub-subsistence wages. If all these pass as "capitalism," we shall have to draw our distinctions more finely before we can say anything interesting.

Within "capitalism" is "the free market," another vague term. A totally free market cannot exist, at least not above the level of a tiny isolated village. The state—some sort of government—has to set laws and market rules, establish and protect currency, provide security, enforce contracts, provide courts for litigation in cases of uncertainty or fraud, and generally create the whole shell in which the market lives. States can and do influence "free" markets, making them produce small farms, giant agribusinesses, or reactionary landlords, as politics directs. Mexico, for instance, provides special subsidies and infrastructure advantages for foreign agribusiness firms, but often unleashes its army to shoot at and rob its own small farmers (notably in Guerrero in the 1970s and Chiapas in the 1990s)—all this under "free market" policies.

On the other side of the political divide, communist experiments in the twentieth century made it clear that massive communization and forced industrialization of agriculture were counterproductive (to use the mildest possible word). Marxism was then largely abandoned—perhaps prematurely, since Marxism does not necessarily imply the sort of thing seen in Stalin's USSR and Mao's China. A milder leftism of that period often was characterized by a general opposition to globalization, a general interest in local political solutions, and a general disinterest in basic environmental issues. Some on the Left were dismissive of such problems as water supply, soil erosion, vegetation decline, and genetic erosion. Some writers seemed to think that all one had to do was end the global economy and destroy the multinational corporations. Yet such a change—if taken literally—would return us to the status quo of 1850, hardly a desirable outcome. Just to mention one problem: recall that only seven or eight countries are exporting large amounts of food. What will the others do if global trade is ended, or even cut back?

In general, all solutions based heavily on political gimmicks fail to take into account the fact that politics is basically about relative power and status, which are inherently limited. Politics is normally a zero-sum (or negative-sum) game: if I win, you lose. Food production has to be positive-sum: we must play—ideally, by cooperating—to produce more. Trying to get politicians and would-be politicians to think this way is difficult, to put it mildly. Technicians, farmers, and ordinary citizens are better at it.

Fortunately, there are ways to cooperate and build. Writers such as Brown and Smil do say at least something about politics and institutions. More has been said by environmentalists such as David Roodman (1998) and Norman Myers (1998), and by food security experts like Johan Pottier (1999). Their frameworks allow us to use the undeniably good ideas of the above-cited schools.

All this gives very little comfort to political dogmatists, left or right. The solutions proven to work come from both left and right. Both left and right have also produced many solutions and ideas that clearly fail. One must keep an open mind, and look at facts and results, not at rhetoric and political smear campaigns.

7

I end this book in the midst of the brightest and darkest hour in the history of food.

Never before has the planet produced enough food to feed all its children. But, also, never before has the planet been faced with such dangers. The holocaust produced by the meteorite that ended the dinosaurs, even the Permian extinction event that wiped out more than 90 percent of all living species, are dwarfed by the horrors to come within the present century—unless humans change their ways. Not only humanity and its crops but all life on earth is directly and seriously menaced.

Will people change their ways, and survive? We could, easily, at any time; but there are few signs of hope in the world's current political system. World leaders are fighting against even the most token restrictions on devastation and pollution.

Yet, humans are surprising animals. When the leaders fail, ordinary people take over. As they have given us food and a safe environment in the past, so they may again. They need only the opportunity. An end to oppression and exploitation would unleash the forces that can save us all.

The message of this book is that food, in the last analysis, is inseparable from emotion and meaning. We cannot solve the world's food problems without taking that into account.

This is the time to remember the millions—billions—of unsung human beings who have created the foods we eat and the foodways we love. Few of them are named in history. The vast majority—the creators of bread, of lime-processed corn dough, of potatoes, of chicken soup, of noodles and dumplings and chapatis—are nameless. They have disappeared in the vast world. Nutritional anthropology's greatest value lies in its recalling to mind the accomplishments of these countless, unknown heroes and geniuses. We owe them our lives, and we do not even know their names.

Let us now praise famous men. . . .

There be of them, that have left a name behind them, that their praises might be reported.

And some there be, which have no memorial; who are perished, as though they had never been; and are become as though they had never been born; and their children after them.

But these were merciful men, whose righteousness hath not been forgotten. . . .

Their seed shall remain for ever, and their glory shall not be blotted out.

—Ecclesiasticus 44:1, 8–13 (Ecclesiasticus provides the ideal conclusion to this chapter, but, reader, please recall that "men" meant "people"—both genders—in King James's day.)

Appendix

Explaining It All: Nutritional Anthropology and Food Scholarship

What could I tell you, my lady, of the secrets of Nature which I have discovered while cooking? . . . Lepezio Leonardo was right in saying that it is possible to philosophize and prepare dinner at the same time. And I could also add: if Aristotle had known how to cook he would have written even more than he did.

—Sor Juana Ines de la Cruz (eighteenth-century Mexico)

1

Research on food in culture was, until recently, a rare pastime. The only country where food was taken seriously was, of course, France. There, gourmetship and food scholarship had always flourished together. Starting in the 1920s, the "Annales School" of historians, a group associated with the journal *Annales: Economies, Sociétés, Civilisations,* devoted particular attention to food and its effect on history (see Forster and Ranum 1979). Classic research in the tradition includes Fernand Braudel's work on France and the Mediterranean (e.g. Braudel 1973) and Emmanuel Le Roy Ladurie's writings on Provence (notably Le Roy Ladurie 1971). In general, the Annales historians stuck close to basics: ecology, economy, trade. These they considered to be the major determinants of foodways over the long term, a time frame that Braudel made famous as the *longue durée.* They were, however, acutely aware of the role of culture and style; how could French eaters be otherwise?

Thanks to them, and to historians more concerned with shifting styles, food history became more and more respectable, even outside of the French cultural sphere. The United States was the last to follow; food studies were still dismissed as frivolous until the 1980s. Studies of food consumption, in particular, were relegated to the academic Siberia of a "women's field." (By contrast, food production—agricultural science— was a "men's field," in fact one of the last bastions of almost-all-male academic departments. Thus it got many times the funding of food-consumption studies.) Women's liberation probably had more effect than Annales School influence on the rise of food research.

In the 1990s and since, an explosion of superb scholarship on food has occurred, spearheaded as usual by historians (see below) but also by cookbook writers, sociologists, psychologists, and anthropologists.

Nutritional anthropology is the study of food in human ecology and in culture. It starts from the biological needs of the human organism and from the study of human evolution and prehistory, and progresses onward to study the ways that human groups construct cultural foodways. It takes us from the relatively simple and straightforward needs of the body for nutrients to the marvelously diverse ways that human societies have found to get those nutrients. As far as basic needs, such as dietary iron, are concerned, "biology is destiny"; we have to have iron or die. Culture enters in determining where we get it: some human groups obtain their iron largely from caribou meat, others from millet, still others from iron-supplement pills, and some from the rust on cast-iron cooking vessels

Nutritional anthropology is thus, by definition, biocultural and biosocial. It cannot separate biology and genetics from cultural and social studies. In any study of actual foodways, these approaches must be combined.

Anthropologists studied food right from the beginning of the discipline. Lewis Henry Morgan (widely called the "father of anthropology" in the United States) built his theories of culture on "modes of livelihood"—subsistence technologies, such as fishing, hunting, herding, and farming (Morgan 1877). Influenced by Morgan, Frank Cushing carried out the first extensive field work in anthropology, inventing the methodology later known as "participant observation." Cushing lived with the Zuni of New Mexico for four years, learning, among other things, everything about their foodways. His still unexcelled account of Zuni foods was published in 1920, but the research was done in the 1870s. The great anthropologist Franz Boas assembled and published George Hunt's three-hundred-page collection of "Kwakiutl" (Kwakwaka'wakw) recipes from British Columbia (Boas 1921). Such epochal studies were often dismissed at the time as mere trivia; today we recognize them as invaluable sources of information. Both Cushing and Boas recognized that foods could not be seen in isolation. They supplied information on the social context of production and consumption, the relevant religious beliefs, the myths, the etiquette of feasting—everything one would need to understand food production and consumption in those societies.

Following them, Bronislaw Malinowski in the first half of the twentieth century stressed the importance of biological needs (at a time when most anthropologists were concentrating on society and religion). His own studies of food were impressive enough, but were largely embedded in longer ethnographic works (Malinowski 1922, 1935). His students, however, concentrated more specifically on food. Raymond and Rosemary Firth produced exemplary ethnographies (Raymond Firth 1936, 1959, 1962; Rosemary Firth 1966), but the true leader in the field was Audrey Richards.

A British lady in the grand tradition, Richards went to one of the most remote, harsh, and food-stressed parts of Africa. Here she studied villages in drought areas and in areas impacted by copper mines that drew off adult males and left the farming to women and children. Her studies make harrowing reading, especially when one realizes that conditions in "Rhodesia"—now Zambia—have not greatly changed since she wrote (as my wife and I were recently able to observe). She describes children starving, women desperately seeking scattered seeds, men lying near-motionless for months on end because they did not have enough food to get up and move around. She dedicated her life to bringing economic and agricultural progress to Africa, and was able to accomplish a great deal. Perhaps fortunately, she did not live to see that progress reversed by AIDS and evil governments. In the process, she launched nutritional anthropology and defined a focus on how social, economic, and cultural conditions impact the food situation. Her major works (Richards 1939, 1948 [orig. 1932]) remain foundational in the field.

On the American side of the Atlantic, a similar role was played by John Bennett. Bennett remains one of the least appreciated historic fathers of anthropology. During World War II, he worked with Margaret Mead and others to see how anthropology could contribute to the war effort (Committee on Food Habits 1943; it did not help Bennett find appreciation that his work often came out under such anonymous headings as this). He found a niche in the question of nutrition on the home front. One of the startling findings of World War I was that many, if not most, draftees were so poorly nourished that they were unfit for service. This was more true in England than in the United States, but it was bad enough everywhere (Drummond and Wilbraham 1958). It led to crash programs in nutrition and, ultimately, to studies by Bennett and others of the cultural matrix that allowed a rich country to malnourish its children (Bennett 1946). Bennett did not stop with malnutrition, however. He went on to develop a career of comprehensive studies of agriculture and food use.

Peace brought hopeful efforts to rebuild war-torn areas and, by extension, to develop areas that had always been poor. This brought Richards back to Africa; it also brought to Latin America such workers as Nevin and Mary Scrimshaw, and their daughter Susan (who has lived an entire lifetime in nutritional and public health). The Scrimshaws introduced nutritional supplements in Guatemala (Scrimshaw 1995).

From the above researches came the concept of the food system (see Goody 1982 for a classic formulation of this idea).

The "world food problem" was extremely serious during the 1950s and 1960s; more and more attention was devoted to it by governments and individuals. Anthropological studies grew apace. By the 1960s, "nutritional anthropology" was a buzzword. The Council on Nutritional Anthropology began life in 1975. I was there, a green kid, in awe of the Scrimshaws and other leaders in the field who organized the society. By 1977, a book, *Nutrition and Anthropology in Action*, edited by Thomas Fitzgerald and with preface by Audrey Richards, set the seal on the field; it was real and was oriented not only toward understanding foodways but also toward coping with malnutrition worldwide.

By 1984, Ellen Messer's comprehensive review could turn up 340 titles in a selective review of the field (Messer 1984; cf. Messer 1997). Subsequent work extends the universe of nutritional anthropology to archeology (Bray 2003; Dietler and Hayden 2001; Gosden and Hather 1999), gender issues and their relation to power and community (Counihan 1999, 2000), and many other realms (see e.g. such collections as Bringéus 2001; Dietler and Hayden 2001; Sharman 1991). Above all, anthropologists have examined the social order. Classic works in this area include Jack Goody's *Cooking, Cuisine, and Class* (1982), and Sidney Mintz's *Sweetness and Power* (1985).

Nutritional anthropology is founded on the premise—going back to Cushing and Boas—that one cannot understand foodways, and thus cannot really succeed in feeding the hungry, unless one understands the full range of meanings that become attached to food in traditional and modern cultures. Food must be produced; farming has its own traditions and ways. Food consumption, everywhere, is associated with home, family, and security. Food also can symbolize wealth and power, or sophistication, or identification with particular groups. Cooking can be a fine art, regarded as highly as painting and poetry; conversely, fine food can be seen as evil and sinful, a mark of vaunting pride or degeneracy and corruption.

Even though such matters are cultural, they have biological roots that cannot be ignored. Human food sharing, for instance, has its primate analogues (see e.g. de Waal 1996; Strier 1999) and its own evolutionary history (Barkow et al. 1992; Cronk 1999; Ridley 1996).

Nutritional anthropology fuses at its margins with other areas of food research, including sociology of food (Mennell et al. 1992; Murcott 1984), history of food (Albala 2002; Braudel 1973; Flandrin and Montanari 1999; Toussaint-Samat 1992), agricultural and plant science studies (Salaman 1985), food science (McGee 1984), and much else. There is a large and active field of food psychology (Capaldi 1996; Conner and Armitage 2002; Logue 1986; Lyman 1989), which has found, for instance, that most or all mammals avoid food that has made them vomit, even if only once. Humans display this trait. (I still cannot even bear the sight of a certain type of hard candy. My parents bought, and hid, a whole pound of it, just before my sixth Christmas. You can guess the rest. . . .) Mammals even avoid foods first tried at a time when they were nauseated for other reasons. Even historians of science (Laudan 1998) and philosophers (Curtin and Heldke 1992) have deigned to sully their usually pure hands with such lowly, earthy matters.

Even cookbook writing lies close to food anthropology. The better ethnic cookbooks are true ethnographies, describing the social and historical causes of foodways as well as giving recipes. An early exemplar of this breed was George Lang's *Cuisine of Hungary*; the tradition continues with works like Scharfenberg's *Cuisines of Germany*. Sometimes, as in the cases of Clifford Wright's *A Mediterranean Feast* (1999) or Diana Kennedy's books on Mexican food (e.g. Kennedy 1998), we have a serious historical work that has some recipes in it, rather than a "cookbook." Sometimes one is clearly dealing with the latter case. Medievalists in particular have been busy in recent years taking cookbooks and food writing very seriously indeed, as a major source of insight into medieval society. For instance, Dembínska's *Food and Drink in Medieval Poland* (1999) is a formal piece of historical research that includes carefully reconstructed recipes. Appropriately, it was published by a scholarly press rather than by a cookbook publisher. Mary Ella Milham's recent translation of

Platina's classic Italian Renaissance cookbook *De Honeste Voluptate* (Milham 1998) is also solidly in the "scholarly" camp. So is Paul Buell and E. N. Anderson's edition of the medieval Mongol/Chinese cookbook *Yinshan Zhengyao* (Buell et al. 2000), and Charles Perry's collection of medieval Arabic foodlore (Rodinson et al. 2001). The Society for Creative Anachronism, not usually noted for its ivory-tower bookishness, has been a leader in developing serious scholarship on medieval foodways. Food is no longer a trivial matter.

What sets nutritional anthropology off from these disciplines is, above all, our focus on explaining foodways in terms of root causes—especially the biocultural matrix. For a historian of Spanish food, it may be enough to show that potatoes entered Spain from Peru and Chile, and spread slowly as they became locally adapted and accepted. For anthropologists (and "virtual" anthropologists like Salaman 1985), it is necessary to explain why potatoes spread at all: why they are nutritionally and agriculturally advantageous. Only this can explain their unique level of acceptance in Spain, where they have been far more successful than any other New World crop.

Anthropologists are, however, not always unique in this. Where we are really unique is in our focus on cross-cultural comparison. No other discipline systematically compares the ways of all human groups. Anthropologists not only take all these societies into account; they also study nonhuman primates. Rare is the food historian who is an expert on two non-neighboring societies, but anthropologists are expected to be experts on the whole world.

Obviously, this means that anthropologists often have less knowledge of most (or all!) of the societies they talk about than historians do. Similarly, we usually know less about the biological side of eating than do the professional nutritionists. But, since our task is general explanation rather than specific detail, we are usually content to make the tradeoff. Different goals lead to different strategies.

On the other hand, anthropologists often specialize in the study of small, isolated, highly traditional societies—Australian aborigines, Bangladeshi villagers, Maya farmers, Chinese fisherfolk. This is an area of research that has been left to us. It is *not* true that anthropologists study primarily such groups; the majority of anthropological research is done in modern industrial societies. What is true is that few people other than anthropologists acknowledge the existence and importance of the small, tradition-oriented groups that still survive in this contemporary world.

It is often difficult to figure out the home discipline of a writer of articles for, say, the food journal *Petits Propos Culinaires*. Anthropologists, historians of science or of culture, sociologists, cookbook writers, medical nutritionists, agriculturalists, and ordinary food-lovers cheerfully share their knowledge, and one usually has to look at the author's work address if one cares to know what is the author's home discipline. Typical edited volumes today have titles such as *Food: Multidisciplinary Perspectives* (Harriss-White and Hoffenberg 1994) and *Food and the Status Quest: An Interdisciplinary Perspective* (Wiessner and Schiefenhövel 1996). In these book, anthropologists, sociologists, historians, biologists, and others all find a place.

2

The reader will perhaps find it interesting to see how anthropologists do research on these matters.

Assessing the nutritional status of a community is a specialized and rather difficult art (see Dufour and Teufel 1995; Jelliffe 1966; Jerome et al. 1980; Shils et al. 1999). Food composition can be roughly estimated from food composition tables (e.g. Pennington 1998), but chemical analysis is needed for serious research.

The main method used in anthropological research is *participant observation*. This involves living with people and doing, more or less, what they do. We are lucky, studying food; in most cases, we can cook and eat with our informants. True participant observation is normally impossible in studies of sexual behavior, and by definition is impossible in studies of people's inner spiritual lives. But it is the way to find out about food. Without living for months in Chinese households, cooking as they did, I would not have understood Chinese fuel economy, water economy, patterns of moving around—things that Chinese homemakers cannot easily talk about because so much of the behavior is "overlearned" to the point of being done quite unconsciously or preattentively. There is no substitute for participant observation, and it must be done for a long time.

With it go several standard techniques. The *twenty-four-hour recall* is perhaps the most widely used. This involves simply asking people what they have eaten in the last twenty-four hours. After they tell all they can remember, one may prompt a bit. One-week or two-week recalls may be used for finding out about shopping, bulk purchases, and the like. Recalls are less than ideal. First, people forget minor snacks and drinks. An extreme case is Anne Fleuret's finding in Tanzania (Fleuret, personal communication ca. 1978) that—judging from their twenty-four-hour recalls—her informants had all starved to death years ago. Since they were alive and talking to her, she naturally doubted their twenty-four-hour recalls. Following them around, she found they were continually nibbling on leaves and berries as they worked and walked to and from fields. They got critical calories and *most* of their vitamins this way. When they went to the city, they naturally failed to eat all these trivial little things, and consequently were in extreme danger of death from malnutrition.

Second, people are not always fully honest. Alcohol sales figures in the United States are several times as high as the alcohol consumption reported by people answering questionnaires. One study found that their interview data agreed with local stores' sales figures for meat, milk, vegetables, and so on, but when it came to alcohol the sales were five times the reported consumption! I suspect that this was not just lying. Ninety percent of the alcohol drunk in the United States is drunk by 10 percent of the drinkers, and I fear that these were in no shape to fill out a questionnaire or answer an interview!

Some of my students, working with a religious sect that has very strict food laws, happened to notice that the food cabinets of their informants were stocked with many cans and boxes (some open and obviously recently used) that contained forbidden items—items that the informants did not mention in their recalls and interviews!

In this modern world of dieting, people can be unrealistic about their calorie consumption. This is more true of women than men (Poehlman and Horton 1999:100).

Following people around is standard. Christine Wilson resorted to "child following" in Malaysia (personal communication, 1971) because children could not recall all the snacks they had at various houses they visited during the day. The best people to do "child following" are, of course, children.

Grownup following is also useful, but behavior of the research subjects is bound to be affected. I have talked to fledgling anthropologists who were amazed at the care and health consciousness of American shoppers they studied. I asked, "Don't you think it might have made a difference in their behavior that they were being watched and taped by a couple of university experts?"

Interviews in anthropology may be structured—written out in detail beforehand—or open ended and unstructured. The interviewer must know what she wants to find out, and ask it in the most culturally appropriate way.

In calculating nutrition, one can weigh the food people eat, and then look up in a table how much food value it has. A pound of potatoes has so many calories, so much vitamin C, etc. This method is broadly adequate, but in many situations it has problems. The people may be growing a special variety that is quite different from the samples used in preparing the tables. Guatemalan peasants, who appeared to be getting far too little lysine, were actually growing a local high-lysine corn variety. Local varieties of greens and berries often run higher in vitamins than commercial varieties. Salmon at the rivermouth are much fatter than salmon at the headwaters; they use all their stored fat to swim up the stream. Therefore, the specialist will always collect extensive samples, freeze them immediately, and rush them to a lab for analysis. (Vitamin C and other nutrients disappear quickly, hence the care.) The ordinary anthropologist will find this difficult to arrange and impractical, and will fall back on the food tables most of the time. But beware: when studying salmon fishermen way upstream, allow for that fat loss.

Specimens of unknown foodstuffs must be collected and identified (ideally, by local biologists at local universities). Photograph, tape, and videotape documentation of foods, food preparation, and eating transactions is highly desirable and frequently necessary. Building up a file of photos, for identification and teaching, should be done early.

Anthropologists never get the full story. In fact, no human can possibly know ultimate truth about anything. On the other hand, the extreme phenomenological position (we can't know the truth, so anything goes and any belief is equally valid) is a contemptible cop-out in medical and nutritional work. We know enough to save lives, and we can easily find out enough to save a lot more. The correct mix is proper humility about one's knowledge; constant search for more; constant testing of knowledge against reality. The latter really requires that different people check each other's findings.

3

Forces that change foodways are thus complex and contingent. Even so, there is enough order and predictability to allow us to plan. Biology, economics, social roles, and traditional cultural ways are all reliable enough determinants to provide sharply defined and usually quite limited contexts for change and agency. People react predictably to certain forces. This is most obvious when decreasing income leads to consumption of cheaper food, but we can also observe the universal appeal of high-status foods or, more precisely, the foods of high-status people; the universal use of food to mark festivals and celebrations; the great stability of religious rules over time and space; and many other generalizations apparent in preceding chapters. One can usefully (if a bit simplistically) model this process by saying that people must first satisfy very wide nutritional constraints and innate taste biases; then satisfy much sharper and more immediate ecological and economic ones; then satisfy social pressures to conform and to mark their station; then go on to create individual plans according to taste. Anyone explaining foodways will naturally gravitate to the appropriate level of generalization; those interested in very broad, overall determinants will look to biology, while those interested in very specific foodways will look to local history. Knowing that people generally like the effects of alcohol is one thing; knowing about that Napa vineyard that produces three different wines on three different soil types is another.

In short, to paraphrase Marx's observations on history, *people construct their foodways, but not in a vacuum; rather, they optimize nutrition given the constraints of income, labor, time, and environment they face, and given the cultural knowledge and practice they bring to the table.* "Cultural construction" is not only not arbitrary; it is enormously influenced by interaction with the world out there. It is comprehensible only when one knows what the constructors know, and understands the limits and possibilities they face.

Notes

NOTES TO THE INTRODUCTION

1. The original of this is a line by the early-nineteenth-century chef Louis Ude: "It is very remarkable, that in France, where there is but one religion, the sauces are infinitely varied, whilst in England, where the different sects are innumerable, there is, we may say, but one single sauce. Melted butter . . ." (quoted in Clifton and Spencer 1993:88).

2. The full verse is, "Ye are the salt of the earth: but if the salt have lost his savour, wherewith shall it be salted? It is thenceforth good for nothing, but to be cast out, and to be trodden under foot of men." The reference is to impure salt gathered from the ground, as opposed to sea salt. Sea salt is all soluble; "salt of the earth" includes a substantial amount of carbonates and other less soluble material. If it is stored carelessly, dew or other moisture will leach the salt out of it, leaving only the worthless residue behind.

I wonder what biblical literalists make of this verse . . . ?

3. Thus I can spare myself from heavy-duty coverage of areas I do not know well and that are covered very well in existing textbooks (see Beardsley and Keil 1997; Bryant et al. 1985). As this book is in the final stages, I am informed that Carol Bryant and her associates are coming out with a long-awaited new edition of the classic textbook, *The Cultural Feast* (Bryant et al. 1985). This will surely be the book of choice, when it appears, for anyone needing a full textbook rather than a question-raising essay.

4. This is the place to acknowledge some of the people who have helped me understand food over the years, and thus perhaps help a small amount in saving them from the general obscurity of those who have fed the world. I wish I could extend this list indefinitely; I would like to include everyone who has ever cooked for me or grown food that I ate. My mother and my father's mother were the first of these; they taught me the joys of eating. I thank my wife Barbara, my children, and all my family. But, to keep things manageable, let me restrict the rest of this list to my friends and advisors among the serious scholars of foodways. In addition to those singled out in my dedication, I am grateful especially to Marja Anderson; Myra Appell; Marilyn Beaudry-Corbett; Alan Davidson;

Alan Fix; Rachel Laudan; Françoise Sabban; Ellen Messer; Charles Perry; Nevin, Mary, and Susan Scrimshaw; Penny van Esterik; Christine Wilson. Special thanks to Sid Mintz, who undertook the awful task of reading the entire manuscript, on which he made perceptive and insightful comments. Anonymous reviewers also helped. I apologize to friends and colleagues for not devoting more attention to their work, but space is limited. Thanks also to Ilene Kalish and the wonderful editing staff of New York University Press!

NOTES TO CHAPTER I

1. This is especially true in species like ours. We are too large to be easy prey for most predators. Moreover, we are pair-bonded (in spite of not a little switching of partners; see above) and relatively egalitarian (Boehm 1999). Species like deer and elephant seals, in which the strongest or toughest male has a whole harem of females, can afford to lose many males in battles over harems. However, even among these species, the weaker males prefer to stay alive and hang around the fringes of the harem in case some female strays—as they often do. Among humans, peaceable groups can outbreed warlike ones.

Coyotes are loners or paired and forage on small, widely distributed bits of food, while African hunting dogs are social and go for large animals. Scrub jays live in pairs and forage for widely distributed resources while the closely related pinyon jays seek out fruiting pinyon-pine groves (Marzluff and Balda 1992).

2. This is not disproved by the tendency of some humans to step out on occasion. So do other pair-bonded animals. Claims in the literature that "most" human societies are "polygamous" are irrelevant; almost always, it is only the rich that can afford more than one mate. There are a few societies where genuine polygamy is common, and a few in China and Venezuela in which a given individual has many lovers rather than one mate. These are specialized, rare cases. The vast majority of humans exists in a state of monogamy—sloppy monogamy, sometimes, but monogamy. Even "swingers" and other sexually promiscuous individuals frequently marry and stay married, often in explicitly "open marriages," proving that something is going on that is deeper and more complex than mere sex.

Within a given society, men show a range of behaviors that show individual rationality recapitulating evolutionary ecology: middle-class men who need to invest a lot in their children form stable marriages, while males in disturbed or underclass situations form transient pair-bonds and often do not care for their children. On pair-bonding issues, see the excellent, thoughtful review by David Geary (2000).

3. At least not in any very meaningful sense. The final, tiny detail that "makes it language" by some highly arbitrary definition may have been added recently. The only communicative skill that all humans share, and that no other

animal has been shown to share, is the ability to formulate long, complex, hierarchically nested grammatical strings of symbols, i.e., the sort of thing we now call "sentences." (Many languages have structures quite unlike English sentences, but similarly complex.) Other animals, even complex communicators like mockingbirds, bower-birds, dolphins, and chimpanzees, do not get above the level of the simple phrase. They can be far more impressive phrase makers than we usually think. They can handle complex symbols and relations thereof, as well as integration of gesture and vocal sign, and many other complexities. But they cannot nest these in more and more complex hierarchic structures that are then systematically varied, as wholes, to make "questions" or "passive constructions" or the like. See Noam Chomsky's classic work *Syntactic Structures* (1957; see also Pinker 1997), as well as Barkow, Cosmides, and Tooby (1992), David Kronenfeld (1979), and Lewis Petrinovitch (1995). The ability to create elaborately structured sentences may indeed be late, but it would have followed a long, slow evolution of more and more complex communication (Pinker 1997), both gestural and vocal.

A related question is that of how music evolved, since many scientists still think (as did Gianbattista Vico 250 years ago; Vico 1948 [1744]; Wallin et al. 2000) that people sang before they talked, or at least that music and speech differentiated from a common source. I do not believe this, but at any rate music remains close to language in many key features (cf. Dissanayake 2000).

4. One odd corner of human tool use concerns toothpicks. People were using them two million years ago (Holden 2000) and chimpanzees not only use them but give each other dental care (McGrew 2000).

5. For instance, for the Diegueno and Cahuilla, groups I know reasonably well, he estimates 40 percent land-animal meat, 50 percent plant food, 10 percent fishing and 40 percent meat, 60 percent plant foods, respectively. Recent research makes it clear that the ratio was more like 10 percent meat to 70 percent vegetables and 10–20 percent fish for the Diegueno, 10 percent meat and 90 percent vegetable foods for the Cahuilla. These groups live largely in the desert, where game is almost nonexistent. What they did get came largely from hunting in the mountains. I do not mean to blame Kelly, an excellent authority; he did the best he could with poor sources

The Cahuilla and "Diegueno" (properly, Kumeyaay) were not really "hunter-gatherers," since they practiced agriculture. Their agriculture supplied only a fraction of their diet, however; most of their food came from gathering. Their game resources were so poor that if they had hunted intensively they would have exterminated the game in short order. This is not an unrealistic possibility; the interior Northwest Coast peoples apparently hunted deer and elk into rarity (cf. Krech 1999). The continued existence of deer and mountain sheep in Cahuilla-Kumeyaay country proves that hunting was very light. The Kumeyaay had access to the ocean; hence the small amount of fish.

Another source of a pro-meat bias in Kelly's data is that many societies were changed by contact with the modern world. The heavy dependence on meat in the Great Plains—Kelly (1995:67) lists 90 percent for some societies—is a post-contact phenomenon, created by access to horses and guns. Before these came, the Plains were lightly inhabited. The few residents seem to have eaten more plant foods than they did in later times—though meat was always a staple in that land of bison.

6. One of the mistakes made by Dawkins (e.g. 1976) and his ilk is assuming that natural selection has fine-tuned us for a very specific lifestyle, and that everything we do is optimal from the genes' point of view. However, recall that what matters (to the gene) is being able to leave more descendents than one's competition. This means that some very poor solutions are acceptable, as long as the other solutions around are even worse. Humans have to put up with a lower back only partially re-engineered for upright stance, an appendix good only for hosting appendicitis, a lot of useless body hair, and many other disproofs of the "argument by design." Genes not only fail to specify everything; they specify a lot of less-than-optimal end results. Mutation, recombination, and other genetic changes guarantee that this situation will never quite be resolved. Perfection does not belong to this world.

On these matters, see the classic work *The Adapted Mind* (Barkow et al. 1992). The various authors of this book point out that natural selection works on particular abilities, not on the brain as a whole. The brain as a whole did enlarge and increase its ability in all sectors. It had to; you can't run a mainframe computer off a flashlight battery and a worn-out extension cord. However, what mattered were the particular abilities that allowed us to win: route finding, talking, sharing, recognizing, calculating where the best feeding chances were, and the like. Above all, it is obvious from the work of A. and H. Damasio (Damasio 1994) that our greatest and most important ability is integrating emotion and cognition. This permits complex social life; it is *the* social faculty.

The most recent controversy along these lines is between Eliot Sober and David Sloan Wilson on the one hand (Sober and Wilson 1999) and several critics on the other (Buss and Duntley 1999; Nunney 1998). Sober and Wilson maintain that people are so social that they must have been selected for it by massive selection for social groups and against unsocial ones. The members of the groups have to be related for this to work (otherwise, no Darwinian selection), but most members of a typical foraging band are indeed more or less related. Buss, Nunney, and many other critics argue that individual selection is quite adequate to explain what we see. What we see is, after all, not self-sacrificing worker bees, but people calculating very sharply and closely how much they are getting out of a social exchange. (Did Joe give me a present last year? How big was it? Do I have to reciprocate?) People cheerfully sacrifice their lives for others—even for strangers, and even for strangers' pets—so we are not the calculating cynics that

Buss, at his worst, makes us out to be; however, kin selection within an already-social group can explain self-sacrifice. So Buss and Nunney have the best of it, so far. But the issue is far from settled.

7. An interesting case in point: identical twins are routinely assumed to be literally "identical," and there are some stories—highly specious! (Marks 2002)—of identical twins reared apart who still have remarkable (indeed, preposterous) similarities. Yet my little twin nieces differ notably. One of them got short-changed in the womb; she was in a cramped position and got starved for nutrients. She was born small and feeble. In such situations, the human body is programmed by an impeccable genetic mechanism to play catch-up and play it fast. The small twin thus grew fast and furiously, and is taller, stronger, heavier, and more rapidly maturing than her sister. This fed into behavior; neither of them is a shrinking violet—they are of the healthy, soccer-playing subspecies of American girl—but the once-starved twin is definitely the assertive, athletic one of the pair, while her sister is more "traditionally feminine." They are still very, very similar, but far from identical, in spite of identical genomes. Thus do genes code for *development,* not traits.

NOTES TO CHAPTER 2

1. A calorie is the amount of heat it takes to raise a kilogram of water one degree Celsius at average sea-level air pressure. Technically, this is a "large calorie" or "Calorie" with capital C; a small calorie is the amount of heat required to raise a gram of water one degree Celsius. Food is thus evaluated, here, in terms of its energy value. The body "burns" food very efficiently, if slowly.

2. Sugars are short-chain carbohydrates; starches are longer; celluloses, lignins, etc., are even longer. Very long-chain carbohydrates, including the celluloses, lignins, etc., can be broken down only by certain microorganisms. Humans actually have some in their lower gut and can get up to 10 percent of calories from the by-products of microorganismal digestion (Milton 2000s), but normally humans must eat sugars, starches, proteins, and fats. Cows and other herbivores have ways of getting more from the microorganisms; the various extra "stomachs" of a cow are really microorganism farms, in which the tenants busily ferment celluloses and such into materials the cow can use. Hence cows can thrive not only on grass and hay but even on wood, while mere humans cannot even handle the grass. The flip side is that digesting cellulose—even with microorganismal help—is so demanding that it limits the cow's brain power. Humans live on a very easily digested, high-energy diet, which allows us to outperform a cow in that realm.

3. Long before Szent-György discovered vitamin C and its effects, a widely known American folk song about the horrors of Arkansas (sorry, Arkansas readers!) contained the significant lines:

He fed me on corn dodgers, as hard as any rock;
My teeth began to loosen and my knees began to knock.
Within my memory, American children suffered "green apple fever" in spring—after a winter of dry foods, they were desperate for fresh ones, and would make themselves sick eating green apples and the like. Greens eaten "to clean the blood" were also popular; the symptoms of unclean blood were precisely the symptoms of scurvy. Little did my elders know that the problem was not something in the blood, but rather something not in the blood.

NOTES TO CHAPTER 4

1. "Volatile oil" is used in two senses: to refer to specific compounds, or (more typically) to refer to the complex mixes of compounds that constitute the actual distillate of the plant or other substance in question. Many volatile oils in this latter sense are mixes of two or three dozen chemicals, often similar to each other but sometimes including quite different types of molecules. There are several chemical classes of volatile oils. Volatile oils are very common in nature, but a given plant (or other substance) usually has very little volatile oil. Rarely do volatile oils comprise even 5 percent of leaf tissues.

Some volatile oils with antiseptic properties include the aromatic oils of the following (Claus 1956; Tyler et al. 1981): anise, camphor, chile, cardamom, cinnamon, clove, cubeb, cumin, eucalyptus, juniper, lavender, lemon, oregano, peppermint, pine, rosemary, sandalwood, thyme, wintergreen. See fuller discussion in Billings and Sherman's papers.

2. It was believed by many in previous eras that the *scent* of the volatile oils in question had directly therapeutic properties (Corbin 1986). These scents were used in medieval Europe to counter the effluvia that were formerly thought to cause plague (see e.g. Nohl 1961:62–66). In later centuries, an entire science of countering stenches by beneficial scents evolved (Corbin 1986). It almost disappeared in the decades following the discoveries of Pasteur and Koch (Corbin 1986), but it did not quite die out.

Aromatherapy, a medical tradition developed by Edward Bach, still uses scents—almost all of them spicy, herbal, and floral volatiles—to cure diseases (Tisserand 1977, 1988). Aromatherapy is generally dismissed as quackery, but this may be premature. Scents such as lavender and eucalyptus have pronounced effects on human EEG wave patterns (Lorig and Schwartz 1988). Many people feel cheered and relaxed by experiencing many of the odors in question, especially herbal ones; thus aromatherapy for moods may turn out to have some scientific value (Ehrlichman and Bastone 1992). Lawless (1991) has provided some evaluation, noting, for example, that lavender scent has been reported to be relaxing by some researchers (Torii et al. 1988), but not by others. One study showed some contradiction between self-report and EEG action in individuals' responses to lavender (Lorig and Schwartz 1988).

3. Humans use fragrances in communication, but only insofar as culture has "constructed" such uses. There is no close relationship or resemblance between spicy and floral smells and the chemicals that serve as pheromones in nonhuman primates. Evidence on human pheromones is equivocal, and research is needed (Engen 1981:139–44; Serby and Chobor 1992, passim, esp. Ehrlichman and Bastone 1992). Humans recognize individual smells, as when infants recognize their mother's body scent (Schmidt and Beauchamp 1992). See, for example, the attempt by Wright (1994) to find reliable accounts of human pheromone activity; none was forthcoming. The famous scent of truffles is a mimic of boar sexual pheromones (Maugh 1982), because truffles are distributed by pigs. The pig is attracted by the scent and, finding no other pig, it eats the truffle (presumably to console itself). Humans have a similar-scented sex pheromone, and this very possibly explains the human fondness for truffles (Ackerman 1990; Maugh 1982). If so, pheromones do influence food tastes, in at least one (rather trivial) case.

However, when humans wish to announce their sexual interest and/or availability, or when they simply wish to smell good, they seem to use perfumes and the like—typically floral and spice smells. This appears to be true in every culture for which such matters are documented, though research is needed.

The use of these botanicals in skin and hair care has clearly led to their being "natural symbols" (*sensu* Douglas 1970) for health, physical fitness, and/or sensuality.

4. On the other hand, some studies show that young children like the smells of feces and spices about equally well (Kneip and Young 1931); but these studies are rather inconclusive, since young children are apt to be unclear and inconsistent in responses, and the experiments are not always easy to do or interpret (see discussion in Engen 1981, passim, esp. pp. 130–37). It has been pointed out (Schmidt and Beauchamp 1992:387) that animals such as the skunk, and many plants as well, produce many scents specifically to repel enemies, and these smells must be widely perceived as unpleasant if they are to be effective. If Engen were correct that skunk smell is not naturally disliked (Engen 1991:44), skunks would not use it so successfully in defense against people and other potential predators.

5. This chapter began life as a paper by Silver Damsen (a graduate student) and myself. Otherwise uncredited observations above come largely from my field work, including observations in many cultures around the world. I am deeply grateful for advice, assistance, and suggestions of Mary Baker, Peter Brabant, Nina Etkin, Alan Fix, Alexandra Maryanski, Daniel Moerman, Paul Rozin, and especially Paul Sherman. Remaining errors are strictly mine.

NOTES TO CHAPTER 5

1. As we shall see later, new mothers are particularly vulnerable to certain deficiencies, as we have seen, and traditional cultures have thus found many ways to feed them. The Chinese, for instance, devote many resources to pregnant and nursing women. Women who otherwise must live on little more than rice are given chicken, pig's liver (rich in iron and B vitamins), ginger, rice wine, sesame oil, and other high-nutrient, high-protein, high-calorie foods, to keep them in health and able to nurse (see Anderson 1988).

2. One reader of this work has complained about the lack of agrobiology. An adequate treatment of this subject would take a book much larger than the present one—which is about food, not crop growth. Moreover, there is a plethora of books on agrobiology and on agriculture and its invention; see the sources cited above.

NOTES TO CHAPTER 6

1. There are more than five senses. Temperature awareness, for instance, is a separate sense on its own, and the alternation of hot and cold dishes in certain cuisines caters to it. Pain is really a separate sense from touch, and has its own slightly masochistic foodway in the adoration of stimulants like chile, black pepper, ginger, mustard, horseradish, and smartweed (*Polygonum* species, the Vietnamese *rau ram*). Otherwise bland Japanese food is spiked with ginger and *wasabi* (*Wasabia wasabi,* a horseradish) to give it a potent "mouthfeel."

NOTES TO CHAPTER 8

1. The author, a meat eater, is frequently faced with the line, "If you saw animals being butchered, you would never eat meat again." In fact, thanks to my rural past in a simpler, more subsistence-oriented age, I have not only seen many animals butchered; I have butchered animals myself. Reminiscing about this to vegetarians does not always go over well.

NOTES TO CHAPTER 9

1. The term "junk food" (now translated into various languages, e.g. *comida chatarra* in Spanish) is both vague and pejorative, though it has a certain use. Everyone seems to agree on a core of cheap candy, salty snacks, and mass-produced cheap sweets of all kinds. Most would add soft drinks. Some use the term to include reasonably nutritious items like hamburgers and pizza, largely because these are cheap and easily available in "fast food" restaurants. I prefer to enclose the terms "junk food" and "fast food" in scare quotes. Among other things, "fast

food" (cf. Schlosser 2001) seems truly wrong as a label for what it usually covers. The street stalls of Singapore and Mexico, the pizzerias and "bars" of Italy, the old-time *daipaidongs* of Hong Kong, and countless other venues around the world provide superb, nutritious, excellently cooked food that is actually "faster" than that found in certain well-known chain restaurants. This being said, fast food has elicited a reaction in the "slow food" movement of Italy, which has now spread beyond Italian borders (I am told there is now a U.S. branch). In Italy in 2002 I found that restaurants sometimes advertise "slow food"—in English as well as Italian!—to lure the modern (post-Schlosserian?) tourist.

NOTES TO CHAPTER 11

1. I know this largely from my own interviews of people from the relevant areas, but see also Hamad Ammar (1954).

2. This comes from my interviews in France; I too can taste the differences between French bread in 1974 (when I first visited France) and ordinary supermarket bread now; the Poilâne breads are indeed like the old-time small-bakery product. There are equivalent "artisanal" bakeries now in most affluent countries. The irony of the former peasant breads becoming expensive luxuries gets more pronounced by the year.

3. To be exact, the commonest and best recipe—I have recorded it among Finns, in Mexico, and elsewhere—is one cup of milk, three eggs, one stick of butter, six cups of flour (more or less), and aromatic seeds and/or citrus peel and dried fruit, as you choose. The Finns use cardamom, the Mexicans prefer anise; I mix both.

Scald the milk, melting the butter in it. Cream three packets of dry yeast in that, when it cools to lukewarm. Then mix this and the eggs into the flour, adding more flour if the dough is too wet to work. Knead twenty-five minutes. Let rise 1 1/2 hours. Knock down, knead quickly, let rise half-hour or so. Knock down, knead briefly, braid, let rise till doubled in bulk. Bake at 350 degrees for about twenty-five minutes, till the surface just begins to brown; watch out—it burns easily. You can glaze it with egg, or a sugar glaze, or anything else you want. In Oaxaca they make beautiful sculptures out of the dough—birds, animals, and so on—but these usually become unrecognizable when they rise or when they are baked. To keep them looking pretty, you have to use a much stiffer dough, which results in an almost inedibly solid bread. Beauty or taste—not both!

NOTES TO CHAPTER 12

1. *Boronía*, originally *buraniya*, takes its name from Buran, an early queen in Iraq; she was the wife of Caliph al-Ma'mun in Baghdad in the ninth century

(Nasrallah 2003:225). Countless versions exist in the Arab world as well as in Spain. Significantly, it still contains fruit in the most interesting version to cross my stove. This version, found in an obscure local cookbook from Cordoba (Spain), deserves wider circulation. Here is a translation, somewhat augmented:

    1 lb. eggplants (young, tender ones)
    1 lb. summer squash (young, tender ones)
    6 tbsp. oil (originally olive oil, but any light oil will do)
    1 lb. green or red peppers
    2 lb. tomatoes
    1 tsp. vinegar
    2 quinces
    Salt to taste
    1 white onion

Peel and core the quinces. Cut them up into medium-sized pieces, and boil in salted water. Peel the eggplant and squash it if you wish, cut it up, and add it to the water when the quinces soften. Boil briefly, till all are soft but not mushy. Note that the eggplants are *not* first salted and drained—their slight bitterness balances the sweetness of the quince.

Heat the oil in a frying pan. When it is hot, throw in the onion, finely chopped, and the peppers, seeded and cut in thin strips. Scald the tomatoes, peel, remove the seeds, chop, add to frying pan. Cover and simmer.

When nearly done, add the cut-up vegetables. Add some salt and the vinegar. Cover and cook briefly. (Morales Rodríguez and Martínez García 1999:153–54; this cookbook provides several other recipes for the dish.)

It is also possible to omit the separate boiling. Start by frying the onion, then add the eggplant and quince, then the pepper, then the squash, then the water, then the tomato, then the vinegar—this is a lazy way to do it, but produces a tolerable result.

2. The following paragraphs are *not* intended to be full coverage of Italian food in America; I am dealing only with pizza. For the Italian story, see Diner (2002).

NOTES TO CHAPTER 13

1. This is not a book of techniques, but a footnote may be worthwhile. Among general types of traditional practices, the following seem to me particularly valuable, and particularly often neglected.

Ecology constrains our choices. Tropical coasts will never have Greenland's seal-hunting opportunities. However, plant breeding and selective trade can do wonders. A culturally conservative group, far from home, can often manage to retain a staple food that is not ecologically optimal. With enough time and plant-breeding expertise, they can make it optimal far beyond its previous scope of habitats. Wheat was originally limited to Mediterranean-steppe hill country with warm, moist winters and rainless summers. It now grows from central Canada to southern Mexico and from north China to the Asian tropics. Adapting the wheat plant to the blizzard-swept high plains of North America was an almost impossible task, heroically carried out; yet that region is now the world's wheat basket. Even more difficult was the development of wheats adapted to Mexico's and China's dry summer-rain zones, yet these too are major sources today.

Wanting more diversity. The biggest difference between the modern west and the traditional world is that traditional peoples usually use, or used to use, a wide range of plants and animals. We have grown more and more dependent on a very few strains of a very few. This is discussed elsewhere in the present work.

Tree crops. When I read J. Russell Smith's classic work *Tree Crops: A Permanent Agriculture* (1950), I wondered why no one was adopting his ideas. I eventually learned. Tree crops require several years to mature. Thus, if the orchard dies, the farmer has lost years of work and investment, and will probably starve or go bankrupt before a new orchard can grow. By contrast, grains and vegetables mature in a few months; the farmer can replant and survive. But there are many ways around this—from crop insurance to diversifying one's plantings—and tree crops do sustain the economy in much of California and elsewhere. We need to work on this. Tree crops (when not too heavily pesticided) create a wonderful environment, hold the soil, attract birds, and allow agriculture on places far too barren or rough for annual crops. Old olive orchards abandoned in deserts for sixty years still bear fruit.

Suburbanites should remember that any trees are infinitely preferable to a lawn, and that home fruit orchards are—along with natives—the best of trees. I am totally mystified as to why my neighbors grow so few fruit trees, especially since I live in an area where at least some of them do much better than almost any other garden plants. By the same token, I wonder why native trees are so unpopular, given that they thrive in a climate so harsh that few other trees survive at all. The goal of reforesting the suburbs with native and food trees should be pursued as far as possible.

Hedgerows and windbreaks. The wildlife benefits, protective functions, and diversity-maintaining values of hedges are so well known that it is really incredible that they continue to vanish.

Multicropping and diversity-maintaining farming, composting, small-field systems, low-tillage agriculture, and soil erosion controls such as terracing. This varied list is usually treated as a single agenda.

Integrated pest management. This approach is not totally organic, but uses pesticides only as a last resort, and relies preferentially on cropping methods and natural predators to control pests. This not only prevents pollution, it gives—in the long run—far better control than heavy pesticide use.

All this can supplement the nontraditional concerns with more efficient machinery, more efficient and low-polluting fuel use, and other aspects of sustainable and efficiency-promoting development. This whole matter has been thoroughly covered in Daly and Cobb (1994) and other standard sources, and need not be pursued.

2. The United States has dealt with its well-known decline in education levels by focusing more and more on such meaningless rote memorization, and drifting farther and farther from any attention to useful skills, let alone matters of serious concern such as the environment. Meanwhile, funding cutbacks guarantee that schools continue to deteriorate physically. Many are literally falling down around the children. The children, being no fools, take very seriously the contrast between schools and shopping malls. They can see where American society's priorities are. No wonder American children don't want to study.

3. Historically, the settlers of the Midwest were as badly off as the moderns; they lived on pork, corn, game, and not much else. Vegetables and fruits came in later, and exploded in popularity in the early twentieth century, as modern nutritional knowledge added itself to marketing options and wonderful new offerings from the nurseries. Urbanization and agribusiness progressively eliminated most vegetable and fruit farms in the late twentieth century. Even back-yard vegetable gardens, common in my youth, have become rare.

References

Achaya, K. T. 1994. *Indian Food: A Historical Companion*. Delhi: Oxford (in India) University Press.

———. 2002. *A Historical Dictionary of Indian Food*. New Delhi: Oxford (in India) University Press.

Ackerman, Diane. 1990. *A Natural History of the Senses*. New York: Random House.

Adamson, Melitta Weiss. 2002. *Regional Cuisines of Medieval Europe: A Book of Essays*. London: Routledge.

Albala, Kenneth. 2000. "Southern Europe." In *The Cambridge World History of Food*, ed. Kenneth Kiple and K. Ornelas. Cambridge: Cambridge University Press. Pp. 1203–10.

———. 2002. *Eating Right in the Renaissance*. Berkeley: University of California Press.

Al-Biruni. 1971. *Al-Biruni's India*. Tr. Edward C. Sachau. (Arabic orig., eleventh century.) New York: Norton.

Allen, Jane E. 2002. "Snack Makers Targeting Trans Fats." *Los Angeles Times*, Sept. 30, pp. S1, S5.

Ammar, Hamed. 1954. *Growing Up in an Egyptian Village*. London: Routledge & Kegan Paul.

Anderson, E. N. 1987. "Why Is Humoral Medicine So Popular?" *Social Science and Medicine* 25:331–37.

———. 1988. *The Food of China*. New Haven, CT: Yale University Press.

———. 1990. "Up against Famine: The Chinese Diet in the Early Twentieth Century." *Crossroads* 1:11–24.

———. 1996. *Ecologies of the Heart*. New York: Oxford University Press.

———. 2003. "Caffeine and Culture." In *Drugs, Labor, and Colonial Expansion*, ed. William Jankowiak and Daniel Bradburd. Tucson: University of Arizona Press. Pp. 159–76.

Anderson, E. N.; M. L. Anderson; John Ho. 1978. "Environmental Background of Young Chinese Nasopharyngeal Cancer Patients." In *Nasopharyngeal Carcinoma: Etiology and Control*, ed. G. Dethe and Y. Ho. Geneva: World Health Organization. Pp. 231–40.

Anderson, E. N., and Chun-hua Wang. 1987. "Changing Foodways of Chinese Immigrants in Southern California." *Annals of the Chinese Historical Society of the Pacific Northwest,* 1985–1986, 63–69.

Angyal, A. 1941. "Disgust and Related Aversions." *Journal of Abnormal and Social Psychology* 36:393–412.

Anholt, Robert R. H. 1992. "Molecular Aspects of Olfaction." In *Science of Olfaction,* ed. Michael J. Serby and Karen L. Chodor. New York: Springer-Verlag. Pp. 51–79.

Apicius. 1958. *The Roman Cookery Book.* Tr./ed. Barbara Flower and Elisabeth Rosenbaum. London: Peter Nevill.

Arberry, A. J. 1939. "A Baghdad Cookery-Book." *Islamic Culture* 13:22–47, 189–214.

———. 1959. *The Romance of the Ruba'iyat.* London: George Allen and Unwin.

Arens, William. 1979. *The Man-Eating Myth.* New York: Oxford University Press.

Ascher, William. 1999. *Why Governments Waste Natural Resources.* Baltimore, MD: Johns Hopkins University Press.

Atran, Scott. 2002. *In Gods We Trust.* New York: Oxford University Press.

Axel, Richard. 1995. "The Molecular Logic of Smell." *Scientific American* 273:154–59.

Azar, Beth. 2001. "Blueberries + Exercise = Healthy Minds?" *Monitor on Psychology,* Dec. 2001:26–28.

Baer, Roberta. 1998. *Cooking—and Coping—among the Cacti: Diet, Nutrition, and Available Income in Northwestern Mexico.* Amsterdam: Gordon and Breach.

Bailey, Robert C.; Genevieve Head; Mark Jenike; Bruce Owen; Robert Rechtkman; Elzbieta Zechenter. 1989. "Hunting and Gathering in Tropical Rain Forest: Is It Possible?" *American Anthropologist* 91:59–82.

Baker, Mary. 1995. "Medicinal Plant Use by Capuchin Monkeys (*Cebus capucinus*)." *American Journal of Primatology* 38:263–70.

Balter, Michael. 1995. "Did *Homo erectus* Tame Fire First?" *Science* 268:1570.

Barkow, Jeffrey; Linda Cosmides; John Tooby (eds.). 1992. *The Adapted Mind.* New York: Oxford University Press.

Beardsworth, Alan, and Teresa Keil. 1997. *Sociology on the Menu: An Invitation to the Study of Food and Society.* London: Routledge.

Bell, David, and Gill Valentine (eds.). 1997. *Consuming Geographies: We Are What We Eat.* London: Routledge.

Bell, Rudolph. 1985. *Holy Anorexia.* Chicago: University of Chicago Press.

Benavides-Barajas, L. 1996. *Al Andalus, La Cocina y su Historia. Reinos de Taifas, Norte de Africa, Judios, Mudéjares y Moriscos.* Motril, Spain: Dulcinea.

Benedek, Thomas G. 2000. "Food as Aphrodisiacs and Anaphrodisiacs?" In *The Cambridge World History of Food*, ed. Kenneth Kiple and K. Ornelas. Cambridge: Cambridge University Press. Pp. 1523–34.

Bennett, John. 1946. "An Interpretation of the Scope and Implications of Social Scientific Research in Human Subsistence." *American Anthropologist* 48:553–73.

———. 1969. *Northern Plainsmen: Adaptive Strategy and Agrarian Life*. Chicago: Aldine.

Billing, Jennifer, and Paul Sherman. 1998. "Microbial Functions of Spices: Why Some Like It Hot." *Quarterly Review of Biology* 73:3–49.

Blackburn, Susan Tucker, and Donna Lee Loper. 1992. *Maternal, Fetal, and Neonatal Physiology: A Clinical Perspective*. Philadelphia: Saunders.

Blumenschine, Robert J., and John A. Cavallo. 1992. "Scavenging and Human Evolution." *Scientific American*, Oct. 1992:90–96.

Boas, Franz. 1888. *The Central Eskimo*. Washington, DC: Bureau of American Ethnology. 6th Annual Report, for 1884–1885. Pp. 390–669.

———. 1921. *Ethnology of the Kwakiutl*. Washington, DC: Bureau of American Ethnology. 35th Annual Report, for 1913–1914.

Boehm, Christopher. 1999. *Hierarchy in the Forest: The Evolution of Egalitarian Behavior*. Cambridge, MA: Harvard University Press.

Bolens, Lucie. 1990. *La cuisine andalouse, un art de vivre Xie–XIIIe Siècle*. Paris: Albin Michel.

Bordo, Susan. 1997. "Anorexia Nervosa: Psychopathology as the Crystallization of Culture." In *Food and Culture: A Reader*, ed. Carole Counihan and Penny Van Esterik. Pp. 226–50.

Boserup, Ester. 1965. *The Conditions of Agricultural Growth*. Chicago: Aldine.

Bottéro, Jean. 1995. *Textes culinaires mésopotamiens*. New York: Eisenbrauns.

Bourdieu, Pierre. 1977. *Outline of a Theory of Practice*. Cambridge: Cambridge University Press.

———. 1990. *The Logic of Practice*. Tr. Richard Nice. (Fr. orig. 1980.) Stanford, CA: Stanford University Press.

Bovard, James. 1991. *The Farm Fiasco*. San Francisco: Institute for Policy Studies.

Braudel, Fernand. 1973. *The Mediterranean and the Mediterranean World in the Age of Philip II*. Tr. Sian Reynolds. (Fr. orig. 1966.) New York: Harper and Row.

Bray, Tamara (ed.). 2003. *The Archaeology and Politics of Food and Feasting in Early States and Empires*. New York: Kluwer Academic/Plenum Publishers.

Brillat-Savarin, Jean Anthelme. 1925. *The Physiology of Taste*. London: Peter Davies. (Fr. orig. 1825.)

Bringéus, Nils-Arvid. 2001. *Man, Food and Milieu: A Swedish Approach to Food Ethnography*. East Linton (Scotland): Tuckwell.

Bromage, Timothy, and Friedemann Schrenk (eds.). 1999. *African Biogeography, Climate Change, and Human Evolution.* New York: Oxford University Press.

Brown, Cecil. 1996. "A Widespread Marking Reversal in Languages of the Southeastern United States." *Anthropological Linguistics* 38:439–60.

Brown, Lester. 1995. *Who Will Feed China? Wake-up Call for a Small Planet.* Washington, DC: Norton for Worldwatch Institute.

———. 1996. *Tough Choices: Facing the Challenge of Food Scarcity.* New York: Norton.

Brown, Paul, and Donald Tuzin. 1983. *The Ethnography of Cannibalism.* Washington, DC: Society for Psychological Anthropology, Special Publication.

Brown, Peter, and Melvin Konner. 1998. "An Anthropological Perspective on Obesity." In *Understanding and Applying Medical Anthropology,* ed. Peter J. Brown. Mountain View, CA: Mayfield. Pp. 401–13.

Bruch, Hinde. 1978. *The Golden Cage: The Enigma of Anorexia Nervosa.* Cambridge, MA: Harvard University Press.

Bryant, Carol A.; Anita Courtney; Barbara A. Markesbery; Kathleen M. DeWalt. 1985. *The Cultural Feast: An Introduction to Food and Society.* St. Paul, MN: West Publishing.

Buell, Paul D.; E. N. Anderson; Charles Perry. 2000. *A Soup for the Qan.* London: Kegan Paul International.

Burton, Robert. 1932. *The Anatomy of Melancholy.* New York: Dutton.

Burton, Sharon. 1990. Unpublished research data from uncompleted Ph.D. thesis directed by myself.

Buss, David, and Joshua Duntley. 1999. "Individuals or Selfish Groups?" (Review of Sober and Wilson 1998). *Contemporary Psychology* 44:327–29.

Cain, William S.; J. Enrique Cometto-Muniz; Rene A. de Wijk. 1992. "Techniques in the Quantitative Study of Human Olfaction." In *Science of Olfaction,* ed. Michael J. Serby and Karen L. Chobor. New York: Springer-Verlag. Pp. 279–308.

Cao Xueqin. 1973–1986. *The Story of the Stone.* Tr. David Hawkes and John Minford. (Chinese orig. eighteenth century) London: Penguin.

Capaldi, Elizabeth (ed.). 1996. *Why We Eat What We Eat: The Psychology of Eating.* Washington, DC: American Psychological Association.

Carney, Judith. 2001. *Black Rice.* Cambridge, MA: Harvard University Press.

Casas, Penelope. 1996. *Delicioso! The Regional Cuisines of Spain.* New York: Knopf.

Certeau, Michel de. 1984. *The Practice of Everyday Life.* Tr. Steven Rendell. Berkeley: University of California Press.

Chang Chung-ching. 1981. *Shang Han Lun,* ed. Otsuka Keisetsu. Tr. Hong-yen Hsu and William Peacher. (Chinese orig. second century AD.) Los Angeles: Oriental Healing Arts Press.

Chang, K. C. (ed.). 1977. *Food in Chinese Culture.* New Haven, CT: Yale University Press.

Chanot-Bullier, C. 1983. *Vieii receto de cousino prouvençalo/vieilles recettes de cuisine provençale.* Marseille: Tacoussel.

Chapple, Christopher Key (ed.). 1998. *Jainism and Ecology.* Cambridge, MA: Harvard University Press for Center for the Study of World Religions.

Chase-Dunn, Christopher, and Kelly Mann. 1998. *The Wintu and Their Neighbors: A Very Small World-System in Northern California.* Tucson: University of Arizona Press.

Childe, V. Gordon. 1951. *Man Makes Himself.* New York: New American Library.

Chobor, Karen L. 1992. "A Neurolinguistic Perspective of the Study of Olfaction." In *Science of Olfaction,* ed. Michael J. Serby and Karen L. Chobor. New York: Springer-Verlag. Pp. 355–77.

Chomsky, Noam. 1957. *Syntactic Structures.* Hague: Mouton.

Chong, Key Ray. 1990. *Cannibalism in China.* Wakefield, NH: Longwood Academic.

Claus, Edward P. 1956. *Gathercole and Wirth's Pharmacognosy.* 3rd ed. Philadelphia: Lea and Febiger.

Clifton, Claire, and Colin Spencer. 1993. *The Faber Book of Food.* London: Faber and Faber.

Coe, Sophie. 1994. *America's First Cuisines.* Austin: University of Texas Press.

Coe, Sophie, and Michael Coe. 1996. *The True History of Chocolate.* London: Thames and Hudson.

Cohen, Mark R., and George Armelagos. 1984. *Paleopathology and the Origins of Agriculture.* New York: Academic Press.

Committee on Food Habits. 1943. *The Problem of Changing Food Habits.* Washington, DC: National Research Council. Bulletin 109.

Conis, Elena. 2003. "Chips for Some, Tofu for Others." *Los Angeles Times,* Aug. 4, health section.

Conner, Mark, and Christopher J. Armitage. 2002. *The Social Psychology of Food.* Philadelphia: Open University Press.

Conner, Wm. E. 2001. "N-3 Fatty Acids from Fish and Fish Oil: Panacea or Nostrum?" *American Journal of Clinical Nutrition* 74:415–16.

Coon, Carleton. 1958. *Caravan.* Rev. ed. New York: Henry Holt.

Cooper, John. 1993. *Eat and Be Satisfied: A Social History of Jewish Food.* Northvale, NJ: Jason Aronson.

Corbin, Alain. 1986. *The Foul and the Fragrant.* Cambridge, MA: Harvard University Press.

Cordain, Loren; Janette Brand Miller; S. Boyd Eaton; Neil Mann; Susanne H. A. Holt; John D. Speth. 2000. "Plant-animal Subsistence Ratios and

Macronutrient Energy Estimations in Worldwide Hunter-Gatherer Diets." *American Journal of Clinical Nutrition* 71:682–92.

Counihan, Carole. 1999. *The Anthropology of Food and Body: Gender, Meaning, and Power.* New York: Routledge.

———. 2000. "The Social and Cultural Uses of Food." In *The Cambridge World History of Food,* ed. Kenneth Kiple and K. Ornelas. Cambridge: Cambridge University Press. Pp. 1513–22.

Counihan, Carole, and Penny van Esterik (eds.). 1997. *Food and Culture: A Reader.* London: Routledge.

Cowan, C. Wesley, and Patty Jo Watson (eds.). 1992. *The Origins of Agriculture.* Washington, DC: Smithsonian Institution Press.

Crone, Patricia. 1987. *Meccan Trade and the Rise of Islam.* Princeton, NJ: Princeton University Press.

Cronk, Lee. 1999. *That Complex Whole: The Evolution of Human Behavior.* Boulder, CO: Westview.

Cudel, Evelyn. 1994. "High Incidence of Diabetes in the O'odham: Community Approach in Prevention and Control for a Native American Tribe." Ph.D. dissertation, Dept. of Anthropology, University of California, Riverside.

Cunningham, A. S.; Derrick B. Jelliffe; E. F. P. Jelliffe. 1991. "Breast-feeding and Health in the 1980s: A Global Epidemiologic Review." *Journal of Pediatrics* 118:659–66.

Curtin, Deane W., and Lisa M. Heldke (eds.). 1992. *Cooking, Eating, Thinking: Transformative Philosophies of Food.* Bloomington, IN: Indiana University Press.

Cushing, Frank. 1920. *Zuni Breadstuffs.* New York: Museum of the American Indian, Heye Foundation.

Dahlberg, Frances (ed.). 1981. *Woman the Gatherer.* New Haven, CT: Yale University Press.

Dalby, Andrew. 1997. *Siren Feasts: A History of Food and Gastronomy in Greece.* London: Routledge.

———. 2000. *Dangerous Tastes.* Berkeley: University of California Press.

———. 2003. *Food in the Ancient World from A to Z.* London: Routledge.

Daly, Herman, and John Cobb. 1994. *For the Common Good.* 2nd ed. Boston: Beacon.

Daly, Martin, and Margo Wilson. 1999. *The Truth about Cinderella: A Darwinian View of Parental Love.* New Haven, CT: Yale University Press.

Damasio, Antonio. 1994. *Descartes' Error.* New York: Putnam's.

Damsen, Silver. 1993. "Human Odor Preferences and Aversions." *Ms.*

Darby, William; Louis Grivetti; Paul Ghalioungi. 1977. *Food: The Gift of Osiris.* New York: Academic Press.

Davidson, Alan. 2000. *The Oxford Companion to Food.* Oxford: Oxford University Press.

Dawkins, Richard. 1976. *The Selfish Gene*. Oxford: Oxford University Press.

DeLauro, Rosa L. 2003. "Imported Drugs: FDA Suddenly Gets 'Concerned.'" *Los Angeles Times*, Nov. 5, p. B15.

Dembínska, Maria. 1999. *Food and Drink in Medieval Poland: Rediscovering Cuisine of the Past*. Tr. Magdalena Thomas. Revised and adapted by William Woys Weaver. Philadelphia: University of Pennsylvania Press.

Deutsch, R. 1977. *The New Nuts among the Berries*. Palo Alto, CA: Bull Publishing.

DeVore, Sally, and Thelma White. 1978. *The Appetites of Man: An Invitation to Better Nutrition from Nine Healthier Societies*. Garden City, NY: Doubleday.

De Waal, Franz. 1996. *Good Natured*. Cambridge, MA: Harvard University Press.

Diamond, Jared. 1997. *Why Is Sex Fun?* New York: HarperCollins.

Diener, Paul, and Eugene Robkin. 1978. "Ecology, Evolution, and the Search for Cultural Origins: The Question of Islamic Pig Prohibition." *Current Anthropology* 19:3:493–540.

Dietler, Michael, and Brian Hayden (eds.). 2001. *Feasts: Archaeological and Ethnographic Perspectives on Food, Politics, and Power*. Washington, DC: Smithsonian Institution Press.

Dilthey, Wilhelm. 1985. *Introduction to the Human Sciences*. Tr./ed. Rudolf Makkreel and Frithjof Rodi. (German orig. late nineteenth century.) Princeton, NJ: Princeton University Press.

Diner, Hasia R. 2002. *Hungering for America: Italian, Irish and Jewish Foodways in the Age of Immigration*. Cambridge, MA: Harvard University Press.

"Dinner in a Mound." 2001. *Science* 291:587.

Dissanayake, Ellen. 2000. "Antecedents of the Temporal Arts in Early Mother-Infant Interaction." In *The Origins of Music*, ed. Nils Wallin, Bjorn Merker, and Steven Brown. Cambridge, MA: MIT Press. Pp. 389–410.

Dobkin de Rios, Marlene, and Brian Hayden. 1985. "Odourous Differentiation and Variability in the Sexual Division of Labour among Hunters/Gatherers." *Journal of Human Evolution* 14:219–28.

Dodd, G. H. 1988. "The Molecular Dimension in Perfumery." In *Perfumery*, ed. Steve Van Toller and George H. Dodd. New York: Chapman and Hall. Pp. 19–46.

Dolhinow, Phyllis. 1999. Review of "Demonic Males: Apes and the Origins of Human Violence" by Richard Wrangham and Dale Peterson. *American Anthropologist* 101:445–46.

Doniger, Wendy, and Brian Smith (ed./tr./introduction). 1991. *The Laws of Manu*. New York: Penguin.

Doty, Richard L. 1991. "Olfactory Function in Neonates." In *The Human Sense of Smell*, ed. D. G. Laing, R. L. Doty, and W. Breipohl. New York: Springer-Verlag. Pp. 155–65.

Douglas, Mary. 1966. *Purity and Danger.* New York: Praeger.

———. 1970. *Natural Symbols.* London: Barrie and Rockliff.

———. 1975. *Implicit Meanings.* London: Routledge & Kegan Paul.

Draper, H. H. 2000. "Human Nutritional Adaptation: Biological and Cultural Aspects." In *The Cambridge World History of Food,* ed. Kenneth Kiple and K. Ornelas. Cambridge: Cambridge University Press. Pp. 1466–76.

Drexler, Madeline. 2003. "Some Cipro with That Burger?" *Los Angeles Times,* June 29, p. M2.

Drucker, Philip, and Robert Heizer. 1967. *To Make My Name Good.* Berkeley: University of California Press.

Drummond, John, and Anne Wilbraham. 1958. *The Englishman's Food.* Rev. ed. London: J. Cape.

Dufour, Darna L., and Nicolette I. Teufel. 1995. "Minimum Data Sets for the Description of Diet and Measurement of Food Intake and Nutritional Status." In *The Comparative Analysis of Human Societies: Toward Common Standards for Data Collection and Reporting,* ed. Emilio L. Moran. Boulder, CO: Lynne Rienner. Pp. 97–128.

Dunbar, Robin. 1993. "Coevolution of Neocortical Size, Group Size and Language in Humans." *Behavioral and Brain Sciences* 16:681–735.

———. 1996. *Grooming, Gossip, and the Evolution of Language.* Cambridge, MA: Harvard University Press.

Duran, Fray Diego. 1994. *The History of the Indies of New Spain.* Tr./ed. Doris Heyden. (Spanish orig. sixteenth century.) Norman: University of Oklahoma Press.

Durkheim, Emile. 1995. *The Elementary Forms of the Religious Life.* Tr. Karen E. Fields. (Fr. orig. 1912.) New York: Simon & Schuster.

Eaton, S. Boyd; Stanley B. Eaton III; Loren Cordain. 2002. "Evolution, Diet, and Health." In *Human Diet: Its Origin and Evolution,* ed. Peter S. Ungar and Mark F. Telford. Westport, CT: Bergin and Garvey. Pp. 7–18.

Eberwine, Donna. 2002. "Globesity: The Crisis of Growing Proportions." *Perspectives in Health* 7:3:6–11.

Effros, Bonnie. 2002. *Creating Community with Food and Drink in Merovingian Gaul.* New York: Palgrave Macmillan.

Ehrlichman, Howard, and Linda Bastone. 1992. "Olfaction and Emotion." In *Science of Olfaction,* ed. Michael J. Serby and Karen L. Chobor. New York: Springer-Verlag. Pp. 410–38.

Eichenwald, Kurt. 2000. *The Informant.* New York: Broadway Books.

Eléxpuru, Inés. 1994. *La cocina de al-Andalus.* Madrid: Alianza Editorial.

Engen, Trygg. 1981. *The Perception of Odors.* New York: Academic Press.

———. 1988. "The Acquisition of Odour Hedonics." In *Perfumery,* ed. Steve Van Toller and George H. Dodd. New York: Chapman and Hall. Pp. 79–90.

———. 1991. *Odor Sensation and Memory.* New York: Praeger.

Etkin, Nina (ed.). 1986. *Plants in Indigenous Medicine and Diet: Biobehavioral Approaches.* Bedford Hills, NY: Redgrave.
———— (ed.). 1994. *Eating on the Wild Side.* Tucson: University of Arizona Press.
Evans, L. T. 1998. *Feeding the Ten Billion: Plants and Population Growth.* Cambridge: Cambridge University Press.
Fairbanks, Virgil F. 1999. "Iron in Medicine and Nutrition." In *Modern Nutrition in Health and Disease,* ed. Maurice Shils, James Olson, Moshe Shike, A. Catharine Ross. Philadelphia: Lippincott Williams and Wilkins. Pp. 193–221.
Farley, Maggie. 2002. "World Hunger on the Rise Again." *Los Angeles Times,* Oct. 16, p. A4.
Faroqhi, Suraiya. 2000. *Subjects of the Sultans: Culture and Everyday Life in the Ottoman Empire from the Middle Ages until the Beginning of the Twentieth Century.* London: I. B. Tauris.
Feely-Harnik, Gillian. 1994. *The Lord's Table: The Meaning of Food in Early Judaism and Christianity.* Washington, DC: Smithsonian Institution Press.
Feld, Steven, and Keith Basso. 1996. *Senses of Place.* Santa Fe, NM: School of American Research.
Firth, Raymond. 1936. *We the Tikopia.* London: George Allen and Unwin.
————. 1959. *Social Change in Tikopia.* London: George Allen and Unwin.
————. 1962. *Economics of the New Zealand Maori.* London: George Allen and Unwin.
Firth, Rosemary. 1966. *Housekeeping among Malay Peasants.* London: Athlone Press.
Fischler, Claude. 1990. *L'homnivore.* Paris: Editions Odile Jacob.
Fitzgerald, Thomas K. (ed.). 1977. *Nutrition and Anthropology in Action.* Leiden: Van Gorcum.
Flandrin, Jean-Louis, and Massimino Montanari (directors). 1996. *Histoire de l-alimentation.* Paris: Fayard.
———— (eds.). 1999. *Food: A Culinary History.* Tr. Albert Sonnenfeld. (Fr. orig. 1996.) New York: Columbia University Press.
Forster, Robert, and Orest Ranum (eds.). 1979. *Food and Drink in History: Selections from the* Annales: Economies, Sociétés, Civilisations. Baltimore, MD: Johns Hopkins University Press.
Foster, George. 1994. *Hippocrates' Latin American Legacy.* Amsterdam: Gordon and Breach.
Foucault, Michel. 1970. *The Order of Things.* New York: Random House.
Foundation of Chinese Dietary Culture. 1998. *Fifth Symposium on Chinese Dietary Culture.* Taipei, Taiwan: Foundation of Chinese Dietary Culture.
Fox, Vickers. 1997. *Spoiled.* New York: Basic Books.

Frake, Charles. 1980. "The Ethnographic Study of Cognitive Systems." In *Language and Cultural Description*, ed. Anwar S. Dil. Stanford, CA: Stanford University Press. Pp. 1–17.

Frankl, Viktor. 1959. *Man's Search for Meaning*. Boston: Beacon Press.

———. 1978. *The Unheard Cry for Meaning*. New York: Simon & Schuster.

Gade, Daniel W. 1976. "Horsemeat as Human Food in France." *Ecology of Food and Nutrition* 5:1–11.

Galen. 2000. *Galen on Food and Diet*. Tr./ed. Mark Grant. London: Routledge.

———. 2003. *Galen on the Properties of Foodstuffs*. Tr./ed. Owen Powell. Cambridge: Cambridge University Press.

Gardner, Martin. 1957. *Fads and Fallacies in the Name of Science*. New York: Dover.

Geary, David C. 2000. "Evolution and Proximate Expression of Human Paternal Investment." *Psychological Bulletin* 126:55–77.

Geertz, Clifford. 1963. *Agricultural Involution*. Berkeley: University of California Press.

Georgakas, Dan. 1980. *The Methuselah Factor*. New York: Simon & Schuster.

Georges, Robert. 1981. "You Eat What Others Think You Are." Paper, Southern California Academy of Sciences Annual Meeting, Los Angeles, CA.

Gibbons, Boyd. 1986. "The Intimate Sense of Smell." *National Geographic* 170:514–25.

Gibbons, Euell. 1962. *Stalking the Wild Asparagus*. New York: David McKay.

Gleick, Peter. 1998. *The World's Water*. Washington, DC: Island Press.

Goldschmidt, Walter. 1947. *As You Sow*. New York: Harcourt, Brace.

Gombrich, E. H. 1984. *The Sense of Order: A Study in the Psychology of Decorative Art*. Ithaca, NY: Cornell University Press.

Goodman, Alan, and Thomas Leatherman (eds.). 1998. *Building a New Biocultural Synthesis*. Ann Arbor: University of Michigan Press.

Goodman, Alan H.; Darna L. Dufour; Gretel H. Pelto. 2000. *Nutritional Anthropology: Biocultural Perspectives on Food and Nutrition*. Mountain View, CA: Mayfield.

Goody, Jack. 1982. *Cooking, Cuisine, and Class*. Cambridge: Cambridge University Press.

———. 1993. *The Culture of Flowers*. Cambridge: Cambridge University Press.

Gosden, Chris, and Jon Hather. 1999. *The Prehistory of Food: Appetites for Change*. Cambridge: Cambridge University Press.

Gould, Stephen Jay. 2002. *The Structure of Evolutionary Theory*. Cambridge, MA: Harvard University Press.

Gray, Patience. 1997. *Honey from a Weed*. Devon: Prospect Books.

Green, Emily. 2002. "The Temptation Is Back." *Los Angeles Times*, Oct. 23, pp. F1, F4.

Green, Peter. 1990. *Alexander to Actium: The Historical Evolution of the Hellenistic Age.* Berkeley: University of California Press.

Greene, Lawrence. 1977. *Malnutrition, Behavior, and Social Organization.* New York: Academic Press.

———. 1980. *Social and Biological Predictors of Nutritional Status, Physical Growth, and Neural Development.* New York: Academic Press.

Gregoire, Jean-Pierre. 1998. "Major Units for the Transformation of Grain: The Grain-grinding Households (e2-HAR.HAR) of Southern Mesopotamia at the End of the Third Millennium BCE." In *Prehistory of Agriculture: New Experimental and Ethnographic Approaches,* ed. Patricia Anderson. Los Angeles: Institute of Archaeology, UCLA. Pp. 223–37.

Grieve, M. 1931. *A Modern Herbal.* New York: Harcourt, Brace.

Grove, A. T., and Oliver Rackham. 2001. *The Nature of Mediterranean Europe: An Ecological History.* New Haven, CT: Yale University Press.

Gundel, Karoly. 1964. *Hungarian Cookery Book.* Budapest: Athenaeum.

Hanger, Catherine. 2000. *World Food: Morocco.* Hawthorn, Australia: Lonely Planet.

Hanks, William. 1990. *Referential Practice.* Chicago: University of Chicago Press.

Harlow, Mary, and Wendy Smith. 2001. "Between Fasting and Feasting: The Literary and Archaeobotanical Evidence for Monastic Diet in Late Antique Egypt." *Antiquity* 75:758–69.

Harner, Michael. 1977. "The Ecological Basis for Aztec Sacrifice." *American Ethnologist* 4:117–35.

Harris, Judith Rich. 1998. *The Nurture Assumption.* New York: Free Press.

Harris, Marvin. 1966. "The Cultural Ecology of India's Sacred Cattle." *Current Anthropology* 7:51–66.

———. 1974. *Cows, Pigs, Wars, and Witches: The Riddles of Culture.* New York: Random House.

———. 1985. *Good to Eat: Riddles of Food and Culture.* New York: Simon & Schuster.

———. 1987. *The Sacred Cow and the Abominable Pig: Riddles of Food and Culture.* New York: Simon & Schuster.

Harris, Marvin, and Eric B. Ross (eds.). 1987. *Food and Evolution: Toward a Theory of Human Food Habits.* Philadelphia: Temple University Press.

Harriss-White, Barbara, and Sir Raymond Hoffenberg (eds.). 1994. *Food: Multidisciplinary Perspectives.* Oxford: Blackwell.

Hartman, Louis F., and A. L. Oppenheim. 1950. *On Beer and Brewing Techniques in Ancient Mesopotamia.* Supplement to the *Journal of the American Oriental Society,* No. 10.

Hattox, Ralph S. 1985. *Coffee and Coffeehouses: The Origins of a Social Beverage in the Medieval Near East.* Seattle: University of Washington Press.

Hawkes, Kristen. 1993. "Why Hunter-Gatherers Work: An Ancient Version of the Problem of Public Goods." *Current Anthropology* 34:341–63.

Hayami, Yujiro, and Vernon Ruttan. 1985. *Agricultural Development.* 2nd ed. Baltimore, MD: Johns Hopkins University Press.

Headland, Thomas N., and Lawrence A. Reid. 1989. "Hunter-Gatherers and Their Neighbors from Prehistory to the Present." *Current Anthropology* 30:43–66.

Heiser, Charles. 1976. *The Sunflower.* Norman: University of Oklahoma Press.

———. 1990. *Seed to Civilization.* 3rd ed. Cambridge, MA: Harvard University Press.

Heldke, Lisa. 1988. "Recipes for Theory Making." *Hypatia* 3:15–29.

Henkin, Robert I. 1967. "Abnormalities of Taste and Olfaction in Various Disease States." In *The Chemical Senses and Nutrition,* ed. Morley Kare and Owen Maller. Baltimore, MD: Johns Hopkins University Press. Pp. 95–114.

Herbert, Victor. 1999. "Folic Acid." In *Modern Nutrition in Health and Disease,* ed. Maurice Shils, James A. Olson, Moshe Shike, and A. Catherine Ross. 9th ed. Philadelphia: Lippincott Williams and Wilkins. Pp. 443–46.

Herodotus. 1954. *The Histories.* Tr. Audrey de Selincourt. (Greek orig. fifth century BC.) Harmondsworth, Middlesex: Penguin.

Hess, Karen. 1992. *The Carolina Rice Kitchen.* Columbia: University of South Carolina Press.

Hill, Kim, and Hillard Kaplan (with response by Kristin Hawkes). 1993. "On Why Male Foragers Hunt and Share Food." *Current Anthropology* 34:701–10.

Hippocrates (ascribed). 1978. *Hippocratic Writings.* Ed. G. E. R. Lloyd. London: Penguin.

Hoberg, Eric P.; Nancy L. Alkire; Alan de Queiroz; Arlene Jones. 2001. "Out of Africa: Origins of the *Taenia* Tapeworms in Humans." *Proceedings of the Royal Society of London* 268:781–87.

Holden, Constance. 2000. "Man, the Toothpick User." *Science* 288:607.

Holley, David. 2002. "Europe's Food Regions Fight to Keep Their Good Names." *Los Angeles Times,* Sept. 16, pp. A1, A8.

Hopkins, Jerry. 1999. *Strange Foods.* Tokyo: Tuttle.

Horden, Peregrine, and Nicholas Purcell. 2000. *The Corrupting Sea: A Study of Mediterranean History.* Oxford: Blackwell.

Howell, David G., and Jonathan P. Swinchatt. 2000. "A Discussion of Geology, Soils, Wines, and History of the Napa Valley Region." *California Geology* 53:3:4–12.

Hughes, R. E. 2000. "Scurvy." In *The Cambridge World History of Food,* ed. Kenneth Kiple and K. Ornelas. Cambridge: Cambridge University Press. Pp. 988–1000.

Hume, David. 1992. "Of the Immortality of the Soul." In *Writings on Religion,* ed. Antony Flew. Chicago: Open Court.

Hung Tzu-Ch'eng. 1959. *A Chinese Garden of Serenity.* Tr. Chao Tze-ch'ang. (Orig. sixteenth century, *Cai Gen Tan,* "discussing vegetable roots.") New York: Peter Pauper Press.

Hunn, Eugene. 1979. "The Abominations of Leviticus Revisited." In *Classifications in the Social Context,* ed. Roy Ellen and D. Pearson. New York: Academic Press. Pp. 103–18.

Ibn Khaldun. 1958. *The Muqaddimah.* Tr. Franz Rosenthal. New York: Pantheon.

International Food Policy Research Institute. 2002. *Sustainable Food Security for All by 2020.* Washington, DC: International Food Policy Research Institute.

Isaac, Glynn. 1978. "The Food-sharing Behavior of Protohuman Hominids." *Scientific American* 238:4:90–108.

———. 1979. "Food Sharing and Human Evolution: Archaeological Evidence from the Plio-Pleistocene of East Africa." *Journal of Anthropological Research* 34:311–25.

Ishige, Naomichi. 2001. *The History and Culture of Japanese Food.* London: Kegan Paul.

Jacob, H. E. 1944. *Six Thousand Years of Bread.* New York: Doubleday, Doran.

Jantzen, Daniel. 1998. "Gardenification of Wild Nature and the Human Footprint." *Science* 279:1312–13.

Jelliffe, D. B. 1966. *The Assessment of the Nutritional Status of the Community.* Geneva: World Health Organization.

Jerome, Norge; Randy Kandel; Gretel Pelto. 1980. *Nutritional Anthropology.* Pleasantville, NY: Redgrave.

Johns, Timothy. 1991. *With Bitter Herbs They Shall Eat It.* Tucson: University of Arizona Press.

Johnson, Samuel. 1963. *Johnson's Dictionary: A Modern Selection.* Ed. E. L. McAdam, Jr., and George Milne. New York: Pantheon.

Jones, Evan. 1981. *American Food.* 2nd ed. New York: Random House.

Jones, Peter J. H., and Stanley Kubow. 1999. "Lipids, Sterols, and Their Metabolites." In *Modern Nutrition in Health and Disease,* ed. Maurice Shils, James Olson, Moshe Shike, A. Catharine Ross. Philadelphia: Lippincott Williams and Wilkins. Pp. 67–94.

Jourdain, Robert. 1997. *Music, the Brain, and Ecstasy.* New York: William Morrow.

Joyce, James. 1961. *Ulysses.* New York: Modern Library.

Kallas, John. 2002. *The Wild Food Primer.* Portland, OR: Institute for Wild Food Education.

Kant, Immanuel. 1978. *Anthropology from a Pragmatic Point of View.* Tr.

Victor Lyle Dowdell. (Ger. orig. 1796.) Carbondale: Southern Illinois University Press.

Kaplan, Stephen. 1992. "Environmental Preference in a Knowledge-Sharing, Knowledge-Using Organism." In *The Adapted Mind*, ed. Jerome H. Barkow, Leda Cosmides, and John Tooby. New York: Oxford University Press. Pp. 588–98.

Katan, M. B., and Nicole M. de Roos. 2003. "Toward Evidence-Based Health Claims for Foods." *Science* 299:206–7.

Katz, Solomon; M. Hediger; L. Valleroy. 1974. "Traditional Maize Processing Techniques in the New World." *Science* 184:765–73.

Katz, Solomon, and William Woys Weaver (eds.). 2003. *Encyclopedia of Food and Culture*. New York: Scribner's.

Kearney, Michael. 1996. *Reconceptualizing the Peasantry*. Boulder, CO: Westview.

Keeley, Lawrence. 1998. "Use of Plant Foods among Hunter-Gatherers: A Cross-cultural Survey." In *Prehistory of Agriculture: New Experimental and Ethnographic Approaches*, ed. Patricia Anderson. Los Angeles: Institute of Archaeology, UCLA. Monograph 40. Pp. 6–14.

Kelly, Robert L. 1995. *The Foraging Spectrum: Diversity in Hunter-Gatherer Lifeways*. Washington, DC: Smithsonian Institution Press.

Keys, Ancel. 1980. *Seven Countries*. Cambridge, MA: Harvard University Press.

Kennedy, Diana. 1998. *My Mexico: A Culinary Odyssey with More Than Three Hundred Recipes*. New York: Random House/Clarkson Potter.

Khare, R. S. 1976a. *Culture and Reality*. Simla: Indian Institute of Advanced Study.

———. 1976b. *The Hindu Hearth and Home*. Durham, NC: Carolina Academic Press.

——— (ed.). 1992. *The Eternal Food: Gastronomic Ideas and Experiences of Hindus and Buddhists*. Albany: State University of New York Press.

King, J. R. 1988. "Anxiety Reduction Using Fragrances." In *Perfumery*, ed. Steve Van Toller and George H. Dodd. New York: Chapman and Hill. Pp. 227–33.

Kinsella, Thomas (ed./tr.). 1970. *The Tain*. New York: Oxford University Press.

Kiple, Kenneth, and Kriemhild C. Ornelas. 2000. *The Cambridge World History of Food*. Cambridge: Cambridge University Press.

Klatsky, Arthur L. 2003. "Drink to Your Health?" *Scientific American*, Feb.: 75–81.

Kniep, E. H., and P. T. Young. 1931. "Studies in Affective Psychology, XII: The Relation between Age and Affective Reactions to Odors." *American Journal of Psychology* 43:406–21.

Koenig, Walter D., and Ronald L. Mumme. 1987. *Population Ecology of the Cooperatively Breeding Acorn Woodpecker*. Princeton, NJ: Princeton University Press.

Kohn, Livia. 1993. *The Taoist Experience*. Albany: State University of New York Press.

Kortlandt, Adriaan. 1978. "The Ecosystems in Which the Incipient Hominines Could Have Evolved." In *Recent Advances in Primatology*. Vol. 3, *Evolution*, ed. D. J. Chivers and K. A. Jaysey. London: Academic Press. Pp. 503–6.

Kotchen, Theodore A., and Jane Morley Kotchen. 1999. "Nutrition, Diet, and Hypertension." In Shils et al. 1999. Pp. 1217–27.

Kottak, Conrad Philip. 2003. *Cultural Anthropology*. 10th ed. New York: Mc-Graw-Hill.

Kovacs, Maureen Gallery (tr.). 1985. *The Epic of Gilgamesh*. Stanford, CA: Stanford University Press.

Kramer, S. N. 1955. "Sumerian Myths and Epic Tales." In *Religions of the Ancient Near East: Sumero-Akkadian Religious Texts and Ugaritic Epics*, ed. Isaac Mendelsohn. New York: Liberal Arts Press. Pp. 11–16.

Krech, Shepard. 1999. *The Ecological Indian: Myth and Reality*. New York: Norton.

Kroes, Robert, and J. H. Weisburger. 2000. "Nutrition and Cancer." In *The Cambridge World History of Food*, ed. Kenneth Kiple and Kriemhild C. Ornelas. Cambridge: Cambridge University Press. Pp. 1086–96.

Kronenfeld, David B. 1979. "Innate Language?" *Language Sciences* 1:209–39.

Laderman, Carole. 1981. "Symbolic and Empirical Reality: A New Approach to the Analysis of Food Avoidances." *American Ethnologist* 8:468–93.

Lakoff, George, and Mark Johnson. 1999. Philosophy in the Flesh. New York: Basic Books.

Lang, George. 1971. *The Cuisine of Hungary*. New York: Atheneum.

Lang, James. 2001. *Notes of a Potato Watcher*. College Station: Texas A & M Press.

Langer, Ellen. 1983. *The Psychology of Control*. Beverly Hills, CA: Sage.

Lappé, Frances Moore. 1971. *Diet for a Small Planet*. New York: Ballantine.

Lappé, Frances Moore, and Joseph Collins. 1971. *Food First*. San Francisco: Institute for Food and Development Policy.

Laudan, Rachel. 1998. *The Food of Paradise*. Honolulu: University of Hawaii Press.

Laufer, Berthold. 1919. *Sino Iranica*. Chicago: Field Museum.

Laurin, Asunción, and Edith Couturier. 1979. "Dowries and Wills: A View of Women's Socioeconomic Role in Colonial Guadalajara and Puebla, 1640–1790." *Hispanic-American Historical Review* 59:280–304.

Lave, Jean. 1988. *Cognition in Practice*. Cambridge: Cambridge University Press.

Lawless, H. 1991. "Effects of Odors on Mood and Behavior: Aromatherapy and Related Effects." In *The Human Sense of Smell*, ed. D. G. Laing, R. L. Doty, and W. Breipohl. New York: Springer-Verlag. Pp. 361–86.

Leach, Edmund. 1964. "Anthropological Categories of Verbal Abuse." In *New Directions in the Study of Language,* ed. Eric Lenneberg. Cambridge, MA: MIT Press. Pp. 23–64.

Lee, Richard, and Irven Devore (eds.). 1962. *Man the Hunter.* Cambridge, MA: Harvard University Press.

Lentz, Carola (ed.). 1999. *Changing Food Habits: Case Studies from Africa, South America, and Europe.* Newark, NJ: Gordon and Breach.

Le Roy Ladurie, Emmanuel. 1971. *Times of Feast, Times of Famine: A History of Climate Change since the Year 1000.* Tr. Barbara Bray. Garden City, NY: Doubleday.

Lévi-Strauss, Claude. 1958. *Anthropologie structurale.* Paris: Plon.

———. 1962. *La Pensee sauvage.* Paris: Plon.

———. 1964. *Le Cru et le Cuit.* Paris: Plon. (Translation: 1969. *The Raw and the Cooked.* Tr. John and Doreen Weightman. New York: Harper and Row.)

———. 1964–72. *Mythologiques.* Paris: Plon.

Lewis, Walter, and Memory Elvin-Lewis. 1976. *Medical Botany.* New York: Wiley.

Liu, Xin. 2000. *In One's Own Shadow.* Berkeley: University of California Press.

Logue, Alexandra W. 1986. *The Psychology of Eating and Drinking.* New York: W. H. Freeman.

LoMonte, Mimmetta. 1990. *Mimmetta LoMonte's Classic Sicilian Cookbook.* New York: Simon & Schuster.

Long, Janet. 2000. "Tomatoes." In *The Cambridge World History of Food,* ed. Kenneth Kiple and K. Ornelas. Cambridge: Cambridge University Press. Pp. 351–58.

Lorig, Tyler S., and Gary E. Schwartz. 1988. "Brain and Odor: I. Alternation of Human EEG by Odor Administration." *Psychobiology* 16:281–84.

Lovejoy, C. Owen. 1981. "The Origin of Man." *Science* 211:341–50.

Lyman, Bernard. 1989. *A Psychology of Food: More Than a Matter of Taste.* New York: Van Nostrand Reinhold.

MacNeish, Richard S. 1992. *The Origins of Agriculture and Settled Life.* Norman: University of Oklahoma Press.

Malinowski, Bronislaw. 1922. *Argonauts of the Western Pacific.* New York: Dutton.

———. 1935. *Coral Gardens and Their Magic.* Cincinnati, OH: American Book Company.

———. 1944. *A Scientific Theory of Culture.* Chapel Hill: University of North Carolina Press.

Mallory, Walter. 1926. *China: Land of Famine.* New York: American Geographic Society. Special Publication No. 6.

Mann, Alan E. 1987. "Diet and Human Evolution." In *Omnivorous Primates,* ed. Robert S. O. Harding and Geza Teleki. New York: Columbia University Press. Pp. 10–36.

Marks, Jonathan. 2002. *What It Means to Be 98 Percent Chimpanzee: Apes, People, and Their Genes.* Berkeley: University of California Press.

Marks, Robert. 1997. *Tigers, Rice, Silk, and Silt: Environment and Economy in Late Imperial South China.* Stanford, CA: Stanford University Press.

Marr, K. L., and C. S. Tang. 1992. "Volatile Insecticidal Compounds and Chemical Variability of Hawaiian *Zanthoxylum* (Rutaceae) Species." *Biochemical Systematics and Ecology* 20:209–17.

Marx, Karl. 1986. *Karl Marx: A Reader.* Ed. Jon Elster. Cambridge: Cambridge University Press.

Marzluff, John, and Russell Balda. 1992. *The Pinyon Jay.* London: Poyser.

Maslow, Abraham. 1970. *Motivation and Personality.* 2nd ed. New York: Harper and Row.

Mason, Sarah L. R.; Jon G. Hather; Gordon C. Hillman. 1994. "Preliminary Investigation of the Plant Macro-remains from Dolni Vestonice II and Its Implications for the Role of Plant Foods in Palaeolithic and Mesolithic Europe." *Antiquity* 68:48–57.

Matalas, Antonia L., et al. 2001. *The Mediterranean Diet: Constituents and Health Promotion.* Boca Raton, FL: CRC Press.

Maugh, Thomas H., II. 1982. "The Scent Makes Sense." *Science* 215:1224.

McCartney, William. 1968. *Olfaction and Odors.* New York: Springer-Verlag.

McCay, Bonnie. 1998. *Oyster Wars and the Public Trust.* Tucson: University of Arizona Press.

McCorriston, Joy. 2000. "Wheat." In *The Cambridge World History of Food,* ed. Kenneth Kiple and K. Ornelas. Cambridge: Cambridge University Press. Pp. 158–74.

McGee, Harold. 1984. *On Food and Cooking.* New York: Scribner's.

McGovern, Patrick E.; Stuart J. Fleming; Solomon H. Katz. 1996. *The Origins and Ancient History of Wine.* Amsterdam: Gordon and Breach.

McGovern, Thomas; Gerald Bigelow; Thomas Amorosi; Daniel Russell. 1988. "Northern Islands, Human Error, and Environmental Degradation." *Human Ecology* 16:225–70.

McGrew, W. C. 2000. "Dental Care in Chimps." (Letter.) *Science* 288:1747.

Mead, George Herbert. 1964. *The Social Psychology of George Herbert Mead.* Ed. Anselm Strauss. Chicago: University of Chicago Press.

Médecin, Jacques. 1972. *La bonne cuisine du Comté de Nice.* Paris: Solar.

The Medieval Health Handbook: Tacuinum Sanitatis. 1976. Tr./ed. Luisa Cogliati Arano. New York: George Braziller.

Meigs, Anna. 1997. "Food as a Cultural Construction." In *Food and Culture: A Reader,* ed. Carole Counihan and Penny van Esterik. New York: Routledge. Pp. 95–106.

Mennell, Stephen; Anne Murcott; A. H. Van Otterloo. 1992. *The Sociology of Food: Eating, Diet, and Culture.* London: Sage.

Mensink, Ronald P.; Peter L. Zock; Arnold D. M. Kester; Martijn B. Katen. 2003. "Effects of Dietary Fatty Acids and Carbohydrates on the Ratio of Serum Total to HDL Cholesterol and on Serum Lipids and Apolipoproteins: A Meta-analysis of 60 Controlled Trials." *American Journal of Clinical Nutrition* 77:1146–55.

Menzel, Peter, and Faith D'Aluisio. 1998. *Man Eating Bugs: The Art and Science of Eating Insects.* Berkeley, CA: Ten Speed Press.

Messer, Ellen. 1984. "Anthropological Perspectives on Diet." *Annual Review of Anthropology* 13:205–49.

———. 1997. "Intra-Household Allocation of Food and Health Care: Current Findings and Understandings—Introduction." *Social Science and Medicine* 44:1675–84.

Mestel, Rosie. 2000. "The Food Pyramid: Does It Miss the Point?" *Los Angeles Times,* Sept. 1, pp. 1, 30.

———. 2002. "Chimps May Have Something to Tell Us." *Los Angeles Times,* April 12, pp. A1, A20.

Milham, Mary Ella. 1998. *Platina on Right Pleasure and Good Health.* Tempe: Arizona State University Press.

Miller, Geoffrey. 2000. "Evolution of Human Music through Sexual Selection." In Wallin et al. 2000. Pp 329–60.

Miller, J. Innes. 1969. *The Spice Trade of the Roman Empire.* Oxford: Oxford University Press.

Milton, Katharine. 1993. "Diet and Primate Evolution." *Scientific American* 269:86–93.

———. 2000a. "Back to Basics: Why Foods of Wild Primates Have Relevance for Modern Human Health." *Nutrition* 16:480–83.

———. 2000b. "Hunter-gatherer Diets: A Different Perspective." *American Journal of Clinical Nutrition* 71:665–67.

———. 2000c. "Quo Vadis? Tactics of Food Search and Group Movement in Primates and Other Animals." In *On the Move: How and Why Animals Travel in Groups,* ed. Sue Boinski and Paul A. Garber. Chicago: University of Chicago Press. Pp. 375–417.

"Minty Insecticide." 2000. *Scientific American,* Feb., p. 24.

Mintz, Sidney. 1985. *Sweetness and Power.* New York: Viking Penguin.

———. 2002. "Food for Thought." In *The Globalization of Chinese Food,* ed. David Wu and Sidney Cheung. Richmond, Surrey: Curzon Press. Pp. xii–xx.

Moncrief, R. W. 1966. *Odour Preferences.* New York: Wiley.

Morales Rodríguez; María Teresa; Juana Rosa Martínez García. 1999. *La cocina tradicional cordobesa.* Córdoba: Ateneo de Córdoba.

Morgan, Lewis Henry. 1877. *Ancient Society.* New York: Holt.

Murcott, Anne (ed.). 1984. *The Sociology of Food and Eating.* Aldershot, Hants, England: Gower.

Murton, Brian. 2000. "Famine." In *The Cambridge World History of Food,* ed. Kenneth Kiple and K. Ornelas. Cambridge: Cambridge University Press. Pp. 1411–27.

Myers, Norman, with Jennifer Kent. 1998. *Perverse Subsidies: Tax Dollars Undercutting Our Economies and Environments Alike.* Winnipeg: International Institute for Sustainable Development.

Nash, J. Madeleine. 2002. "Cracking the Fat Riddle." *Time,* Sept. 2, pp. 45–55.

———. 2003. "Obesity Goes Global." *Time,* Aug. 25, pp. 53–54.

Nasrallah, Nawal. 2003. (Orig. 1999.) *Delights from the Garden of Eden: A Cookbook and a History of the Iraqi Cuisine.* N.p.: author.

National Academy of Sciences. 2002. "Report Offers New Eating and Physical Activity Targets to Reduce Chronic Disease Risk." Press release, Sept. 5.

National Research Council. 1989. *Lost Crops of the Incas.* Washington, DC: National Academy Press.

———. 1996. *Lost Crops of Africa.* Vol. 1, *Grains.* Washington, DC: National Academy Press.

Naylor, Audrey. 1997. *The Impact of Breastfeeding on Long-Term Health Outcomes Worldwide.* (5-page paper.) Washington, DC: Wellstart International.

Nestle, Marion. 2002. *Food Politics: How the Food Industry Influences Nutrition and Health.* Berkeley: University of California Press.

Netting, Robert. 1993. *Smallholders, Householders.* Stanford, CA: Stanford University Press.

Newall, Virginia. 1971. *An Egg at Easter.* Bloomington: Indiana University Press.

Nijveldt, Robert J., et al. 2001. "Flavonoids: A Review of Probable Mechanisms of Action and Potential Applications." *American Journal of Clinical Nutrition* 74:418–25.

Nissenbaum, Stephen. 1980. *Sex, Diet, and Debility in Jacksonian America: Sylvester Graham and Health Reform.* Westport, CT: Greenwood.

Nohl, Johannes. 1961. *The Black Death.* London: Unwin.

Norman, Barbara. 1972. *Tales of the Table.* New York: Prentice-Hall.

Nunn, John. 1996. *Ancient Egyptian Medicine.* Norman: University of Oklahoma Press.

Nunney, Leonard. 1998. "Are We Selfish, Are We Nice, or Are We Nice Because We Are Selfish?" (Review of Sober and Wilson 1998.) *Science* 281:1619–20.

Nyerges, Christopher. 1995. *In the Footsteps of Our Ancestors: Guide to Wild Foods.* 4th rev. ed. Los Angeles: Survival News Service.

O'Brien, Eileen M., and Charles R. Peters. 1999. "Landforms, Climate, Ecogeographic Mosaics, and the Potential for Hominid Diversity in Pliocene Africa." In *African Biogeography, Climate Change, and Human Evolution,*

276 | *References*

ed. Timothy Bromage and Friedemann Schrenk. New York: Oxford University Press. Pp. 115–37.

Ohnuki-Tierney, Emiko. 1993. *Rice as Self*. Princeton, NJ: Princeton University Press.

Oldenburg, Ray. 1989. *The Great Good Place*. New York: Paragon House.

Orans, Martin. 1975. "Domesticating the Functional Dragon: An Analysis of Piddocke's Potlatch." *American Anthropologist* 77:312–28.

Orians, Gordon, and Judith Heerwagen. 1992. "Evolved Responses to Landscapes." In *The Adapted Mind*, ed. Jerome H. Barkow, Leda Cosmides, and John Tooby. New York: Oxford University Press. Pp. 555–79.

Ortiz de Montellano, Bernard R. 1990. *Aztec Medicine, Health, and Nutrition*. New Brunswick, NJ: Rutgers University Press.

Ott, Sandra. 1981. *The Circle of Mountains*. London: Oxford University Press.

Patterson, K. David. 2000. "Lactose Intolerance." In *The Cambridge World History of Food*, ed. Kenneth Kiple and K. Ornelas. Cambridge: Cambridge University Press. Pp. 1057–62.

Pelto, Gretel. 2000. "Perspectives on Infant Feeding: Decision-Making and Ecology." In *Nutritional Anthropology: Biocultural Perspectives on Food and Nutrition*, ed. Alan Goodman, Darna Dufour, and Gretel Pelto. Mountain View, CA: Mayfield. Pp. 298–311.

Pennington, Jean. 1998. *Bowes and Church: Food Values of Potions Commonly Used*. 17th ed. Philadelphia: Lippincott-Raven.

Pennisi, Elizabeth. 1999. "Did Cooked Tubers Spur the Evolution of Big Brains?" *Science* 283:2004–5.

Perry, Charles. 2001. "Elements of Arab Feasting." In *Medieval Arab Cookery*, ed. Maxime Rodinson, A. J. Arberry, and Charles Perry. London: Prospect Books. Pp. 225–32.

Petrinovich, Lewis. 1995. *Human Evolution, Reproduction, and Morality*. New York: Plenum.

Peyton, James. 1994. *La Cocina de la Frontera*. Santa Fe, NM: Red Crane.

Piddocke, Stuart. 1965. "The Potlatch System of the Southern Kwakiutl: A New Perspective." *Southwestern Journal of Anthropology* 21:244–64.

Pilcher, Jeffrey M. 1998. *Que vivan los tamales! Food and the Making of Mexican Identity*. Albuquerque: University of New Mexico Press.

Pinker, Steven. 1997. *How the Mind Works*. New York: Norton.

Piperno, Dolores, and Deborah Pearsall. 2000. *Origins of Agriculture in the Neotropics*. New York: Academic Press.

Poehlman, Eric T., and Edward S. Horton. 1999. "Energy Needs: Assessment and Requirements in Humans." In Shils et al. 1999. Pp. 95–104.

Pollock, Nancy J. 1992. *These Roots Remain: Food Habits in Islands of the Central and Eastern Pacific since Western Contact*. Honolulu: University of Hawaii Press.

Post, John. 1976. *The Last Great Subsistence Crisis in the Western World.* Baltimore, MD: Johns Hopkins University Press.

Pottier, Johan. 1999. *Anthropology of Food: The Social Dynamics of Food Security.* Cambridge, England: Polity Press.

Potts, Richard. 1996. *Humanity's Descent: The Consequences of Ecological Instability.* New York: William Morrow.

Prescott, Heather Munro. 2000. "Anorexia Nervosa." In *The Cambridge World History of Food,* ed. Kenneth Kiple and K. Ornelas. Cambridge: Cambridge University Press. Pp. 1057–62.

Pritchard, John. 1977. "Economic Development among the Haisla." Ph.D. dissertation, Dept. of Anthropology and Sociology, University of British Columbia.

Profet, Margie. 1992. "Pregnancy Sickness as Adaptation: A Deterrent to Maternal Ingestion of Teratogens." In *The Adapted Mind,* ed. Jerome H. Barkow, Leda Cosmides, and John Tooby. New York: Oxford University Press. Pp. 327–66.

Purseglove, J. W.; E. G. Brown; C. L. Green; S. R. J. Robbins. 1981. *Spices.* London: Longmans.

Quandt, Sarah. 2000. "Infant and Child Nutrition." In *The Cambridge World History of Food,* ed. Kenneth Kiple and K. Ornelas. Cambridge: Cambridge University Press. Pp. 1444–53.

Ramos-Elorduy, Julieta. 1998. *Creepy Crawly Cuisine: The Gourmet Guide to Edible Insects.* Photographs by Peter Menzel. Rochester, VT: Park Street Press.

Ramos-Elorduy, Julieta, and José Manuel Pino Moreno. 1989. *Los insectos comestibles en el México antiguo.* Mexico: AGT Editor.

Ramos-Elorduy de Conconi, Julieta. 1991. *Los insectos como fuente de proteínas en el futuro.* Mexico: Limusa.

Rasmussen, Knud. 1927. *Across Arctic America.* New York: Putnam's.

———. 1931. *The Netsilik Eskimo.* Reports of the Fifth Thule Expedition, VIII. Copenhagen: n.p.

Rebar, Robert W. 1994. "The Breast and the Physiology of Lactation." In *Maternal-Fetal Medicine: Principles and Practice,* ed. Robert Creasy and Robert Resnik. Philadelphia: Saunders. Pp. 144–61.

Redon, Odile; Françoise Sabban; Silvano Serventi. 1991. *La Gastronomie au Moyen Âge.* Paris: Stock.

Reynor, Hollie A., and Leonard H. Epstein. 2001. "Dietary Variety, Energy Regulation, and Obesity." *Psychological Bulletin* 127:325–41.

Richards, Audrey. 1939. *Land, Labor, and Diet in Northern Rhodesia.* London: Routledge.

———. 1948. (Orig. 1932.) *Hunger and Work in a Savage Tribe.* Glencoe, IL: Free Press.

Ridley, Matt. 1996. *The Origins of Virtue*. New York: Viking Penguin.

Rifkin, Jeremy. 1992. *Beyond Beef: The Rise and Fall of the Cattle Culture*. New York: Dutton.

Robertson, D. G. 1896. *The Kafirs of the Hindu Kush*. London: Lawrence and Bullen.

Rodinson, Maxime; A. J. Arberry; Charles Perry. 2001. *Medieval Arab Cookery*. Totnes, Devon: Prospect Books.

Roodman, David. 1998. *The Natural Wealth of Nations*. Washington, DC: Island Press.

Root, Waverly. 1958. *The Food of France*. New York: Random House.

———. 1971. *The Food of Italy*. New York: Random House.

Roseberry, William. 1996. "The Rise of Yuppie Coffees and the Reimagination of Class in the United States." *American Anthropologist* 98:762–75.

Rosner, Fred. 1997. *Medicine in the Mishneh Torah of Maimonides*. Northvale, NJ: Jason Aronson.

Ross, Catharine. 1999. "Vitamin A and Retinoids." In Shils et al. 1999. Pp. 305–27.

Rouby, Catherine (ed.). 2002. *Olfaction, Taste, and Cognition*. Cambridge: Cambridge University Press.

Rousseau, Jean-Jacques. 1983. *On the Social Contract*. Tr. Donald A. Cress. (Fr. orig. 1782.) Indianapolis: Hackett.

Rozin, Elisabeth. 1983. *Ethnic Cuisine: The Flavor-Principle Cookbook*. Lexington, MA: Stephen Greene Press.

Rozin, Paul. 1982. "Human Food Selection: The Interaction of Biology, Culture, and Individual Experience." In *The Psychobiology of Human Food Selection*, ed. Lewis M. Barker. Westview, CT: AVI. Pp. 225–54.

———. 1987. "Sweetness, Sensuality, Sin, Safety, and Socialization: Some Speculations." In *Sweetness*, ed. John Dobbing. London: Springer-Verlag. Pp.99–111.

———. 1988. "Social Learning about Food by Humans." In *Social Learning: Psychological and Biological Perspectives*, ed. Thomas R. Zentall and Bennett G. Galef, Jr. Hillsboro, NJ: Erlbaum. Pp. 165–87.

Rozin, Paul, and April E. Fallon. 1981. *The Acquisition of Likes and Dislikes for Foods*. Unpaginated pamphlet offprinted from *Criteria of Food Acceptance*, ed. J. Solms and R. L. Hall. Zurich: Foster Verlag.

Rozin, Paul; Linda Millman; Carol Nemeroff. 1986. "Operation of the Laws of Sympathetic Magic in Disgust and Other Domains." *Journal of Personality and Social Psychology* 50:703–12.

Rozin, Paul, and Deborah Schiller. 1980. "The Nature and Acquisition of a Preference for Chili Pepper by Humans." *Motivation and Emotion* 4:77–101.

Rummel, Rudolph. 1998. *Statistics of Democide*. Munster: Lit.

Sabban, Françoise, and Silvano Serventi. 1997. *La Gastronomie à la Renais-sance.* Paris: Stock.

———. 1998. *La Gastronomie au Grand Siècle.* Paris: Stock.

Sacks, Oliver. 1987. *The Man Who Mistook His Wife for a Hat.* New York: Harper and Row.

Sahagun, Bernardino de. 1950–1982. *Codex Florentinus.* Tr. A. Anderson and Charles Dibble. (Sp. orig. mid-sixteenth century.) Salt Lake City: University of Utah Press.

Sahlins, Marshall. 1976. *Culture and Practical Reason.* Chicago: University of Chicago Press.

Salaman, Redcliffe. 1985. *The History and Social Influence of the Potato.* Cambridge: Cambridge University Press.

Sauer, Carl. 1952. *Agricultural Origins and Dispersals.* Berkeley: University of California Press.

Scharfenberg, Horst. 1989. *The Cuisines of Germany.* New York: Poseidon Press.

Schlosser, Eric. 2001. *Fast Food Nation.* New York: HarperCollins.

Schmidt, Hilary J., and Gary Beauchamp. 1992. "Human Olfaction in Infancy and Early Childhood." In *Science of Olfaction,* ed. Michael J. Serby and Karen L. Chobor. New York: Springer-Verlag. Pp. 378–95.

Schulz, Richard. 1976. "Some Life and Death Consequences of Perceived Control." In *Cognition and Social Behavior,* ed. John S. Carroll and John Payne. New York: Academic Press. Pp. 135–53.

Schwabe, Calvin. 1979. *Unmentionable Cuisine.* Charlottesville: University of Virginia Press.

Scrimshaw, Nevin (ed.). 1995. *Community-Based Longitudinal Nutrition and Health Studies: Classical Examples from Guatemala, Haiti, and Mexico.* Boston: International Foundation for Developing Countries.

Scully, Terence. 1995. *The Art of Cookery in the Middle Ages.* Woodbridge, Suffolk: Boydell and Brewer.

Seely, Stephen. 2000. "The Cardiovascular System, Coronary Artery Disease, and Calcium: A Hypothesis." In *The Cambridge World History of Food,* ed. Kenneth Kiple and K. Ornelas. Cambridge: Cambridge University Press. Pp. 1109–20.

Sen, Amartya. 1984. *Resources, Values, and Development.* Cambridge, MA: Harvard University Press.

———. 1992. *Inequality Reexamined.* Cambridge, MA: Harvard University Press and Russell Sage Foundation.

Serageldin, Ismail. 2002. "World Poverty and Hunger: The Challenge for Science." *Science* 296:54–58.

Serby, Michael J., and Chobor, Karen L. (eds.) 1992. *Science of Olfaction.* New York: Springer-Verlag.

Serventi, Silvano, and Françoise Sabban. 2002. *Pasta: The Story of a Universal Food.* Tr. Anthony Sugaar. (Fr. orig. 2000.) New York: Columbia University Press.

Shankman, Paul. 1969. "Le Rôti et le Bouilli: Lévi-Strauss' Theory of Cannibalism." *American Anthropologist* 71:54–69.

Sharman, Anne. 1991. *Diet and Domestic Life in Society.* Philadelphia: Temple University Press.

Sheridan, Thomas. 1995. *Where the Dove Calls.* Tucson: University of Arizona Press.

Sherman, Paul, and Jennifer Billing. 1999. "Darwinian Gastronomy: Why We Use Spices." *BioScience* 4:453–63.

Sherman, Paul, and Samuel M. Flaxman. 2001. "Protecting Ourselves from Food." *American Scientist* 89:142–51.

Shils, Maurice; James Olson; Moshe Shike; A. Catharine Ross. 1999. *Modern Nutrition in Health and Disease.* Philadelphia: Lippincott Williams and Wilkins.

Shipman, Pat. 2001. "A Worm's Eye View of Human Evolution." *American Scientist* 90:508–10.

Shiva, Vandana. 1997. *Biopiracy: The Plunder of Nature and Knowledge.* Boston: South End Press.

Simeti, Mary Taylor. 1989. *Pomp and Sustenance: Twenty-Five Centuries of Sicilian Food.* Hopewell, NJ: Ecco Press.

Simon, Stephanie. 2002. "Hope Has Dried Up on Farms." *Los Angeles Times,* Sept. 16, pp. A1, A10.

Simoons, Frederick. 1994. *Eat Not This Flesh.* 2nd ed. Madison: University of Wisconsin Press.

———. 1998. *Plants of Life, Plants of Death.* Madison: University of Wisconsin Press.

Smartt, J., and N. W. Simmonds (eds.). 1995. *Evolution of Crop Plants.* London: Longman.

Smil, Vaclav. 2000. *Feeding the World.* Cambridge, MA: MIT Press.

Smith, Andrew F. 2002. *Peanuts: The Illustrious History of the Goober Pea.* Urbana: University of Illinois Press.

Smith, Eric Alder. 1991. *Inujjuamiut Foraging Strategies.* New York: Aldine de Gruyter.

Smith, Eric Alder, and Bruce Winterhalder (eds.). 1992. *Evolutionary Ecology and Human Behavior.* New York: Aldine de Gruyter.

Smith, J. Russell. 1950. *Tree Crops: A Permanent Agriculture.* New York: Devin Adair.

Smith, Robertson. 1894. *Lectures on the Religion of the Semites.* London: A. & C. Black.

Sober, Elliot, and David Wilson. 1999. *Unto Others.* Cambridge, MA: Harvard University Press.

Sokolov, Raymond. 1981. *Fading Feast.* New York: Farrar Straus Giroux.

Solway, Jacqueline, and Richard B. Lee. 1990. "Foragers, Genuine or Spurious?" *Current Anthropology* 31:109–46.

Spencer, Herta. 2000. "Calcium." In *The Cambridge World History of Food,* ed. Kenneth Kiple and K. Ornelas. Cambridge: Cambridge University Press. Pp. 785–97.

Squires, Sally. 2002. "When It Comes to Food, We Fudge a Little." *Los Angeles Times,* Sept. 16, p. S4.

Stager, Kenneth. 1964. *The Role of Olfaction in Food Location by the Turkey Vulture* (Cathartes aura). Los Angeles: Los Angeles County Museum of Natural History. Contributions to Science, no. 81.

Stanford, Craig B., and Henry T. Bunn (eds.). 2001. *Meat-eating and Human Evolution.* New York: Oxford University Press.

Staub, Ervin. 1989. *The Roots of Evil: The Origins of Genocide and Other Group Violence.* Cambridge: Cambridge University Press.

Stevenson, Richard J., and Robert A. Boakes. 2003. "A Mnemonic Theory of Odor Perception." *Psychological Review* 110:340–64.

Stobart, Tom. 1970. *Herbs, Spices, and Flavorings.* London: International Wine and Food Publishing Co.

Stoddart, D. M. 1988. "The Biological Underpinnings of Scents." In *Perfumery,* ed. Steve Van Toller and George H. Dodd. New York: Chapman and Hall. Pp. 3–17.

Stoddart, Michael D. 1990. *The Scented Ape.* New York: Cambridge University Press.

Stokstad, Erik. 2003. "The Vitamin D Deficit." *Science* 302:1886–88.

Stone, Glenn Davis. 2002. "Both Sides Now: Fallacies in the Genetic-Modification Wars, Implications for Developing Countries, and Anthropological Perspectives." *Current Anthropology* 43:611–30.

Stonich, Susan. 1993. *"I Am Destroying the Land!" The Political Economy of Poverty and Environmental Destruction in Honduras.* Boulder, CO: Westview.

Strang, Jeanne. 1991. *Goose Fat and Garlic.* London: Kyle Cathie.

Strier, Karen. 1999. *Primate Behavioral Ecology.* Needham Heights, MA: Allyn and Bacon.

Suttles, Wayne. 1985. *Coast Salish Essays.* Seattle: University of Washington Press.

Sutton, Mark. 1988. *Insects as Food: Aboriginal Entomophagy in the Great Basin.* Socorro, NM: Ballena Press.

Syrotuck, William G. 1971. *Scent and the Scenting Dog.* Rome, NY: Arner.

Tain, The. 1983. Tr. Thomas Kinsella. Harmondsworth, Middlesex: Penguin.

Thibaut-Canelade, Eliane. 1995. *La Table medievale des Catalans.* Montpellier: Les Presses de Languedoc.

Tisserand, Robert. 1977. *The Art of Aromatherapy.* New York: Inner Traditions.

———. 1988. "Essential Oils as Psychotherapeutic Agents." In *Perfumery,* ed. Steve Van Toller and George H. Dodd. New York: Chapman and Hall. Pp. 167–81.

Torii, S., et al. 1988. "Contingent Negative Variation (CNV) and the Psychological Effect of Odour." In *Perfumery,* ed. Steve Van Toller and George H. Dodd. New York: Chapman and Hall. Pp. 107–20.

Toussaint-Samat, Madelon. 1992. *History of Food.* Tr. Anthea Bell. (Fr. orig. 1987.) Oxford, England: Basil Blackwell.

Trease, George Edward, and William Charles Evans. 1978. *Pharmacognosy.* 11th ed. London: Bailliere Tindall.

Tuma, E. 1965. *Twenty-Six Centuries of Agrarian Reform.* Berkeley: University of California Press.

Turnbull, Colin. 1972. *The Mountain People.* New York: Simon & Schuster.

Turner, Jonathan, and Alexandra Maryanski. 1979. *Functionalism.* Menlo Park, CA: Benjamin Cummings.

Tyler, Varro; Lynn R. Brady; James E. Robbers. 1981. *Pharmacognosy.* 8th ed. Philadelphia: Lea and Febiger.

Ungar, Peter S., and Mark F. Teaford (eds.). 2002. *Human Diet: Its Origin and Evolution.* Westport, CT: Bergin and Garvey.

UNICEF (United Nations Children's Fund). 2002. *The State of the World's Children, 2002: Leadership.* New York: UNICEF.

Van Esterik, Penny. 1989. *Beyond the Breast-Bottle Controversy.* New Brunswick, NJ: Rutgers University Press.

———. 1992. *Women, Work, and Breastfeeding.* Cornell International Nutrition Monograph No. 23. Ithaca, NY: Cornell University Press.

———. 1997. "The Politics of Breastfeeding: An Advocacy Perspective." In *Food and Culture: A Reader,* ed. Carole Counihan and Penny Van Esterik. New York: Routledge. Pp. 370–83.

Van Gelder, Geert Jan. 2000. *God's Banquet: Food in Classical Arabic Literature.* New York: Columbia University Press.

Velez-Ibañez, Carlos. 1996. *Border Visions.* Tucson: University of Arizona Press.

Vico, Giambattista. 1948. *The New Science of Giambattista Vico.* Tr. Thomas G. Bergin and Max Harold Fisch. (Latin orig. 1744.) Ithaca, NY: Cornell University Press.

Vogel, Gretchen. 1999. "Did Early African Hominids Eat Meat?" *Science* 283:303.

Vrba, Elizabeth; George Denton; Timothy C. Partridge; Lloyd H. Burckle (eds.).

1995. *Paleoclimate and Evolution, with Emphasis on Human Origins.* New Haven, CT: Yale University Press.

Walens, Stanley. 1981. *Feasting with Cannibals.* Princeton, NJ: Princeton University Press.

Waley, Arthur. 1956. *Yuan Mei.* New York: Grove Press.

Wallerstein, Immanuel. 1976. *The Modern World-System.* Vol. 1. New York: Academic Press.

Wallin, Nils; Bjorn Merker; Steven Brown (eds.). 2000. *The Origins of Music.* Cambridge, MA: MIT Press.

Wang, Hai-wei; Charles J. Wysocki; Geoffrey H. Gold. 1993. "Induced Olfactory Receptor Sensitivity in Mice." *Science* 26:998–1000.

Watson, Burton. 1977. *Ryokan: Zen Monk-Poet of Japan.* New York: Columbia University Press.

Watson, James L. (ed.). 1997. *Golden Arches East: McDonald's in East Asia.* Stanford, CA: Stanford University Press.

Weaver, Connie M., and Robert P. Heaney. 1999. "Calcium." In *Modern Nutrition in Health and Disease,* ed. Maurice Shils, James Olson, Moshe Shike, A. Catharine Ross. Philadelphia: Lippincott Williams and Wilkins. Pp. 141–55.

Weckmann, Luis. 1992. *The Medieval Heritage of Mexico.* Tr. Frances M. Lopez-Morillas. (Sp. orig. 1984.) New York: Fordham University Press.

Wellstart International. 1992. *Breastfeeding: A Natural Resource for Food Security.* Washington, DC: Wellstart International.

———. 1996. *Preamble to the U.S. Baby-Friendly Hospital Initiative Guidelines and Criteria.* Washington, DC: U.S. Committee for UNICEF and Wellstart International.

Wheaton, Barbara. 1983. *Savoring the Past: French Kitchens from 1300 to 1789.* Philadelphia: University of Pennsylvania Press.

Wiessner, Polly, and Wulf Schiefenhövel (eds.). 1996. *Food and the Status Quest: An Interdisciplinary Perspective.* Oxford: Berghahn Books.

Willett, Walter. 2002. "The Food Pushers." (Review of Nestle 2002.) *Science* 297:198–99.

Willett, Walter, and Meir J. Stampfer. 2003. "Rebuilding the Food Pyramid." *Scientific American,* Jan.: 64–71.

Williams, Roger. 1956. *Biochemical Individuality.* Austin: University of Texas Press.

Wilmsen, Edwin N., and James R. Denbow. 1990. "Paradigmatic History of San-speaking Peoples and Current Attempts at Revision." *Current Anthropology* 31:489–524.

Woodham-Smith, Cecil. 1962. *The Great Hunger.* New York: Harper and Row.

World Health Organisation. 1994. *Resolution of the World Health Assembly: Infant and Young Child Nutrition.* Geneva: World Health Organization.

Wrangham, R., and Jane Goodale. 1989. "Chimpanzee Use of Medicinal

Leaves." In *Understanding Chimpanzees,* ed. Paul G. Heltne and Linda A. Marquardt. Cambridge: Harvard University Press. Pp. 22–37.

Wrangham, Richard, and Dale Peterson. 1996. *Demonic Males: Apes and the Origins of Human Violence.* Boston: Houghton Mifflin.

Wright, Clifford. 1999. *A Mediterranean Feast.* New York: William Morrow.

———. 2000. "Slippery as a Wet Noodle: The Impossible History of Macaroni." Lecture to Culinary Historians of Southern California, Los Angeles, Nov. 4, 2000.

Wright, Karen. 1994. "The Sniff." *Discover,* April 1994, pp. 60–67.

Wright, R. H. 1982. *The Sense of Smell.* Boca Raton, FL: CRC Press.

Wu, David Y. H., and Tan Chee-beng. 2001. *Changing Chinese Foodways in Asia.* Hong Kong: Chinese University Press.

Wu, David Y. H., and Sidney C. H. Cheung. 2002. *The Globalization of Chinese Food.* London: Curzon.

Yoneda, Soei. 1982. *The Heart of Zen Cuisine.* Tokyo: Kodansha International.

Young, Arthur. N.d. (ca. 1900; orig. 1792). *Travels in France and Italy during the Years 1787, 1788, and 1789.* New York: Dutton.

Zeidler, Judy. 1999. *The Gourmet Jewish Cook.* New York: William Morrow.

Zohary, Daniel, and Maria Hopf. 2000. *Domestication of Plants in the Old World.* 3rd ed. Oxford: Oxford University Press.

Zubaida, Sami, and Richard Tapper (eds.). 1994. *Culinary Cultures of the Middle East.* London: I. B. Tauris.

Index

About the Author

E. N. Anderson is Professor of Anthropology at the University of California, Riverside. His previous books include *The Food of China* and *Ecologies of the Heart.*